THE BAUHAUS REASSESSED

THE BAUHAUS REASSESSED

SOURCES AND DESIGN THEORY

GILLIAN NAYLOR

THE HERBERT PRESS

Copyright © Gillian Naylor 1985
Copyright under the Berne Convention

First published in Great Britain 1985 by
The Herbert Press Limited, 46 Northchurch Road, London N1 4EJ
Reprinted 1993

Designed by Judith Allan
Jacket design by Gillian Greenwood
House editor Anne Kilborn

Printed and bound in Hong Kong by South China Printing Co (1988) Ltd

A CIP catalogue record for this book
is available from the British Library

ISBN 0–906969–30–1

Front cover: Coffee pot in German silver, designed 1923/4, by Wilhelm Wagenfeld.
Jug in German silver, W. Rössger and F. Marby, 1923/4.
Kunstsammlungen, Weimar

Back cover: Cradle by Peter Keler, 1922. Painted wood.
Kunstsammlungen, Weimar

In memory of my son Tom

CONTENTS

Introduction   9

PART I   SOURCES

1   Educational theory   14
2   Craft and industry   25
3   The Werkbund   37

PART II   THE BAUHAUS IN WEIMAR

1   War and revolution   48
2   The Cathedral of Socialism   57
3   The workshops   67
4   Johannes Itten and the Basic Course   75
5   Claims for Art: (1) Kandinsky and Klee   83
                      (2) Van Doesburg and Moholy-Nagy   93
6   Crisis and consolidation   103

PART III   THE BAUHAUS IN DESSAU

1   Dessau: the great transformation   124
2   Dessau and architecture   129
3   From workshop to laboratory   144
4   Hannes Meyer: formalism or functionalism?   165
5   Confrontation and collapse   175

Sources and notes   181
Select bibliography   192
Index   195

INTRODUCTION

'The history of the Bauhaus is a long story, an endless one, I could never reach the end; I have merely traced one strand – let's drop the subject.'

Oskar Schlemmer

Oskar Schlemmer wrote this in 1923, four years after the Bauhaus opened in Weimar and ten years before the school was forced to close. Since then the story of the Bauhaus has been told and re-told: the subject, it seems, will never be dropped. There are various reasons for this obsession with a school of design and architecture which, like the Weimar Republic, survived for only fourteen years. The first, of course, relates to the reputation of the staff who taught there: Feininger, Itten, Kandinsky, Klee, Muche, Moholy-Nagy and Schlemmer, who were brought in to establish a programme, and the former students Albers, Bayer, Breuer and Gunta Stölzl who trained and then became teachers there. The second concerns the nature of the programme and the ideals it represented. As this book attempts to show, these were not necessarily innovatory; other schools of art, design and architecture in Germany had experimented with 'preliminary' courses and an inter-disciplinary approach, and Gropius's preoccupation with 'type-forms' and standardization had a long pre-history in philosophies of manufacture. The school's attempts to establish a methodology for design through what Kandinsky described as 'the new science of art' had their counterparts in Russia and Holland.

What is unique about the Bauhaus, however, is the fact that its ideologies epitomize changing concepts concerning the nature and purpose of design in the early twentieth century. The school inherited, reinterpreted and then rejected the craft ideals of the nineteenth century; it attempted to discover 'laws' in art that could be related to design and architecture, and its fundamental aim was to establish a universal language of form that would represent the elimination of social as well as national barriers.

The pathos and futility of such idealism, which again was not a prerogative of the Bauhaus, was emphasized by the political vendettas that were ultimately to close the school. At the same time, however, the fact that it had so frequently to justify its existence meant that its assumptions were constantly being challenged, both from within and without. Itten, van Doesburg, Moholy-Nagy and Hannes Meyer all acted as catalysts in their attempts to define and redefine its programme. Besides this each workshop (or laboratory) evolved a distinctive approach to material and form, and was supported by German industry during its brief periods of economic recovery: in spite of growing right-wing pressures, Bauhaus concepts of the rationalization of standards for housing and product design were by no means unique in Germany.

Unlike other schools of design and architecture in Germany, however, the Bauhaus was a constant focus for publicity, largely generated, while he was in charge, by Gropius himself. He needed to attract students of the right calibre, he needed funding and he needed protection from the ideological and political campaigns that threatened the school throughout its existence. He built up a prestigious 'Circle of Friends' of the Bauhaus, and he also wrote at length in defence of the school and its achievements. The first book he wrote – *Idee und Aufbau des Staatlichen Bauhauses in Weimar* – was published in 1923 to describe and justify the school's activities in Weimar; several of the Bauhaus Books, edited by Gropius and Moholy-Nagy, and published between 1925 and 1930, also dealt with Bauhaus activities, as, of course, did *The New Architecture and the Bauhaus* (1935) and *Bauhaus 1919–1928*, published in 1938 by the Museum of Modern Art to coincide with the first Bauhaus exhibition in New York. Of these three inter-war books *Bauhaus 1919–1928* (incorporating a translation of *Idee und Aufbau*) provides the most comprehensive first-hand account of the school; in *The New Architecture and the Bauhaus*, the role the painters played there is scarcely acknowledged.

Since its foundation, however, scarcely a year has passed without the publication of books and articles about various aspects of the Bauhaus by its staff, students and by scholars. The most dedicated of these was, of course, Hans M. Wingler, who died whilst this book was in preparation. H. M. Wingler founded the Bauhaus-Archiv in Darmstadt in 1961, a year before the publication of the first edition of his *Bauhaus*, an invaluable and unique source book based on archive material. The Bauhaus-Archiv transferred to West Berlin in 1971 and is now housed in a purpose-built museum, designed according to Gropius's plans, which was opened in 1979. The availability of the source material has naturally contributed to a 'new wave' of publications, as well as catalogues to exhibitions held in Berlin. Research and rehabilitation of the Bauhaus has also continued in East Germany. Dr Karl-Heinz Hüter's *Das Bauhaus in Weimar* (1976) provides, as well as archive material, a valuable analysis of social and economic developments in Weimar; Professor Christian Schädlich, of the *Hochschule für Bauwesen* in Weimar has also, in his *Bauhaus–Weimar 1919–1925* provided a clear and detailed account of the school in its Weimar period. Publications such as these, of course, provide vital economic data which is not easily available in the West.

The prelude to this book – *The Bauhaus Reassessed* – was a short text I published on the Bauhaus in 1968. When I was asked, four years ago, to amend the book for republication, I felt that a complete revision was needed, not only to take account of subsequent research, but also to provide a more detailed commentary and analysis of the activities of the school, particularly in the context of educational reforms in Germany prior to the First World War. I also felt that the role of the painters there needed to be re-examined, and that a less cursory account of the Hannes Meyer period was needed. But as Oskar Schlemmer remarked – 'the history of the Bauhaus is a long story' – and this revised version still only skims over the surface of the subject. There are many omissions, the most regrettable being any discussion of Schlemmer's work for the school. He is quoted frequently, for he was an acute and lively commentator, but lack of time and space forced me to omit references to the Bauhaus Theatre, and concepts of performance, which, of course, were vital to the school's activities.

There are many acknowledgments to be made: first to the work of the late Hans Wingler and the Bauhaus-Archiv in Berlin, which when I visited it was directed by Dr Peter Hahn; I also met Dr Karl-Heinz Hüter in East Berlin, Dr Georg Opitz in Dessau and Dr Christian Schädlich in Weimar. I am grateful for their help, and for their permission to reproduce photographs. Thanks also are due to Michael Collins, of the British Museum, and to the Victoria and Albert Museum for permission to take photographs; to John Heskett who generously provided me with some material from his own research; to my colleagues at the Royal College of Art, particularly the Library; to David Herbert and Ayeshah Haleem for their patience and their support; to Anne Kilborn for her help with the editing; to my mother, and above all to my friends who helped me through the dark days that have nothing to do with this book.

1, 2 (*Left*) Weimar Bauhaus seal 1919–22 (*Right*) Weimar Bauhaus seal from 1922 (design by Oskar Schlemmer)

3 (*Overleaf*) Walter Gropius and the Gropius house, Dessau *Private collection*

PART I   SOURCES

The formation of the Bauhaus in April 1919 has become both a landmark and a legend in the history of design and design education. During its brief lifetime (the school was closed by the Nazis in 1933), its fame and notoriety were based on its seemingly avant-garde teaching methods, and its attempts to relate creativity and changing concepts of craftsmanship to the demands of industrial production. Its ideals, like those of the majority of design reformers, were Utopian and ambiguous. The problems and values that preoccupied the school and its students were to change their character many times, partly in response to social, industrial and political pressures, and partly in response to the emerging dogmas of the Modern Movement, which demanded a new language of form to demonstrate the values of a new age. Developments within the Bauhaus, therefore, reflect in microcosm certain developments within the Modern Movement, and the school's prestige has varied according to subsequent reassessments and revaluations of the priorities and achievements of the avant-garde in the 1920s and 1930s.

In 1919, however, when Walter Gropius took over the school, the nature of the avant-garde, especially in Germany, was difficult to define. For the impact of the war and the revolution, which will be discussed in Part II, both challenged and reinforced certain attitudes to art, design and architecture which had been developing in Germany since the turn of the century, when the *Jugendstil*, Germany's equivalent of Art Nouveau, had flourished in cultural and political centres such as Berlin, Munich, Dresden and Weimar. The *Jugendstil* movement, naturally enough, shared many of the impulses of Art Nouveau: the rejection or reinterpretation of academic standards in art, architecture and design, the exploration of literary and musical analogies, the celebration of the vernacular as well as new spatial and decorative concepts in architecture, and the conviction that art and design were inseparable, reflecting both a social and aesthetic commitment to the 'individual value', as Ruskin put it, 'of every human soul'.

In Germany the challenge and championship of these 'individual values' took many forms, partly because of different patterns of state and regional patronage, and partly because of the uneasy relationships between craftsmen and industry which had led to both political and social tensions, as well as to demands for changes in the priorities for education, especially design and art education.

When it was first founded, therefore, the educational aims and teaching methods of the Bauhaus were by no means unique in Germany, where, from the mid-nineteenth century, demands for relevance, practicality and flexibility at all levels of education had run counter to traditional conceptions and hierarchies of learning. A precedent, perhaps significant as far as the Bauhaus was concerned, for state repression of avant-garde educational methods had been established in Prussia as early as 1851, when Froebel's Kindergarten experiments, first launched in 1839, were banned as 'socialist' institutions.

State control and organization of education to reinforce the power, prosperity and ideology of the state over both educated and educators were consolidated in the latter part of the nineteenth century, especially after unification in 1871, when the Prussian system of education was widely adopted. By 1900 a three-tier pattern of education had been established, through elementary (or *Volk*) schools, middle schools and high schools. The middle schools were intended to serve the needs of the lower middle classes – the tradespeople and craftworkers – while the high schools were dedicated to the study of the classics and the humanities. Education in the high schools formed the basis of university education for the professional classes (including artists and architects), while the middle schools could also lead the students to art, applied art, technical or trade schools. The position of the art academies and trade schools within this hierarchy was ambiguous, for while the trade schools supplemented the guild system of apprenticeship in specific skills, the art academies were conceived to serve a dual purpose, the assumption being that the promotion of Fine Art as an end in itself would inevitably lead to higher standards in applied art. The statutes of the Berlin Academy of Fine Art, drawn up in 1790, give some indication of the utilitarian concepts that inspired it: 'The aim of the institute is . . . to encourage the flowering of the arts in order to inspire and promote the art industry of the fatherland, and so influence trade and manufacture that the native artist will not lag behind his foreign counterparts in tasteful work of every kind.'[1]

Confidence in such explicit links between art and industry, however, was undermined throughout the nineteenth century. On the one hand, the status of the 'academy', and its associations with historicism and state prestige was challenged by new concepts of the nature, role and independence of the artist; again, the problems of a rapidly industrializing nation forced patrons, local and state authorities to re-examine their priorities for design education. In the 1880s several new schools of applied design (*Kunstgewerbeschule*) were established, many of them associated with museums. By the turn of the century, therefore, Germany had a well-established network of design schools, founded to promote German trade in general as well as to maintain and consolidate standards in local craft industries. The Grand Duke of Saxe-Weimar's brief to Henry van de Velde, the Belgian architect and designer who founded the school that Gropius was to take over in 1919, was by no means untypical. Van de Velde was invited to Weimar in order to advise 'on matters pertaining to the arts and crafts, architecture, decorative arts and the like . . .', '. . . to give practical counsel to craftsmen and manufacturers', and to 'provide, through the preparation of designs, models and prototypes . . . artistic suggestions which will take into account the nature and condition of local art practice'.[2]

Institutions such as the *Kunstgewerbeschule* in Weimar, therefore, had a dual role – to inspire as well as consolidate local craftsmanship. This, in one sense, was in keeping with the aims of the *Jugendstil*. For unlike England, Germany had maintained local craft industries throughout the nineteenth century, the guild system of apprenticeship and workshop training providing a practical alternative to the *Kunstgewerbeschule*. By the end of the century, however, Germany's craft workers were threatened by economic recession, by industrialization, and by changes in the social structure. For, at the most simplistic level, those with the means to buy consumer goods looked either to mass production or to 'art industry' to supply demands that local craftsmen could not meet.

The responses among artists, designers, educationalists, and social critics as well as government officials were complex. The majority were aware of, or had absorbed, Marx's theories of alienation, which involved both the product and the producer. 'Alienation,' Marx had written in 1844, 'shows itself not only in the result, but also in the *process, of production*, within *productive activity* itself. . . . The more the worker expends himself in work, the more powerful becomes the world of objects which he creates in face of himself, and the poorer he himself becomes in his inner life, the less he belongs to himself. . . . The *alienation* of the worker in his product means not only that his labour becomes an object, takes on its own existence, but that it exists outside him, independently, and alien to him, and that it stands opposed to him as an autonomous power. The life which he has given to the object sets itself against him as an alien and hostile force.'[3]

More than half a century later, the Surrealists were to provide their own commentary on the alienation of the world of objects. In nineteenth-century Germany, however, Marx's theories, filtered perhaps through the writings of Ruskin and the theory and practice of William Morris, prompted remedial action rather than irony. Ideas and ideals for action ranged from demonstrations of the autonomy of the artist, to pressures for reforms in education in general. Froebel's work, suppressed in 1851, was re-examined prior to the First World War, together with the theories of the Italian doctor, Maria Montessori,[4] whose concepts of child education and self-knowledge through the encouragement and development of creativity were considered vital to the whole educational process. The concept of 'education through art' was widely debated and demonstrated in Germany at the turn of the century. Writing in 1908, for example, J. A. Lux, the first historian of what he described as the 'modern movement' in Germany, maintained that, 'Ten years of the modern movement have fundamentally changed our conception of the school,' and that experiments to encourage and strengthen the 'creative powers' of school children had also stimulated reforms in design education.[5]

EDUCATION THROUGH ART

One pioneer of these reforms at all levels of education was Alfred Lichtwark who, as director of the Hamburg *Kunsthalle*, was involved in practical reforms in that city's *Kunstgewerbeschule*, in education for women, and in the preservation of local art and local culture. In 1887 Lichtwark founded the Art Education Movement in order to consolidate his theories about the nature of art education and its relationship both to the welfare of the individual and the state. Art training, according to Lichtwark, was still dominated by archaic ideas of feudal patronage; both the art academies and the *Kunstgewerbeschule*, fossilized in 'art towns', were dedicated to lifeless copying and meaningless production. If art were central to life, as well as to education, if as much care were to be given to the training of the eye and the sensibilities (*Empfindungen*) as to the intellect, the problems of German industry would be solved: barriers between producer and product would cease to exist, and the consumer – the general public – likewise 'educated through art' would recognize 'genuine' quality. Lichtwark's theories[6] were to have a significant influence on general education as well as on design and art training before the First World War, and they were reinforced by the formation of other societies, such as Ferdinand Avenarius's *Dürerbund* in 1902, and, of course, the Werkbund in 1907.

The Deutscher Werkbund, whose debates are discussed in Chapter 3, provided a platform for the articulation and implementation of ideas about the relationship of art to design and society. Before its formation, however, several German art and design schools had adopted programmes that challenged traditional conceptions of the role and training of the artist and craftsman. Adolf Hölzel in Stuttgart (whose students included Oskar Schlemmer and Johannes Itten), Anton Ažbè, who ran a private school in Munich (Kandinsky was one of his pupils) and Lothar and Gertrud von Kunowski, who taught in Rome and Florence as well as in Munich and Berlin, all ran art schools that emphasized individual expression and new approaches to colour, line and form.

The intentions, as much as the achievements, of their seemingly radical courses were important not only because of their rejection of traditional methods of instruction and expression, but because they implied a change in the role of the artist and his relationship both to his work and society. They stressed the individuality and autonomy of the artist, but at the same time they urged an empathy with form and structure that united rather than isolated the artist from nature. Writing about drawing, Lothar von Kunowski, in his significantly titled *Durch Kunst zum Leben* (Through Art to Life), published in 1903, encouraged the artist to reveal the essence rather than the appearance of nature and materials (plants, trees, stones, metal) in order to achieve true expression.[7]

This 'identification' with nature, however, was also extended to an identification with national culture and with folk art: the artist's mission, uncorrupted by academicism, was to act as a catalyst for the ideals of the people, so creating a national art and reviving national culture. The most exaggerated (and in view of subsequent developments, the most sinister) expression of these ideals appeared in 1890 with the publication of Julius Langbehn's *Rembrandt Als Erzieher* (Rembrandt as Educator). The book, first published anonymously, ran into several revised editions, with 60,000 copies being printed in the first year of its publication. 'One theme,' writes Fritz Stern, 'dominated the entire book: German culture was being destroyed by science and intellectualism and could be regenerated only through the resurgence of art and the rise to power of great artistic individuals in a new society.'[8] This primacy of the artist would, according to Langbehn, emerge from more liberal attitudes to children's education (which linked his theories to those of the Art Education Movement), and from the people – the peasant – who 'stood for all that remained unpolluted in society, for all that remained fixed and rooted'.[9]

But Langbehn's theories, as Fritz Stern points out, were double-edged. On the one hand they were linked with the general *fin de siècle* rejection of industrialization and mechanization, and with attempts to generate a more humanistic social order. On the other, however, Langbehn's anti-semitism, his call for a *Führer* who would 'set the dead masses into motion . . . by realizing the feelings, aspirations and demands of his people . . .'[10] revealed the ambivalence of much of his mysticism.

At the time of its publication, however, the book's ideal of redemption through art and craftsmanship was a potent one. It demanded programmes for reform at all levels of education, and its message was absorbed by a generation of artists whose work was to be banned as 'degenerate' by the *Führer* that Langbehn had evoked. There are, for example, undertones of Langbehn's philosophies in some of the early letters of Oskar Schlemmer, that most intelligent and humanistic of artists who was to join the staff of the Bauhaus in 1920. Schlemmer was born in 1888, and spent two years as an apprentice in a shop for inlay work before he went to study at the Stuttgart *Akademie der bildenden Künste* in 1906. He volunteered for military service in 1914 and was wounded twice before his demobilization in 1918. His diaries and letters, covering the period from 1910 to his death in 1943, provide a witty, illuminating and tragic commentary on the ambiguities of the ideal of commitment for a German artist during that period. Although one must take into account that they were not intended for publication, Schlemmer's letters and diaries reveal an artist 'thinking aloud' – attempting to make sense of what was going on around him. Writing 'from the field' to Fraulein Martha Luz in June 1918,[11] Schlemmer maintains that 'the isolation of the modern artist cannot be denied'. 'Our times,' he writes, 'lack a great unifying idea or religion. The artists are striving to create one, and the way to it appears to be through absolute individual subjectivity.' At that time Schlemmer believed that the artist would be understood by 'his own kind and . . . among the receptive souls of the simple, uneducated people. When the spark leaps the gap between the complicated, intellectualizing artist and the simple strong soul of the people, the current of cause and effect will be closed.'

In the Utopia Schlemmer envisaged, the artist, whose aim was to make the 'invisible visible', would share his perception with the unsophisticated and the childlike, since the educated, or as he put it 'the half-educated, with their good common sense' were being stultified and compromised, unable to achieve or recognize creativity.

Debates concerning the 'education' of the artist were also extended to the training of the designer. Here the exponents of reform had obvious precedents to draw upon. England had already confronted, though hardly resolved, problems relating to the role of the designer or craftsman in an industrial society; and Germany, as has already been pointed out, had, by the late-nineteenth century, established a network of *Kunstgewerbeschule* whose work was mainly related to local patronage and local trades. Several of these schools, however, had been founded in association with museums, which implied a historicist role, and methods of training there had become as academic and restrictive as those in the art academies.[12] The issues discussed involved the degree of creative freedom allowed to the potential designer and the nature of his training; how far this was to be academic and therefore divorced from the apprenticeship system, how far the stress was to be on traditional craft skills, or on their rejuvenation through the *Jugendstil*, and how much acknowledgment was to be given to the demands of German industry. As in the 'fine art' area, the most experimental of the schools were private establishments, and the most interesting of these, in view of developments in Weimar, was the Debschitz-Schule set up in Munich by Wilhelm von Debschitz and Hermann Obrist in 1902.

OBRIST AND THE DEBSCHITZ-SCHULE

Hermann Obrist is best known, through histories of Art Nouveau, for his work in embroidery, ceramics and sculpture, and for his links with the *Jugendstil* group in Munich (Illus. 4); he is also acknowledged in histories of the Bauhaus as one of van de Velde's

4 Table with tray in oak, designed for the United Workshops for Art in Handicraft, Munich, by Hermann Obrist, *c*.1898 *Munich Stadtmuseum*

nominees as his successor at Weimar in 1914. Obrist, however, played an important role in German design education, first through his work for the Debschitz-Schule,[13] and then through his ambiguous relationships with the Werkbund. He was thirty-nine when the Debschitz-Schule was founded, and by that time he had had a long and varied career. He was born near Zurich where his father was a doctor; his mother, who was descended from Scottish nobility, separated from her husband when Hermann was still a child, and they went to live in Weimar. Obrist studied medicine and botany in Heidelberg and Berlin before deciding to become an artist. He visited England and Scotland in 1887, where he learned of the theories and influence of William Morris, and returned to study in the *Kunstgewerbeschule* in Karlsruhe. The academicism of the school appalled him, however, so he left to work in a rural pottery near Jena. In 1888 he was selling his wares at the Thuringian Autumn Fair in Weimar; in 1889 he was exhibiting them in Paris, where he won a Gold Medal. He stayed in Paris to study sculpture, and then moved to Florence, where, as well as working as a sculptor, he set up an embroidery workshop with Bertha Ruchet. In 1895 he returned to Munich where he established both sculpture and embroidery studios, and met the then pioneers of Munich's *Jugendstil* – August Endell, Bernhard Pankok, Richard Riemerschmid and van de Velde, and, in 1900, Wilhelm von Debschitz.

Von Debschitz was the son of a general; he avoided a military career, however, and arrived in Munich in 1900 in order to study painting. Obrist admired not only the talent of the younger man, but also his organizing abilities. Their school, which was to teach 'free' as well as applied art, opened in 1902 with three students. The numbers gradually increased, and the school began to establish a pattern of teaching and recreation similar to that of the early years at the Bauhaus. The students were taught in workshops and the stress was on craftsmanship (*Handwerk*), and the fusion of fine and applied art. There was to be no specialization: the students were encouraged to participate in all the activities of the school – woodwork, metalwork, textiles and ceramics – as well as sculpture, painting and drawing. Obrist also maintained that the students should spend at least a year on an 'elementary course' (*Elementarunterricht*) in which they would 'joyously swarm' (*jubelnd ausschwärmen*) with the minimum of direction.[14] Obrist, however, who suffered from deafness, gradually began to withdraw from the activities of the school, not only because of his physical affliction, but because he disagreed with von Debschitz's changes in policy. Unlike Obrist, von Debschitz believed that reforms in art and design should be achieved through *Gesellschaft* (partnership) rather than through individual endeavour, and that the school should work towards practical achievements in both craft work and industrial design. He maintained his belief in the workshop system of instruction, the designs produced there being prototypes for craft as well as industrial production. Gropius was aware of the activities of the school, which survived until 1914, and remained in contact with von Debschitz until he left Germany: 'What did we do wrong?' Gropius is reported to have asked in his final meeting with von Debschitz in 1933.

The privately-owned and run Debschitz-Schule, therefore, presented one 'model' for the fusion of art and design education in pre-war Germany. Obrist's conception of the teaching there, with its stress on workshop rather than studio instruction, the abolition of boundaries between art and design, and the idea of a 'preliminary' year for self-discovery anticipate the early years at the Weimar Bauhaus. Again, the change of direction when von Debschitz, despite opposition from Obrist, began to insist on the production of 'marketable' goods also had their parallels in subsequent ideological crises within the Bauhaus.

Between 1900 and 1914, however, several art and design schools in Germany had embarked on programmes of expansion and reform. In the small 'art towns' like Weimar and Darmstadt these were directly influenced by ducal patronage; they tended to serve local needs, establishing 'art' industries and reinforcing local craft traditions. Compared with the situation in Prussia, however, with its social problems and its mixed industrial and agrarian economies, the 'art towns' and the experimental schools seemed like ivory towers, divorced from the realities of commercial life.

BEHRENS: DARMSTADT, NÜRNBERG AND DÜSSELDORF

Prussia's industrial expansion was based on both state and private enterprise; 'art' in the academic sense, and to a certain extent 'applied art' were essential for cultural prestige and hegemony. New and growing industries, however, produced consumer as well as capital goods, and these had to be competitive in home as well as in export markets. Reforms in Prussia's art and design schools are generally associated with Hermann Muthesius's energetic work for the Prussian Board of Trade. Muthesius, who had spent seven years in England (from 1896–1903) studying and reporting on British architecture and design on behalf of his government, joined the Prussian Board of Trade in 1904 and remained an adviser there until 1926, the year before his death. In the period prior to the First World War he was active in the formation of the Werkbund and in recommending appointments to Prussian art and design schools. It is significant, however, that most of Muthesius's 'nominees' were drawn from the *Jugendstil* group in Munich, and that their appointments as teachers, or as heads of schools coincided with or confirmed changing (and sometimes confused) attitudes to the nature of their commitment as artists or designers. Peter Behrens, for example, who was appointed head of the Düsseldorf *Kunstgewerbeschule* in 1903, had trained as a painter, and had lived in Munich in the 1890s; while he was there he had already produced glassware, porcelain (Pl. 1), and carpets, and he designed his own house, together with its furniture and decoration, when he was invited to join the Grand Duke of Hesse's Artists' Colony in Darmstadt in 1901. (The Artists' Colony on the Mathildenhohe in Darmstadt was a latterday example of civic and princely patronage. The impetus for its formation came from the Grand Duke Ernst Ludwig of Hesse, who was determined to make his city a centre of art and culture as well as of commerce. Ernst Ludwig, a grandson of Queen Victoria, succeeded to the Grand Duchy in 1892, at a time when Darmstadt was expanding, with capital goods being produced there, as well as furniture, ceramics and wallpaper.[15] Money was granted for the scheme on the grounds that: 'The encouragement of artistic handicraft is extremely important, not only from the aesthetic point of view but also from that of political economy, as it brings substantially more money to the common people than does so-called "High Art" [painting and sculpture] and creates contented folk.')[16]

During his brief period at Darmstadt, Behrens was asked to teach short courses on applied art at Nürnberg,[17] and it was this experience as a teacher, as well as his growing experience as a designer, that led to his appointment as director of the *Kunstgewerbeschule* in Düsseldorf in 1902. The school, which opened in 1883 and which was the first to be established in Germany, was also one of the first to be influenced by Muthesius's policies for design reform, and Behrens's programme reflected his preoccupation with 'inner laws' that would determine form in architecture, industrial design and craftsmanship. 'Today's school of applied art', he wrote in 1907, 'has to take into account the demands of aesthetic expression in handwork, and industry's need for an artistic impulse'. His students, he claimed, were encouraged to consider 'the intellectual principles of all form-creating work', and to attempt to discover and reconcile 'the laws of art' with those of 'technique and material'.[18]

He established a preliminary course at the school, in which students studied drawing and experimented with exercises in basic design using various materials before deciding on a specialization. He reorganized the architectural course there, and invited Josef

5, 6 Chair, desk and wardrobe (*opposite*) designed by Bruno Paul for Dr Ernst Levin, who was then a student in Munich, *c.* 1907. The wardrobe can be dismantled *Private collection. Photograph: J. K. Wilkie*

Hoffmann from Vienna, Kandinsky from Munich, and H. P. Berlage from Holland to join the staff. This distinguished triumvirate declined, but the painter Josef Bruckmüller, and the architect Max Benirschke, both associated with the Vienna Secession, came to Düsseldorf. More important perhaps, in view of later developments in Germany, was the appointment of J. L. M. Lauweriks (a disciple of both Cuypers and Berlage in Holland) to the architecture department in 1904. This appointment was a significant one, not only because Adolf Meyer, Gropius's first partner, was a pupil of Lauweriks, but because Lauweriks, through his association with Dutch design and architectural reform movements at the turn of the century, was concerned with the achievement and expression of universality in form and structure. Lauweriks was a member of the Theosophical Society, and believed that harmony, on both a practical and metaphysical level, could be established through a geometry of order, and that a systematic approach to design could lead, through rationalization and standardization, to a total unity and harmony of formal expression. Ideas such as these, which were to recur throughout the Werkbund debates, were, of course, fundamental to Bauhaus theory, but their interpretation was to lead to those ideological conflicts that are inherent in any discussion of twentieth-century design theory.

BRUNO PAUL AND BERLIN

Bruno Paul, who was appointed director of the school of design associated with the *Kunstgewerbe Museum* in Berlin in 1907, had a more pragmatic approach to design reform and it was, significantly, the seemingly classical, or classicizing designs for furniture that he exhibited in the Applied Art Exhibition in Dresden in 1906 that gained him this prestigious post. Wilhelm von Bode, then director of the Berlin Museum, was looking for a new principal for its school when he saw Paul's work in Dresden, designs which, in his opinion, exhibited none of the 'vagaries' of the *Jugendstil*, but which were based on 'an original interpretation of earlier forms'.[19]

Paul, like Behrens and van de Velde, had trained as a painter, first in Dresden then in Munich. He settled in Munich, and worked as an illustrator and cartoonist for the magazines *Jugend* and *Simplicissimus* before he began designing furniture, first for himself and then for private clients (Illus. 5 and 6). Again like Behrens and van de Velde, he was self-taught as a designer and as an architect; he was a founder member of the *Vereinigten Werkstätten für Kunst und Handwerk* in Munich in 1898, and pioneered the idea of *Typenmöbel* – furniture that could be produced by semi-mass production techniques (see

below). Paul had no teaching experience when he took over the Berlin school, but he obviously needed considerable political finesse in order to instigate changes there, since it came under the joint administration of the Ministry of Culture and the Ministry of Trade. The practical reforms that he made in the initial stages seem to have been mainly organizational, introducing new staff and timetables, and setting up courses in art history. His teaching theories, however, which he elaborated in articles published between 1917 and 1919[20] are interesting in that they put forward ideas that were implicit in Gropius's first programme for the Bauhaus, as well as in certain aspects of Werkbund educational theory prior to the First World War. (Paul was also a founder member of the Werkbund.)

Like Gropius, Paul doubted, for example, whether 'art' could or should be taught. He had no faith in the current system of specialization in *Technische Hochschule* (for architects), *Kunstakademie* (for artists), and *Kunstgewerbeschule* (for applied artists), and believed that the teaching of all these skills and disciplines should be united in what he called an *Einheitskunstschule*. Training there, like that in the former guilds, should be in workshops; all students should follow a common basic course in the initial stages of their training (they should later be able to move across specializations) and the teaching should be shared between specialists and artists. Only this flexible but rigorous system of training, Paul maintained, could produce 'artists' capable of improving standards in contemporary architecture and design.

Paul's recommendations were essentially practical. They were not inspired by the mysticism (real or assumed) of the first Bauhaus manifesto, but by his own experiences as a self-taught designer in Munich. In the 1890s, Munich, the industrial and cultural capital of Bavaria, had become the focus of the avant-garde and reformist activities of the *Jugendstil*. The magazine *Jugend*, which gave the German movement its name, was founded there in 1896; *Simplicissimus* was also launched in 1896, and *Dekorative Kunst* in 1897. Paul's cartoons for *Jugend* and *Simplicissimus*, however, are interesting in that they satirize both the bourgeoisie and the exaggerations of the avant-garde. A similar rejection of complacency and exaggeration can be seen in his work as a furniture designer. Paul's early designs, as his first biographer, Joseph Popp, pointed out, demonstrate his concern for craftsmanship and his understanding of the nature of wood;[21] he exploits the use of elaborate inlays, veneers and bentwood in chairs and cabinets for public and private commissions. Only a handful of these designs, however, could be characterized as 'Art Nouveau', and it was his reinterpretation rather than rejection of 'earlier forms' that impressed Wilhelm von Bode in 1906. In 1908 Paul consolidated this ideal of simplification by designing a range of *Typenmöbel* ('type-furniture'): cupboards, cabinets, chairs and tables that were made from standardized components and a choice of materials and finishes that could be used throughout the house. This emphasis on standardization could, of course, be justified on various levels. It cut down costs, and at the same time it demonstrated an ideal of unostentatious domestic order and unity (rather than uniformity) that was related to bourgeois rather than aristocratic or élitist values (thus rejecting, both in form and concept, the ethos of the *Jugendstil*). Moreover it implies a new role for the craftsman/designer and demonstrated that 'clear and sober objectivity (*Sachlichkeit*) that is so evident in engineering design'.[22] Such ideals, which implied a transformation of the concept and value of craftsmanship, were, by 1908, firmly established in German design and educational theory: the problems of their practical implementation still remained to be solved.

2 CRAFT AND INDUSTRY

The protagonists of the craft revival in pre-war Germany were obviously influenced by the idealism as well as by the achievements of the English Arts and Crafts Movement. The English had looked to the past for authenticity in design and had attempted to establish a new social order through the redemptive role of craftsmanship in an industrializing society. The ambiguities of this philosophy were demonstrated in the prestige of its products. 'When English creations began to appear,' wrote Samuel Bing, the promoter of Art Nouveau in France, 'a cry of delight sounded throughout Europe. Its echo can still be heard in every country.'[1] The dream, therefore, of 'an art made by the people and for the people' remained a dream that only the rich could indulge in. The revolution that William Morris worked for and, on a more practical level, the state intervention that C. R. Ashbee recommended if craftsmanship was to survive in competitive industry[2] did not materialize, so that in England the craft ideal survived as a commentary on the nature of work and the demands of mass production and mass consumption.

In nineteenth-century Germany, however, because of the complexity of social and economic developments in the various states that were to form the Reich in 1871, the role and status of the craftsman was completely different. The guild system, for example, survived into the twentieth century,[3] with 'master' craftsmen in various occupations allegedly supervising the training of apprentices and journeymen according to standards and statutes laid down by local or state authorities. Very few of these guilds, naturally enough, enjoyed the status or the prestige of their medieval counterparts; they involved the majority of 'trades', and included shop-keepers, butchers, bakers and carpenters. Obviously they resisted industrialization, on economic rather than ideological grounds, but their effectiveness as an alternative to trade unions was weakened by the social divisions within the guilds themselves – the 'masters' being reluctant to relinquish their autonomy in the interests of their workforce. Neither could they be considered custodians of quality, since the majority attempted to undercut the prices of mass-produced goods, and where they were protected by local statutes, apparently abused such privileges as they had. Bismark, describing the situation in Frankfurt in 1853, reported: 'Here the guild system has so far remained intact, and we are spared none of the disadvantages that it brings – that is, excessive prices for manufactured articles, indifference to customers, and therefore careless workmanship, long delays in orders, late beginning, early stopping, and protracted lunch hours when the work is done at home, little choice in ready-made wares, backwardness in technical training, and many other deficiencies.'[4]

After unification in 1871 most of the restrictions imposed by the craft guilds were abolished, but the 'master artisans' still remained a significant political and symbolic force. In 1882, the General Congress of Master Artisans, protesting against proposals to lower the age of majority (when journeymen could achieve independence) from twenty-four to twenty-one, maintained that the handicraft workshop represented all those values that the state was struggling to uphold: tradition, honesty, frugality, piety and order, and that these values should be acknowledged and reinforced in the face of growing industrial unrest. 'This theme was reiterated at every masters' congress,' writes Shulamit Volkov, 'and was cited endlessly in the master artisan journals.'[5] The 1882 congress also resulted in the formation of the General Union of German Artisans (*Allgemeine deutscher Handwerkerbund*) – a state controlled organization which called for the 'legal institution of obligatory guilds, for compulsory masters' examinations, for the introduction of workers' labour books, and for the establishment of handicraft chambers to serve the masters as the supreme organs of their self-administration.'[6] This state control, however, which attempted to clarify the status and the responsibility of the 'master artisans' did not necessarily result in better standards of trade and workmanship. Its main achievement was to provide a platform for the growing conservatism and 'anti-modernism' of a large section of German society.

The English Arts and Crafts Movement, despite the radical politics of several of its supporters, was essentially conservative in that it attempted to preserve or revive traditional methods and values of workmanship. Quality in workmanship, however, was linked to an idealized concept of the quality of life of the workman, and it was these wider social and humanitarian concerns that distinguish the British nineteenth-century craft revival from the politics of the guilds in nineteenth-century Germany. The guilds were essentially reactionary: from the 1880s they were actively promoted as a bulwark against social disorder and revolution, and they came to symbolize, though rarely to demonstrate, the noble forces of genuine human dignity and self-support. 'The German Handicrafts,' said Hitler, 'rooted in a dignified tradition, will proceed to a new blooming, sheltered by *Volk* and *Staat*.' The quotation is from Volkov, who concludes, 'National-Socialist propaganda must have sounded strangely familiar to the small master artisans in Germany of the 1920s. Some of them could actually remember the experience of the late nineteenth century and recall the attitudes of their predecessors. . . . They reacted to objective economic difficulty as well as to their subjective fears of further modernization, an unfulfilled need to belong, and a deep-seated feeling of homelessness.'[7]

THE WERKSTÄTTE AND HELLERAU

There were, of course, other efforts to preserve and revitalize the crafts, among them the growing number of *Kunstgewerbeschule* with their attempts to transform the artist and

7 Glasses and carafe designed by Richard Riemerschmid, *c*. 1905

8 Wine glass designed by Peter Behrens for Benedik and Poschinger, *c.* 1901 *Reproduced by courtesy of the Trustees of the British Museum*

craftsman into the 'art-worker'. The concept of the 'art-worker', however, was challenged before the First World War by a new generation of designers and teachers, Behrens and Paul among them, who rejected the élitism in both *Jugendstil* and academic attitudes, and who, before they became involved in teaching, had contributed to the rejuvenation of the workshop tradition. In 1898 ('the revolutionary year' – as Lux was to call it – 'the official year of the birth of the modern movement in Germany')[8] *Werkstätte* (workshops) were founded in Munich and Dresden. Initially launched to demonstrate the ideal of 'art in handicraft', these organizations soon became involved in designs for semi-mass production, for a middle-class rather than an exclusive market. There were two *Werkstätte* in Munich: the founder members of the better known – the *Vereinigte Werkstätte für Kunst in Handwerk* (United Workshops for Art in Handicraft) – included Richard Riemerschmid and Paul Schultze-Naumburg, as well as Paul and Behrens (Illus. 7, 8 and 9). Also in Munich, Karl Bertsch, an architect, had founded the *Werkstätte für Wohnungseinrichtung*

9 Ceramic plate designed by Richard Riemerschmid for Meissen, *c*. 1906 *Reproduced by courtesy of the Trustees of the British Museum*

(Workshops for Domestic Furniture), and in 1907 both these organizations amalgamated with the most influential of the three, the Dresden *Werkstätte für Kunst in Handwerk*.

The Dresden Workshops were founded by Karl Schmidt who had been trained, in the apprenticeship system, as a carpenter. Schmidt visited England, and when he returned to Dresden in 1896 he completed his training. In 1898 he opened a small carpentry workshop which was so successful that he set up a training school in 1907, and in 1909 embarked on the building of the Garden City of Hellerau for his 'commune' of workers and their families. According to Lux's enthusiastic description,[9] Schmidt was self-taught, clear thinking, creative and sensitive, with 'the nature of a Quaker, a pietist, devout and clever in business'. The philosophy and development of his workshops was clearly influenced by his visit to England, his knowledge of the theories of Ruskin and Morris, and his belief in work that was a joy to the maker and the user. He had no objection, however, to the use of the machine as part of the production process, provided that the quality of the product

29

10 (*Top*) Living room with furniture designed by Richard Riemerschmid. The painting (or photograph) on the left indicates one source for the 'classicizing' ideals of 'type' furniture *Photograph from Werkbund Yearbook 1914*

11 (*Above*) A room in Richard Riemerschmid's own house *Photograph from Werkbund Yearbook 1912*

12 (*Left*) Advertisement for the Dresden Workshops. High-quality furniture is produced for domestic use, as well as for hotels, sanatoria, and ship interiors. Carpets, furnishing material, lighting fittings, etc., are also made there. It is interesting to note that Baillie Scott is one of the designers credited *Photograph from Werkbund Yearbook 1913*

13 (*Right*) Painting and assembling garden furniture in the Dresden Workshops *Photograph from Werkbund Yearbook 1913*

and the quality of the life of the workmen were maintained (for the one was dependent on the other). Like Bruno Paul, the majority of the designers working for the Dresden *Werkstätte* (who included Richard Riemerschmid – Schmidt's brother in law), concentrated on the production of *Typenmöbel* – furniture made from standardized components (Illus. 10, 11, 12, and 13). They were designers, therefore, rather than craftsmen or 'artworkers', and the majority were able to supervise the production of their work. This sense of community was, of course, reinforced by the school and the ideals for Hellerau. Schmidt's *Lehrwerkstätte und Fachschule* (training workshop and trade school), for example, attempted to destroy the barriers between the teachers and the taught: the teaching consisted of demonstrations and discussions; there were no examinations, no grades and no punishments, and with the building of Hellerau, this 'ideal' factory had its own housing, shops and schools, as well as a further spiritual and unifying dimension in music and dance. Emil-Jacques Dalcroze, the Swiss dancer and music teacher, ran a school of eurhythmics in Hellerau (a theatre, designed by Heinrich Tessenow, was built there in 1911), so that this small garden city demonstrated concepts of privilege for the workers – 'an aristocracy of workers', as Schmidt put it, 'that transcended traditional class distinctions.'[10]

The Hellerau workshops, therefore, offered in their organization and production an ideal of order both for the home and work: there were to be no distinctions between 'masters' and workmen; there was to be good housing, good schooling, and the attempt to inspire both body and mind through music and dance. All this was supported by the successful production of unostentatious, rationally-designed furniture: the practical and spiritual embodiment of the ideal of the home, as well as of the workshop.

A PHILOSOPHY OF MANUFACTURE

Concern for rationalization and order, as well as for marketable commodities and profit, had made Germany one of the leading industrial nations before the First World War. Firms like Krupps (armaments and steel), Hoechst and I.G. Farben (chemicals and dyes), Siemens and AEG (electrical equipment) were beginning, through state as well as private enterprise, to dominate world markets. Their expansion and consolidation obviously influenced the production and the demand for consumer goods, and challenged the traditional craft-based industries. Some of the reactions to this challenge have already been discussed: the crafts were supported where they were considered economically viable and because of the values associated with the ideal of craftsmanship.

At the turn of the century, however, the inevitability of industrialization was acknowledged by the majority of Germany's design theorists and reformers, and their debates were concerned first with attempts to define an aesthetic for industrial 'culture', and second with the social implications of industrialization. These efforts to establish a philosophy of design for industrial production involved issues that had been identified by nineteenth-century theorists. Gottfried Semper, for example, in *Wissenschaft, Industrie und Kunst*,[11] an essay describing his reactions to the Great Exhibition in London in 1851 noted that, 'objects, in which the seriousness of their use does not allow for anything unnecessary, e.g., coaches, weapons, musical instruments and their like, sometimes showed a higher degree of soundness in decoration and in the methods by which the value of functionally-defined forms is enhanced.' Such objects had more 'integrity' than the consumer goods on show there, because their forms, following the laws of mechanical selection and construction, were logical rather than arbitrary. Semper's preoccupation in this essay, and in his other writing, was with the nature and evolution of style, and his theories, which influenced both the evaluation and the teaching of applied design in England as well as Germany, will be discussed in other contexts. Semper's main concern, however, was with the determinants for form, rather than with the form-giver: a complex issue which questions the autonomy as well as the role of the designer. According to Semper, the stylistic confusions of the Great Exhibition, which he described as a 'babel of the arts' were 'nothing but a clear expression of certain anomalies in the existing state of society'. Both Ruskin and Morris were to share the conviction that style is a reflection of the society that creates it. Semper, however, in spite of his radical politics (he had come to England as a political refugee from the Dresden uprisings of 1848) believed that design was an evolutionary rather than a revolutionary process, and that the decorative work in the Great Exhibition reflected a state of transition in both the art and the science of design. 'While our art industry will muddle on without direction,' he wrote, 'it will unwittingly perform a noble deed by destroying traditional prototypes with ornamental treatment.' This thirst for ornament, he believed, demonstrated a crisis of confidence: whereas in former cultures design developed according to need (both practical and spiritual), industrialization had created new needs which still had to find formal expression. Form, or style, however, could not be imposed by 'the whims of the artist . . . or powerful patrons';[12] it was determined by material and technique – what Semper called 'means'. 'The machine,' wrote Semper, 'knits, sews, embroiders, carves, paints, invades far into the domain of human art, and puts every human skill to shame. . . . The abundance of means is the first serious danger with which art has to struggle. This term is perhaps a paradox – there is no lack of abundance of means, but rather a lack of ability to master them.'[13] Acquiring the mastery of means, however, came through knowledge of materials and techniques, rather than through the acquisition of taste. The designer of the future, therefore, should not be taught to imitate past forms in academies, but should learn his skills through the apprentice-ship system. 'A brotherly relationship between the master and his journeymen and apprentices will signal the end of the academies and industrial schools, at least as we know them today,'[14] wrote Semper, anticipating the preoccupations of German educationalists at the turn of the century.

BEHRENS AND AEG

This ideal of apprenticeship – the acquisition and transmission of practical skills – was difficult to relate to the factory system, which involved not only the division of labour, but the distancing of the designer from the actual processes of production. During the nine-

14 One of the AEG showrooms designed by Peter Behrens *Photograph from Werkbund Yearbook 1912*

teenth century relationships had been established between the designer and the traditionally craft-based industries (textiles, ceramics, glass, etc.), but the role of the designer in large-scale industrial concerns, whose success was fundamental to economic survival, was more difficult to establish. Peter Behrens's appointment to AEG (*Allgemeine Elektricitäts Gesellschaft*) set the precedent, and marked the emergence of a new type of patron (the 'enlightened' industrialist concerned with every aspect of the design of his empire) as well as a new type of designer: the consultant who was responsible for all those concerns, from posters, advertisements and shop-window displays, through to products and the architecture and housing (including furnishing) of the corporation's workers.

Peter Behrens was appointed as 'artistic adviser' to AEG in 1907, four years after his appointment to the *Kunstgewerbeschule* in Düsseldorf. AEG had been founded by Emil Rathenau in 1887. Rathenau had visited the Paris Electrical Exhibition in 1881, and had formed a joint stock company with the Edison Company in the United States in 1883: the early success of the firm was ensured by the support of German banks, and by the establishment of trading and research agreements with its largest rival, Siemens & Halske.[15] Walther Rathenau, Emil's son and Behrens's patron, described his father's vision. When Emil '. . . saw this little bulb alight for the first time, he had a vision of the whole world covered with a network of copper wires. He saw electric currents flowing from one country to another, distributing not only light but power – energy that would become the blood of the economy and would stimulate its movement and growth. In his mind's eye he saw changes in the structure of populations as communications took on a new form – changes which had not been fully realized. Looking into the future he saw the possibility of extracting metals and other rare materials from the bowels of the earth by the force of electric power. He vowed that he would devote his life to electricity. He saw many things that have not yet come to pass but that will come about in the future. Such was his gift of prophetic vision.'[16] (His 'prophetic vision', sadly, did not extend to the twenties: Walther Rathenau, a liberal and a Jew, was in charge of German economic policy during the war; he became Minister of Reconstruction and then Foreign Minister in the Weimar Republic, and was murdered by a group of nationalists in July 1921.)

Before Behrens's appointment, AEG had already employed architects and designers: Otto Eckmann, who was associated with the *Jugendstil* group in Munich, had designed posters and publicity material; Franz Schwechten (now remembered as the architect of the *Kaiser Wilhelm Gedächtniskirche*, the gaunt ruined church in the centre of West Berlin) had designed several of its factories, and Alfred Messel had designed the firm's headquarters on the Friedrich-Karl-Ufer in 1905.[17] Behrens was initially appointed to design 'artistic shapes for arc lamps and all accessories';[18] the 'accessories' included kettles, tea-pots, window displays and exhibition buildings (Illus. 14, 15, 16, and 17). He then began to work on larger architectural commissions, including the Turbine Factory, which was completed in 1909. Behrens, therefore, was the first designer to be put in charge of a large industry's 'corporate identity'; in spite of the innovative nature of his appointment,

15 Brass electric kettle, designed to imitate handwork. Peter Behrens for AEG, 1908 *Reproduced by courtesy of the Trustees of the British Museum*

16, 17 Electric coffee pot and electric fan both designed by Peter Behrens for AEG, 1908 *Fan photograph Henning Rogge*

34

however, his designs for the domestic market (including the furniture for the workers' housing) followed traditional prototypes, while his industrial design, for the most part, was confined to the modification of existing products. Nevertheless, Le Corbusier, who spent four months in Behrens's office in 1911, described him as 'a powerful, profound, serious genius, gripped by an urge to impose control; he is as if created for these tasks and for this time: most congenial to the spirit of present day Germany'.[19] Behrens's expression of control is demonstrated in the classicizing forms of his architecture, and in the conservative nature of his products. He was neither a radical thinker, nor, after he left Darmstadt, a radical designer; but he was evidently a powerful organizer, and, as at Düsseldorf, he had the ability to identify potential in the appointments he made to his expanding office. Adolf Meyer, his former student, as well as Walter Gropius, joined Behrens soon after his appointment, and Mies van der Rohe began to work there in 1908.

In *The New Architecture and the Bauhaus* Gropius described his debt to Behrens: 'It was Behrens who first introduced me to logical and systematical co-ordination in the handling of architectural problems. In the course of my active association in the important schemes on which he was engaged . . . my own ideas began to crystallize as to what the essential nature of building ought to be. I became obsessed with the conviction that modern constructional technique could not be denied expression in architecture, and that that expression demanded the use of unprecedented forms. Dynamic as was the stimulus of Behrens's masterly teaching, I could not contain my growing impatience to start on my own account. In 1910 I set up in independent practice.'[20] In spite of this accolade, Gropius's 'growing impatience', as Alan Windsor indicates, was also related to tensions between the two architects, of a practical rather than an ideological nature.

Gropius was, of course, writing with hindsight, but his preoccupation at that time with 'modern constructional technique' and 'unprecedented forms' (which were to be interpreted in several ways in his programmes for the Bauhaus) was to be emphasized in the memorandum about housing construction that he wrote to Emil Rathenau in 1910. The memorandum, headed *Programme for the establishment of a company for the provision of housing on aesthetically consistent principles*,[21] blames speculation and bad management for the deterioration 'both in taste and durability' of current buildings in Germany. The solution is 'to implement the concept of industrialization of house construction' by introducing standardized components for both the construction and the equipment of the home. The result would not necessarily mean dull uniformity, since each house would maintain 'an individual personality through variations in form, material and colour'. There would, however, be 'artistic uniformity' – the expression of the *Zeitgeist*: 'a convention, in the best sense of the word, cannot be hoped for by emphasizing individuality. It results, rather, from the achievement of an integration that will develop from the rhythm of repetition and from the uniformity of proven and recurring forms.' Gropius's concept of 'uniformity', however, and of 'proven and recurring forms', bore no relationship to the work that Behrens was producing for AEG. With this memorandum, the first definition of his theories, Gropius was rejecting the craft tradition, and declaring his allegiance to the spirit of the collective, and to ideals that would eventually destroy the Bauhaus. The implications of such theories were to be widely debated in Germany and one focus for these debates was the Werkbund, an energetic and reformist organization which, prior to 1914, had identified many of the conflicts relating to design in inter-war Germany.

3 THE WERKBUND

The Werkbund was formed in Munich on 5 October 1907, and the majority of its twenty-four founder members had been associated with reform movements in Munich and Dresden. The *éminence grise* of the organization, however, was Hermann Muthesius (Illus. 18). Muthesius was the son of a master-mason. Although he was based in Berlin for most of his professional life, he was born in Saxe-Weimar. As well as working for his father, he studied at the *Real-gymnasium* in Weimar, and from there he went to Berlin to read philosophy. From 1883 to 1887 he studied architecture. Before his appointment to the Prussian civil service he had travelled widely; he had worked for a German architectural firm in Tokyo, and had built a German evangelical church there; before returning to Germany he visited China, Siam, India and Egypt. His appointment to the Prussian Board of Trade gave him the opportunity to study and report on British architecture and design, and some bureaucratic influence over the organization of Prussian design schools. He was also the mouthpiece for official attitudes to design reform, and in this capacity he was certainly no sycophant. He was a prolific writer, and developed his ideas in books, speeches and articles. The most influential of his books, prior to the formation of the Werkbund were *Stilarchitektur und Baukunst* (1903), and the three-volume *Das Englische Haus*, published in 1904 and 1905. This thorough documentation of English domestic architecture is now well known following its belated translation into English.[1]

The book is in part a celebration of the English way of life, and an ideal of the home, with its comfort and order, its rituals of tea and toast and its excellent plumbing. At the same time, however, Muthesius felt that this preoccupation with ease and comfort could signal a twilight of the gods for the English, since it had failed to advance the potential of the two traditions – the one domestic and vernacular and the other industrial – on which their reputation and economic survival were based. Most of the houses that Muthesius was writing about were those commissioned by the affluent upper middle classes, who were building themselves a past. Muthesius recognized this and the élitism it implied: 'The curse which lies upon their products' (he was writing about furniture), 'is one of economic impossibility.' In fact Muthesius only seemed to feel really at ease in the English bathroom, where he found 'a completely new sort of beauty . . . the beauty of practical purpose'.[2] 'Here', he wrote, 'we have a really new art which needs no creation to succeed, an art based

18 Hermann Muthesius. Pencil drawing by his son Günther Muthesius *Courtesy Wolfgang Muthesius*

on actual modern conditions and modern achievements, and perhaps one day, when all contemporary fashions purporting to be modern artistic movements have passed away, it will seem to be the most eloquent expression of our age.' He also discusses the nature of 'modernity' in *Stilarchitektur und Baukunst*, which was published before *Das Englische Haus*: it was, he maintained, the British gospel of *Sachlichkeit* and truth to materials that, inspired his demand for 'modern means' to meet 'modern needs'. For 'true modernity', he claimed, lay in 'reason and practicality', and was demonstrated not only by the vernacular traditions of a truly popular culture, but also by the pure forms created by those 'children of the new age', the engineer and the industrialist.[3]

Ideas such as these were to become the stock in trade of 'progressive' design theorists for the next three decades. Muthesius's proto-modern movement pronouncements have tended to be eclipsed, partly by the more rousing iconoclasm of some of his successors' declarations, and partly by his rejection of the new 'expression of the age' when it was demonstrated in the Werkbund Siedlung (housing estate) at Weissenhof in 1927. In 1903, however, Muthesius was anticipating subsequent dogma when he proclaimed the advent of a new style, the 'style of the future', that would emerge from the cultural chaos of his own epoch. Like Adolf Loos and Le Corbusier, he saw in the *Jugendstil* the death throes of historicism rather than the seeds of regeneration, and like the idealists of the twenties he was convinced that the emergence of a new architecture would go hand in hand with the emergence of new spiritual values. Such philosophies were acceptable in Germany in so far as they encouraged the ideal of German supremacy in design and trade (for at its most basic level Muthesius's brief was to improve Germany's standing in her export markets). But when Muthesius attacked the bastions of German culture he aroused a furore that led first to the formation of the Werkbund, and then, when he spelled out the implications of his ideas, to a polarization of ideologies within that organization.

The 'Muthesius case', as the *cause célèbre* which led to the formation of the Werkbund was called, was triggered off by a speech Muthesius made, early in 1907, to the newly-formed Berlin *Handelshochschule* (Trade School). In it he reiterated his condemnation of what he called the 'surrogate' styles of historicism (an attack on the teaching in some of the *Kunstgewerbeschule*) and the *Jugendstil*, and repeated his belief that industry, rather than the artist, had the vigour and the energy to inspire a new cultural revolution: for German art, he declared, was bankrupt. Germany's artists and sculptors were virtually unknown abroad, her architects were among the most reactionary in Europe, and her reputation in artistic matters had sunk so low that 'German' and 'tasteless' were virtually synonymous. In the ensuing débâcle there were lobbies (which went to the Kaiser) for Muthesius's resignation, while his supporters, mainly drawn from the *Werkstätte* and related circles, announced the formation of a Werkbund – an alliance of artists, architects, designers, tradesmen and manufacturers – that would promote Muthesius's cause.

Muthesius himself did not attend the inaugural meeting of the new organization, for fear of compromising it. Its founder members, however, included several small firms, members of the Munich and Dresden *Werkstätte*, Joseph Hoffmann and Josef Olbrich of the prestigious Vienna *Werkstätte*, as well as designers, architects and teachers. The 'founding' firms included Peter Bruckmann & Söhne, who produced silverware (Bruckmann was to be an active and articulate member of the Werkbund, and was its President from 1909–16, and again in 1926), several printers and publishers, including Eugen Diederichs and the

Gebrüder Klingspor, Wilhelm & Co (a metal workshop) and Gottlob Wunderlich, weavers. The individuals represented various aspects of the social, aesthetic and educational theories that had been developing in Germany over the past decade. Peter Behrens, Bruno Paul and Richard Riemerschmid were founder members. Theodor Fischer, the organization's first Chairman, taught architecture at the *Technische Hochschule* in Munich where his pupils included Walter Gropius and Bruno Taut; (the young Dutch architect J. J. P. Oud spent some time in his office in 1911). Fritz Schumacher (who was to die of malnutrition after the Second World War) taught architecture at the *Technische Hochschule* in Dresden where his students included Heckel, Kirchner and Schmidt-Rottluff, founders of the *Brücke* group of painters. The architect Paul Schultze-Naumburg had also been a founder member of the *Deutsche Bund für Heimatschutz* (the *German Society for the Protection of the Homeland*) in 1901. He, like Fischer and Schumacher, was concerned with the conservation of traditional culture; unlike them, his ideals for the promotion of a national art and design led him to join the Nazi party. He was appointed head of the former Bauhaus in Weimar in 1930, and succeeded in obliterating all traces of the Bauhaus there.

MUTHESIUS AND THE WERKBUND

In 1907, therefore, the bitter and conflicting ideologies of the 1920s and 1930s were latent in the aspirations of the Werkbund. When it was first founded, however, the organization was united by the uneasy unanimity of most pioneering gestures. In the period up to 1914, Muthesius was its most powerful protagonist. He was elected Vice-President in 1912, and as Joan Campbell points out, he 'devoted his energies to expanding the Werkbund's influence, provided it with useful government contacts, and to a great extent succeeded in imposing his views on the association.'[4] The aim of the organization according to a statement drawn up in 1910 was to promote the 'best in art, industry, craftsmanship and trade', and to co-ordinate 'all those efforts to achieve quality that are evident in industrial endeavour'. From the outset, therefore, the Werkbund included 'trade' as well as 'industrial endeavour' in its programme for reform (Illus. 19). A theory, however, was needed to define 'best' and 'quality' as well as 'industrial endeavour', and a programme had to be established to implement these ideals. Muthesius had no time for a pragmatic approach: '. . . Eclecticism proves the absence of rigour and organization' he maintained in *Wo Stehen Wir?* (*Where do we stand?*),[5] a major policy statement to the Werkbund Congress in Dresden in 1911. Here, with references to Schinkel, and quoting Greek, Roman, Gothic and eighteenth-century precedents, Muthesius made an impassioned plea for the reinstatement of the mystical and at the same time disciplining ideal of form. The concept of form, which, he claimed – like poetry and religion – was 'a secret creation of the spirit', had been destroyed by the barbarities, both commercial and spiritual, of the nineteenth century. It was the task of the Werkbund, now that the initial battles for quality had been more or less won, to reinstate and demonstrate an ideal of form. 'Until recently', he stated, 'the primary concern of the Werkbund has been with quality; so much so that the need for quality, both in workmanship and material, is now generally accepted throughout Germany. This does not mean that the Werkbund's task has been fulfilled. For spiritual considerations are more important than material ones, and higher than function, material and technique stands form. The first three aspects may be impeccably achieved, but if form is ignored we are still living in a coarse and brutish world. So there

19 Illustrations from the *Werkbund Yearbook 1914*. The Werkbund, as well as illustrating applied design in its publications, also included photographs of ships, planes, etc., to demonstrate its concepts of functionalism.

20 Caricature from *Simplicissimus*, 1914, of the Muthesius/van de Velde confrontation. Van de Velde
has the 'individual' chair, Muthesius has the 'type-chair', and the carpenter, with no drawings or
calculations, has the 'real' chair

remains before us a clear goal, a great and important task: the revival of the feeling for
form, and the revitalization of architectonic sensibility.'

The main thrust of Muthesius's criticism was directed at architecture, for he believed
that design in general, as well as the arts, would be influenced by the 'revitalization of
architectonic sensibility'. Architecture, he maintained, strives towards the typical (*typischen*),
and he spelled this out again in the discussion which followed his speech: 'If a new
conception of today's architecture can be detected then it is this; we are in the process of
returning from an individual to a standard way of thinking.' In Muthesius's philosophy,
therefore, objectivity, reason and intellect replaced intuition, individuality and creativity
as the inspiration for form, and ideal form acquired the classical connotations of the pure,

the absolute and the universal (or the typical). Some Werkbund members, however, for personal as well as ideological reasons, resented Muthesius's assumption of cultural authority. They believed that his motives were political rather than cultural, and they saw his attack on individualism as a threat to creativity and as a denial of the autonomy of the artist. 'Sooner or later', wrote the art critic Robert Breuer, 'it was inevitable that the Individualists who recognized only their inner demon and nothing else in the world, would come into conflict with the Diplomatists of the typical, the organizers of an elevated general standard.'[6] These conflicts came to a head in July 1914, in the Werkbund's seventh annual meeting held before the opening of its first major exhibition in Cologne. Muthesius had prepared a ten-point manifesto as a policy statement and Henry van de Velde, acting as spokesman of the individualist lobby, had overnight, and with the help of willing printers, produced a blow by blow counterblast.[7] Muthesius's statement summarizes and clarifies the theories he put forward in *Wo Stehen Wir?* (Illus. 20).

THE 1914 DEBATE

'Architecture,' he begins, 'together with all the activities of the Werkbund, is moving towards standardization (*Typisierung*). Only by means of standardization can it achieve that universality characteristic of ages of harmonious culture.' Standardization for Muthesius, therefore, was a philosophical as well as a practical imperative; it was a metaphor for universality and the expression of unity in art, architecture and design. It involved the transcendence rather than the suppression of individuality; the re-establishment of a universal language of form that could be related to German ideals and German culture, and at the same time establish the identity of German products in the export market.

Van de Velde's riposte concentrated on the freedom and the hegemony of the artist. 'So long as there are artists in the Werkbund, and so long as they are influenced by its fate, they will protest against the imposition of orders or standardization. The artist is, in essence, a total individualist, a free spontaneous creator: he will never, of his own accord, submit to a discipline which imposes on him a canon or a type.' He believed that the materialistic preoccupation with exports lay like a curse on German industry. Glass by Tiffany, Copenhagen porcelain, silverware by Jensen and the books of Cobden-Sanderson were not designed for export. They were the creation of individuals, first appreciated and sponsored by individuals and finally generally acknowledged. Types and standards evolved through years of individual endeavour and they could never be imposed: the quality of German design (*Kunstgewerbe*) was beginning to be recognized abroad, so it was the Werkbund's task to consolidate what had been achieved, rather than attempt to adopt or superimpose a new and alien mould.[8]

These arguments demonstrate the conflicting theories that the Werkbund and its members had inherited from nineteenth-century polemics. Muthesius's belief in typeforms that would express the spirit of the age is allied to the theories of Semper, who believed that style was determined by need, materials, function and use. Van de Velde's rejection of such determinism was rooted in the Arts and Crafts rejection of the spirit of the age, and its conception of the designer as custodian of humanistic values. The subsequent debate, therefore,[9] reads like a summing up of nineteenth-century attitudes and a rehearsal for subsequent arguments about the nature and the role of the designer in the twentieth century.

21, 22 Interior and exterior of the Fagus Factory, Alfeld-an-der-Leine, designed 1911 by Walter Gropius and Adolf Meyer. The intended 'transparency' of the façade has been destroyed by the necessity for blinds and curtains *Photographs from Werkbund Yearbook 1913*

The 'individualist' lobby – a powerful one which included August Endell and Hermann Obrist from the old guard in Munich, as well as younger men like Bruno Taut and Walter Gropius – urged Werkbund members to be on their guard against the 'great German failing . . . the tendency to fossilize in systems and dogma' (Hermann Obrist); to remember that beauty was the expression of a personal pilgrimage that could have nothing to do with the materialistic demands of the export market (Endell), and to acknowledge the creative artist as the ultimate form-giver and arbiter of standards (Bruno Taut – who also called for a dictatorship of culture rather than profit, nominating van de Velde and Poelzig as

dictators). Walter Gropius's role in this confrontation is an interesting one. He had joined the Werkbund in 1910 while he was working for Behrens and in 1911 had completed, with his partner Adolf Meyer, his first major commission – the shoe-last factory at Alfeld-an-der-Leine (Illus. 21, 22). One might assume from the tone of his memorandum to AEG about standardized housing components that he would be sympathetic to Muthesius's ideals. Gropius's article on the *Development of Modern Industrial Architecture* which was published in the Werkbund Yearbook of 1913 makes it clear, however, that he believed that it was the artist or architect (he uses the terms interchangeably) who would determine the form of these buildings: 'The more freely he (the artist/architect) is allowed to display his originality in the new language the more the building will provide the asset and advertisement the firm desires.' Muthesius's stress on the '*typisch*' in architecture ran counter to Gropius's theories about the architect's role in determining the future development of architecture and concepts of form – so much so that he became one of Muthesius's most outspoken opponents, and wrote to the Werkbund leadership urging that he should be asked to resign. (As Franciscono points out, it may well have been Gropius's attitude at this time that prompted van de Velde to recommend him, along with Endell and Obrist, as his successor at Weimar.)[10]

Support for Muthesius came from Peter Behrens, Richard Riemerschmid and the Munich branch of the Werkbund. Wilhelm Ostwald, the colour theorist, claimed that the artist should work for the nation rather than for himself or an individual patron. Friedrich Naumann, a former Protestant minister and a Christian Socialist who had been associated with Hellerau and who joined the Werkbund when it was founded, also supported Muthesius. (In *Der Deutsche Stil*, published in Hellerau in 1912, Naumann had written: 'Our whole national export planning is dependent upon the machine because the world market will tolerate only standardized goods. . . . What we need is large scale industrial production, not the magic of the small workshop, the zeal of the individual craftsman, and the good old craft traditions.')[11]

In his own defence Muthesius explained that the sacrifices he demanded were in the interests of unity. He wished to see the practical and the ideal reconciled in an architecture that would both serve and express the highest aspirations of society. Such aspirations, he maintained, transcending national boundaries, might be given practical as well as architectonic expression in a style that was truly international. These anticipations on Muthesius's part of what we now call the International Style remained theoretical, however. Some fourteen years later he was to describe Weissenhof, the Stuttgart suburb sponsored by a new Werkbund generation, as 'Cubist' and 'formalistic'.[12] It was the Cologne Exhibition of 1914 which probably provided a more faithful reflection of Muthesius's ideals for a 'universal' architecture. For here 'style' was represented by stripped down classicism in Peter Behrens's Festival Hall and Joseph Hoffmann's Austrian Pavilion, and by the vernacular in workers' housing – the *Niederheimische Dorf* – a rustic settlement designed for industrial workers by Georg Metzendorf, who had designed workers' housing for Krupp.

Ironically, the use of classicism for monumental architecture and the vernacular for domestic building also represented the ideals of the Third Reich, so that the 'modernism' of the pioneers of the 1920s and 1930s became a symbol not only of progress in the Muthesian sense, but of protest.

PART II   THE BAUHAUS IN WEIMAR

The Werkbund exhibition opened in Cologne in July 1914. In August 1914 the First World War broke out, and 'within days, the halls that had housed the finest products of Germany's industry and crafts were converted to receive wounded soldiers from the front'.[1] The war, and the subsequent peace terms were, of course, catastrophic for Germany, although the organization of the war-time economy was to contribute to developments in peace-time industry. Deprived of essential imports of raw materials, German research and industry concentrated on developing substitutes and, as William Carr noted, 'the era of *Ersatz* started in Germany; aluminium formerly imported from Switzerland was extracted from German clays and replaced copper in munitions and electrical fittings; wood-pulp products kept textile mills going: nitrate of cellulose replaced cotton in the manufacture of explosives. . . .'[2] Walter Rathenau, by then director of AEG, was appointed director of a government-sponsored War Raw Materials Department which co-ordinated these activities, so that the major part of production was under state control. Muthesius was also able to demonstrate the practical implications of his ideal of *Typisierung* (standard-ization) when he, together with Peter Behrens, worked on a committee to formulate proposals for industrial standardization (*Normenausschuß der deutsche Industrie*), based on American mass-production methods. The proselytizing for sobriety in design, now con-fined to the home market, continued in 1915 with the publication of the *Deutsche Warenbuch* with illustrations of modestly priced products (Illus. 23).

This preoccupation with the organization of a wartime economy must be contrasted with the human, emotional and social impact of the war and its aftermath. When the armistice was declared on 11 November 1918, Germany had lost two million dead, and was on the verge of revolution. During the week before the signing of the armistice workers and army garrisons in major ports and cities throughout Germany had mutinied, setting up their own army and workers' councils. The Kaiser abdicated on 9 November, and a republic was proclaimed. The German radicals and revolutionaries, the most articulate among them being the Spartacus League led by Karl Liebknecht and Rosa Luxemburg, hoped for a repeat of events in Russia. The German Communist Party was founded in Berlin in December 1918; less than a month later Liebknecht and Luxemburg, together with many Communist Party members, were murdered by a right-wing army faction in

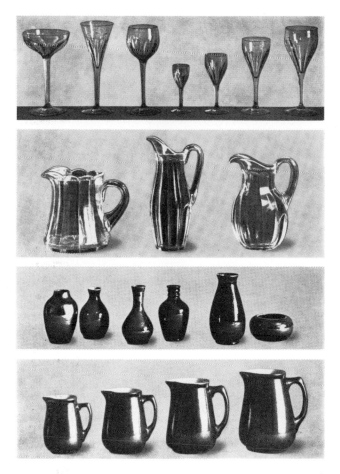

23 A page from the *Deutsches Warenbuch* published in 1915 to illustrate ranges of modestly priced products

Berlin, and in February 1919 Friedrich Ebert, a moderate socialist, was appointed first President of the new republic. The new national assembly was convened in Weimar, a town with liberal traditions, and it was in this explosive political situation that Walter Gropius came to Weimar to form his new school of architecture and design.

Weimar was, and still is, an 'art town'. Bach, the Cranachs, Goethe, Schiller, Herder and Liszt had lived there. The castle, seat of the Dukes of Saxe-Weimar, is now a museum and art gallery (with a Bauhaus collection), its grounds a vast public park, with Goethe's 'garden house' beneath a hill which leads to the Am Horn suburb. To the east is the cemetery, with Gropius's memorial (now restored) to the workers assassinated in the Kapp Putsch of 1920. Another memorial on the outskirts of the town marks the site of Buchenwald.

Before the First World War, the town's income was mainly derived from agriculture. Jena was the only major industrial city in Saxe-Weimar, and Weimar itself, with 40,000 inhabitants, had several small, mainly craft-based industries. An art academy had been established in the town in 1860 under Ducal patronage, and in 1910 this became a *Hochschule für bildende Kunst*, training both painters and sculptors. (Although it was essentially an academic institution Max Beckmann, Hans Arp and Hans Richter had studied there.) In 1902 Grand Duke Wilhelm Ernst invited Henry van de Velde to Weimar with a brief to revitalize both craft and industrial production.[3] Van de Velde began by running a private 'seminar' for drawing, modelling and craft-work. 'The Craft Seminar,' wrote van de Velde to Gropius in 1915, 'was so infrequently consulted that a few years later I founded the School of Arts and Crafts, in order to prepare and develop the younger generation of Weimar in all areas of the crafts.'[4] The school, which was designed by van de Velde, opened in 1907 with printing, weaving, ceramics, book-binding and precious metal workshops; van de Velde also built new premises for the art academy on the same site, so there were practical, if not ideological, links between the two schools. It was, however, an uphill task for van de Velde, who was resented partly because he was a foreigner, and partly because of his avant garde ideas. Weimar preferred to foster its historical and local traditions, and the 'cosmopolitanism' that he represented was suspect, especially with the growing nationalism and xenophobia of the years leading up to the war. By 1915 his position there, as a foreign national, was untenable, and he resigned, nominating Walter Gropius, August Endell and Hermann Obrist as possible successors to his post. When he left for Switzerland in July 1915 the school was closed, its workshops dismantled and the building was used as a military hospital during the war.

GROPIUS AND WEIMAR

In 1915 Gropius was thirty-two and a lieutenant in the army. He had established his reputation as the architect of the Fagus factory and the Model Factory in the Cologne exhibition (Illus. 24), and had also designed furniture and ceramics as well as a diesel locomotive and sleeping car for the railway factory at Königsberg. Born in Berlin, he came from a family of artists, architects, academicians and administrators. Carl Wilhelm Gropius (1793–1870) was a painter and a theatre designer; he was a member of the Berlin Academy, and in 1827 opened a diarama there with paintings by himself, his brother Ferdinand and Schinkel, the neo-classical architect. Martin Gropius, his great uncle, was an architect, and designed the *Kunstgewerbe Museum* in Berlin; his father, also Martin, was its principal in 1877, as well as director of education in Prussia. The *Gebrüder* Gropius and their lineage were therefore well established in Berlin (Illus. 25); Walter Gropius and his partner Adolf Meyer were building up a successful architectural practice before the war, and it seems strange that Gropius, once alerted to the possibility of replacing van de Velde at Weimar, should work with such tenacity to secure his position there. He could not have foreseen, at the outbreak of war, the dearth of architectural work in the immediate post-war years; and in spite of his support for van de Velde in the Werkbund debate of 1914, the attractions of a post in a small art school in a historical but provincial city did not seem to match his ambitions, particularly since the Grand Duke had specified a replacement who would work in the 'new national spirit' which Karl-Heinz Hüter interprets as 'neo-Biedermeier and neo-classical'.[5]

24 Corner detail of Gropius's 'Model' factory at the Cologne Exhibition 1914

25 *The Atelier of the Gebrüder Gropius*, oil, Eduard Gaertner, 1830 *Preussischer Kulturbesitz*
Photograph: Jörg P. Anders

There were two points in Weimar's favour, however. First, van de Velde was an international figure and it was no mean achievement to be asked to replace him, and second, it seemed from the outset that there was a possibility of Gropius's establishing a school of architecture there. After van de Velde's departure the Weimar Academy and State Council began to formulate proposals for the reopening and reorganization of the *Kunstgewerbeschule*. Fritz Mackensen, the director of the academy, wrote to Gropius in October 1915 suggesting that the *Kunstgewerbeschule* should be replaced by a Department of Architecture and Applied Arts, that this should be part of the Academy and that Gropius should direct it. Gropius's reply is brisk and to the point: 'What I envision (*sic*) is an autonomous teaching organism, which of course has to develop from a modest base, but which is artistically *independent* and which perhaps (at first) is administratively *co*-ordinated with the existing academy. . . . On all essential matters I would be able to work well only according to my *own* ideas. . . . The *absence of restrictions* must be an explicit condition. . . .'[6] This was followed by a request from the Weimar State Council for Gropius to expand his ideas about a school of architecture, and for him to give an 'explanation of the kind of influence the crafts would receive from the artistic side and from the giving of instruction in handicrafts to masters, journeymen and apprentices'. Gropius replied from the front, outlining his ideals for a collaboration with art and industry – essentially a Werkbund-inspired statement – but one which consolidates his alignment with Muthesius's opponents in its emphasis on the role of the artist as custodian of culture and the avant garde. Handwork and the applied arts, he maintained, had never entirely lost their 'feeling for art'; concentration in improvements in the crafts, therefore, was no longer essential: the challenge lay in persuading industrialists of the value of art. Industrial products, however, should not imitate craft-made goods. In the past the craftsman combined the skills of the artist, the technician and the retailer. Industry had the advantage of mass-production; it lacked the skill, however, to make this production artistic. Artists must be trained, therefore, to work with industry . . . 'for the artist possesses the ability to breathe soul into the lifeless product of the machine, and his creative powers continue to live within it as a long ferment. His collaboration is not a luxury, not a pleasing adjunct; it must become an indispensable component of the total output of modern industry.'[7]

A school organized to teach artists to collaborate with industry could perhaps be conceived in the spirit of the medieval *Hütten* (lodges) in which artists, architects, sculptors and craftsmen of all kinds worked together towards a common goal. The revival of this spirit, adapted to contemporary requirements, would contribute to the emergence of a new style. This statement, with its emphasis on art rather than architecture, anticipates the ideals that Gropius attempted to achieve when he arrived in Weimar. In 1916, however, the Weimar authorities were somewhat alarmed by it. In theory, they maintained, it was excellent, but Gropius's ideas about handwork were rather vague. Their main concern was with craft, rather than machine production, so perhaps Endell should be persuaded to accept the post.[8]

The war curtailed further negotiations, but in 1918 Gropius began to press his claims again. With the November revolution, the old order in Weimar was (temporarily) discredited; the need for new priorities was acknowledged, and at the same time Gropius's suitability for the post was upheld by Wilhelm von Bode, director of the Berlin Museum, and a pillar of the establishment. In March 1919, in the period of confusion following the revolution, Gropius's position as the head of the school was confirmed. He was given permission to take over the school, which was to be renamed the *Staatliches Bauhaus*. Characteristically, the first memorandum that Gropius wrote to the new authorities was a detailed statement of the budget he required.[9]

THE BAUHAUS MANIFESTO

The negotiations leading up to the formation of the Bauhaus reveal Gropius as a tough administrator and shrewd politician. The Bauhaus manifesto, however, is written by an idealist and a visionary:

> *The ultimate aim of all creative activity is the building!* The decoration of buildings was once the noblest function of the fine arts, and the fine arts were indispensable to great architecture. Today they exist in complacent isolation, and can only be rescued

from it by the conscious co-operation and collaboration of all craftsmen. Architects, painters and sculptors must once again come to know and comprehend the composite character of a building both as an entity and in terms of its various parts. Then their work will be filled with that true architectonic spirit which, as 'salon art', it has lost.

The old art schools were unable to produce this unity; and how, indeed, should they have done so, since art cannot be taught? Schools must be absorbed by the *workshop* again. The world of the pattern-designer and applied artist, consisting only of drawing and painting, must at last and again become a world in which things are *built*. If the young person who takes joy in creative activity begins his career now, as he formerly did, by learning a craft, then the unproductive 'artist' will no longer be condemned to inadequate artistry, for his skills will be preserved for the crafts in which he can achieve great things.

Architects, painters, sculptors, we must all return to the crafts! For these there is no such thing as 'professional art'. There is no essential difference between the artist and the craftsman. *The artist is an exalted craftsman.* By the grace of Heaven and in rare moments of inspiration which transcends the will, art may unconsciously blossom from the labour of his hand, *but a foundation in handicraft is essential for every artist.* It is there that the primary source of creativity lies.

Let us therefore create a *new guild of craftsmen* without the class distinctions that raise an arrogant barrier between craftsman and artist! Let us together desire, conceive and create the new building of the future, which will combine everything – architecture *and* sculpture *and* painting – in a *single form* which will one day rise towards the heavens from the hands of a million workers as the crystalline symbol of a new and coming faith.[10]

It would be simplistic to dismiss this statement, with its stress on craftsmanship, as an attempt by Gropius to ingratiate himself with the Weimar authorities. In the first place it was a revolutionary statement, and the bureaucracy in Weimar was essentially reactionary. Again, in spite of its incantatory tone, it represents Gropius's thinking at that time, and it also contains theories that Gropius was to reiterate, in less exclamatory terms, in later statements about the nature and the work of the school. It is, at its most basic, a demonstration of Gropius's continued support for the ideals of the anti-Muthesius faction following the Werkbund debate of 1914. Gropius's colleagues then included Hermann Obrist, Bruno Taut and Hans Poelzig, and these and other architects, together with the art and architectural critic Adolf Behne, resumed their activities immediately after the end of the war when they founded the *Arbeitsrat für Kunst* in Berlin. The Working Council for Art (there were others in most major cities) was formed in the revolutionary spirit of the Workers' Councils and Soldiers' Councils; the *Novembergruppe*, a similar proselytizing society, was launched at the same time in Berlin, as well as the short-lived 'Glass Chain', a 'correspondence club' initiated by Bruno Taut. All three shared a nucleus of common membership as well as certain common characteristics: first, an allegiance to the revolutionary ideas for a fraternity of the arts that were emerging from Russia; second, a belief that such a fraternity should be committed to the demonstration of a totally new art that would combine painting, sculpture, craftsmanship and invention in a new unity of expression based on spiritual rather than formal properties; and third, the conviction that the culmination of this art would be architecture – 'the crystallized expression of man's noblest thoughts, his human nature, his faith, his religion'.

The quotation is taken from Walter Gropius's contribution to the catalogue of the *Exhibition of Unknown Architects* held in Berlin in 1919. The exhibition was one of the many activities sponsored by the *Arbeitsrat* to promote its ideas and to widen its membership; for after being launched by Bruno Taut and Adolf Behne, the *Arbeitsrat* was reconstructed in April 1919 under the joint presidency of Gropius, Behne and César Klein, the painter. Before the group was disbanded early in 1921, its membership included Max Taut (Bruno's less volatile brother), Otto Bartning (who was to take over the Weimar school when Gropius left), the Expressionist painters Ernst Heckel and Emil Nolde, and the sculptor, Gerhard Marcks, while Adolf Meyer, Hermann Finsterlin and Eric Mendelsohn were among its official 'Friends and Sympathisers'. The *Novembergruppe*, which survived until the late 'twenties, had a similar membership; founded by Max Pechstein, César Klein and Eric Mendelsohn, its members included Lyonel Feininger, Hans Poelzig, Peter Behrens, Mies van der Rohe, the Tauts and the Luckhardt Brothers, while contributors to the 'Glass Chain' included the Tauts, Gropius, Mendelsohn and Finsterlin.

The ideas that Gropius put forward in his founding manifesto for the Bauhaus, which was written at the same time as his *Arbeitsrat* statements, were reflections of *Arbeitsrat* ideologies. The Bauhaus manifesto, in fact, is a collage of sentences and paragraphs from the *Unknown Architects* catalogue, and Gropius's contribution to *Ja! Stimmen des Arbeitsrat für Kunst in Berlin*, a pamphlet which was published to coincide with the exhibition in Berlin.[11]

Gropius's theories in the *Ja! Stimmen* document are also repeated in the first 'Programme for the Staatliches Bauhaus in Weimar' which was issued in April 1919 together with the manifesto.[12] In both he maintains that art cannot be taught, but craftsmanship can, and that architects, painters and sculptors are craftsmen in the fullest sense of the word. In both he says that the school is the servant of the workshop, and will one day be absorbed into it, and in both he proclaims the priority of creativity and individuality. The programme, however, gives practical details about the examination system and the 'Range of Instruction' offered. There were to be 'master and journeyman examinations according to Guild statutes'; fees were to be paid, which 'will gradually disappear entirely with increasing earnings from the Bauhaus'. There were to be six categories of craft training ('the basis of all teaching at the Bauhaus'): sculpture (including stonemasons, woodcarvers, ceramic workers and plaster casters); metal-work (blacksmiths, locksmiths, founders, metal-turners); cabinet-making; painting and decorating (glass-painters, mosaic workers, enamellers); printing (including etchers, wood-engravers, lithographers, art printers) and weaving. Instruction in drawing and painting, which is listed separately from craft-training, included the traditional subjects: 'landscape, still-life, composition and free-hand sketching from memory and imagination'. It also included 'the design of furniture and practical articles', the design of lettering, and 'the design of exteriors, gardens and interiors'. Colour theory, the science of materials and basic business studies were also to be taught, as well as art history – 'not presented in the history of styles, but rather to further an understanding of historical working methods and techniques'.

The programme, to say the least, was over-ambitious, and there were conceptual as well as practical difficulties with a scheme which aimed to achieve a new architecture through the amalgamation of seemingly traditional approaches to teaching art and craftsmanship. Admittedly Gropius maintained in the introductory statement, that the 'unified work of art – the great structure' was the 'ultimate, if distant aim of the Bauhaus'. At the same time there was no indication how the craft and fine art training would be directed to achieve this ultimate aim, how the distinctions between fine art and craftsmanship were to be abolished, how a cross-disciplinary approach could be established if the guild system of training and examination were to be restored, and how the 'priority of creativity' and 'freedom of individuality' were to be reconciled with 'strict study discipline'.

The problem facing Gropius was that of transforming a traditional fine art academy and a defunct *Kunstgewerbeschule* into a 'house of building', which would demonstrate a unity of the arts – the *Gesamtkunstwerk* – in revolutionary rather than reactionary form. Gropius's terminology, which he shared with members of the *Arbeitsrat für Kunst* was revolutionary in intent, but the programme he put forward was related to that of a conventional craft school.

26 Cover for the Bauhaus proclamation; woodcut on coloured paper, Lyonel Feininger, 1919 *Busch-Reisinger Museum, Harvard University*

The Bauhaus manifesto and programme was a recruitment document as well as a statement of intent, and copies were sent to art, craft and architecture schools, as well as to newspapers. If its content, with its stress on craftsmanship, was at that time acceptable to the Weimar authorities, the image chosen to represent these aspirations – the 'Cathedral of the Future' woodcut by Lyonel Feininger – was anathema (Illus. 26): all the more so since Feininger was the first appointment that Gropius made to the newly constituted school. In 1920, Wilhelm von Bode, regretting his earlier support for Gropius, summed up their apprehension: 'Gropius had presented me with a programme that to me appeared a little radical, but was quite acceptable in its essential points. He elucidated it verbally, to the effect that he was primarily concerned, as I am, with the re-establishment of the crafts; that he intended first to enlist only competent craftsmen and to train young people thoroughly in the crafts for some years – fine art would have to come later! And then he started right off with the appointment of Feininger!'[1]

Feininger, whom von Bode described as a 'Cubist', had in fact been associated with Weimar since 1906 when he had set up a studio there. He was born, however, in New York in 1871 and his parents were German. They returned to Germany in 1887 with their sixteen-year-old son, who had intended to train as a musician but who decided, when he reached Germany, to become a painter. He studied at the *Kunstgewerbeschule* in Hamburg and in Berlin and, like Bruno Paul, he first earned his living as an illustrator and a cartoonist. He visited Paris several times while he was establishing himself as a painter and after the war he joined the *Novembergruppe* and the *Arbeitsrat für Kunst*. It was these associations, as well as his painting, that impressed Gropius. Feininger, however, could scarcely be described as a 'Cubist' painter; if he is to be associated with a 'movement' in art, he must, in spite of the delicacy of his work with its muted colours and linear tensions, be categorized as an Expressionist. He drew and painted landscapes, seascapes (Illus. 27) and cities – towns with churches, towers, medieval and modern buildings. This duality, the evocation of the past to transform the present, which is characteristic of Expressionist painting as well as *Arbeitsrat* statements, is also inherent in the Bauhaus manifesto. The cathedral image, as presented by Gropius and represented by Feininger, however, owed nothing to the spirit of Weimar, especially as the three five-pointed stars which crown its

27 *Bathers*, oil, Lyonel Feininger, 1912 *Busch-Reisinger Museum, Harvard University*
28 (*Right*) Terracotta frieze for the entrance hall of Gropius's 'Model' factory in Cologne by Gerhard
   Marcks. Stained glass window by César Klein

spires seemed symbolic, not of the unity of art, architecture and craftsmanship, as Feininger
intended, but of Bolshevism.

When Gropius arrived in Weimar, the spirit of the November Revolution was very
much in evidence there, for although the new National Assembly had chosen the town for
its temporary headquarters because of its cultural and a-political associations, it was some
time before the political and cultural *status quo* was re-established. In January 1919 more
than a thousand workers had demonstrated against the Liebknecht and Luxemburg
murders, and during the following months there were demonstrations against the National
Assembly and unemployment. In March 1920, when right-wing military forces in Berlin,
led by the journalist Wolfgang Kapp, tried to seize power, there were demonstrations in
several German cities, including Weimar, where nine workers were shot by the military
contingent. Gropius's monument to the *Märzgefällene* was commissioned in 1920 and

erected in 1922. By that time, however, the school had few local supporters and Gropius was fighting to keep it in the town.

There were three major sources of opposition to the school's presence in Weimar: the local bureaucracy, the staff of the former art academy, and the representatives of local trades, who regarded its activities as a threat to their livelihood. The first furore about the school's alleged political affiliations is worth examining, since the issues involved anticipate the problems the Bauhaus was to face throughout its existence. In December 1919, a conference, organized by the 'Free Association of Civic Interests' was held in Weimar. The first item on the agenda was *The New Art in Weimar*, and the speaker, Dr Kreubel, attacked the school for its 'Spartakist/Bolshevist' tendencies. One of the students, Hans Gross, spoke at the meeting, and in phraseology that is reminiscent of Langbehn, called for a new leader of German art – a 'man of steel and iron' – who would express 'the German spirit'. 'You have many people who are supposed to be German, but you despise them. . . . The revenge is cruel for a people that renounces itself. Bear in mind that you are German! *Think* and act!'[2] As a result Gross had his grant withdrawn and left the school, together with thirteen other students. The school, said Gropius, was concerned with work not politics. 'If the Bauhaus becomes a playground for political games, it will collapse like a pack of cards. I have always stressed this, and watch like Cerberus to keep politics of any kind out of the school.' The Gross affair was particularly threatening, since it involved nationalism, racism and a rejection of that concept of unity that Gropius had evoked in the foundation manifesto. The implications of the incident were sufficiently serious for the Ministry of Culture in Weimar to order an investigation, and their report is significant in that it describes the Bauhaus as an essentially German institution. The document states that 'only three students from outside the Reich hold scholarships', and that these three were already at the academy when the Bauhaus was formed. Again '. . . concerning the allegation that elements alien to the race, specifically Jews, were unduly pushing themselves into the foreground, and were seeking to lead and dominate the Bauhaus with their ideas . . . it would be strange if seventeen Jews – all the others are of Aryan origin – were able to dominate two hundred other students.'[3] Although the Ministry gave the school a clean bill of health, this is a very ambiguous statement. However, having rid the school of Gross and his colleagues, Gropius clearly wanted to avoid a confrontation on nationalistic and racial grounds. Again, when the teaching programme came under attack when he was fighting for a renewal of his budget in July 1920, his defence was that training in the school was conventional rather than avant garde, and entirely in keeping with developments that were taking place in other schools of art, design and architecture throughout Germany.

THE FIRST APPOINTMENTS

It was inevitable that Gropius would come into conflict with the existing staff at the art academy when he began to implement his programme, for they clearly believed, in spite of the spirit of the manifesto, that they would be concerned with art, while the new appointments would concentrate on the training of craftsmen and draftsmen. The arrival of Feininger, a painter and a 'Cubist' in May 1919 was, as we have seen, disquieting. Gropius had also made two further appointments: Gerhard Marcks and Johannes Itten, who were to start teaching at the school in October 1919. Marcks, a sculptor and a member of the *Arbeitsrat* had, in academic terms, a respectable pedigree. He was a craftsman as well as an

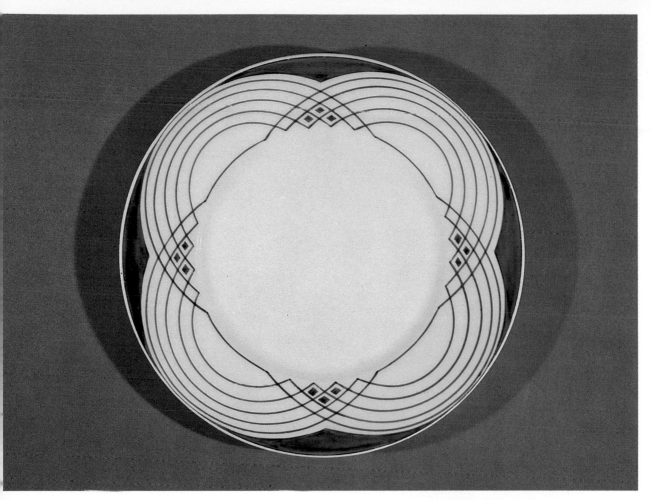

Pl. 1 Plate designed by Peter Behrens, for
Bamscher, Weiden, *c. 1901 Reproduced by
courtesy of the Trustees of the British
Museum*

Pl. 2 Pitcher in earthenware, thrown by Max
Krehan, designed by Gerhard Marcks,
1921/22 Kunstsammlungen, Weimar

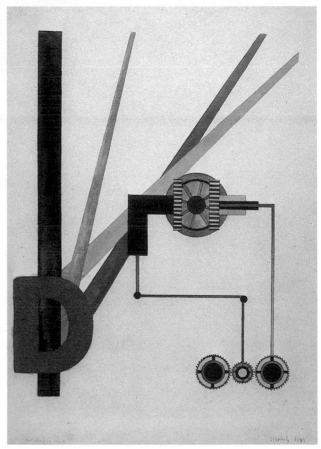

Pl. 4 *Architecture*, oil, Paul Klee, 1923 *Bildarchiv Preussischer Kulturbesitz*

Pl. 5 (*Above right*) *Composition*, collage and gouache, Moholy-Nagy, *c.* 1921 *University of East Anglia Collection*

Pl. 6 (*Right*) Chair in polished cherry, Marcel Breuer, 1922 *Kunstsammlungen, Weimar*

Pl. 3 (*Left*) *Swinging*, oil on board, Wassily Kandinsky, 1925 *The Tate Gallery, London*

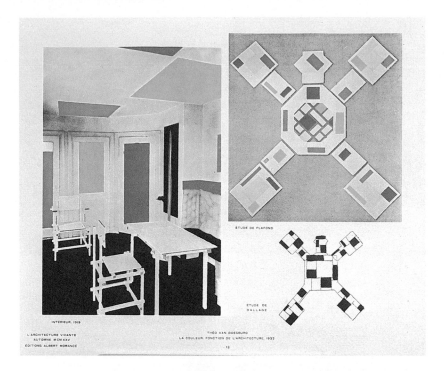

ÉTUDE DE PLAFOND

ÉTUDE DE DALLAGE

INTÉRIEUR, 1919

L'ARCHITECTURE VIVANTE
AUTOMNE MCMXXV
ÉDITIONS ALBERT MORANCÉ

THÉO VAN DOESBURG
LA COULEUR, FONCTION DE L'ARCHITECTURE, 1923

13

artist, and had worked in ceramics (Illus. 28 and 29). He designed ceramic sculpture for the entrance hall of Gropius's 'model' factory at the Cologne Exhibition. Marcks was also a teacher and had worked briefly with Bruno Paul at the Berlin *Kunstgewerbeschule*. Johannes Itten was, at that time, an unknown quantity. He was running his own private school in Vienna, and had been introduced to Gropius by Gropius's charismatic first wife, Alma Mahler, the widow of Gustav Mahler. Before Itten's arrival, however, Gropius had his first confrontation with the old guard of the academy when the students put on an exhibition of their work in June 1919. The majority of the work – painting and graphics – was produced under the direction of the former professors (now masters) of the academy who had rejoined the newly constituted school, and the exhibition, held in order to decide which students should be awarded scholarships, provided Gropius with his first oppor-

29 Animals in earthenware by Gerhard Marcks *Handwerkliche Kunst in Altes und Neues Zeit* Werkbund publication, 1920

Pl. 7 (*Top left*) Interior of Schroeder House, designed by Gerrit Rietveld. From *L'Architecture Vivante*
Pl. 8 (*Far left*) Tea-infuser in bronze, with ebony and silver base and mount. Designed by Marianne Brandt, 1924 *Kunstsammlungen, Weimar*
Pl. 9 (*Left*) Tapestry in wool by Hedwig Jungnick, 1921–22 *Kunstsammlungen, Weimar*

tunity to attack academicism and to restate the aims of the school. Lyonel Feininger, writing to his wife, described how Gropius 'intended to deal harshly with and go against certain elements uncompromisingly', and how Max Thedy's group 'got the worst of it, being represented entirely and without exception by good and dry academic work'.[4] Gropius used his speech at the opening of the exhibition to restate his ideals for art and the artist in a post-war society.[5] 'We are living in chaotic times,' he said, and the exhibition reflected the chaos. He had seen paintings, carefully finished, and in beautiful frames, but who were these paintings for? 'We find ourselves in a colossal catastrophe of world history, in a transformation of the whole of life and the whole of the inner man.' Many of the students had returned from the front; their experiences there had changed them completely, and no one could go back to the certainties of pre-war days. Those days were over and society must be transformed 'not by large spiritual organizations, but from within, by small, secret self-contained groups' (he used words with guild and masonic associations – *Bünde, Logen, Hütten*). Inspired by individuals, individualism will be transcended in the creation of the total work of art 'which will shine its abundance of light on to the smallest objects of everyday life'.

This speech, however heroic in intent, was seen as an attack on the autonomy and the independence of the fine artist as well as on traditional systems of art education, and the New Art in Weimar speech six months later was obviously prompted by the anxieties and intrigues of the teachers in the former art academy, who by then were pressing for Gropius's resignation. Their most articulate supporter in this campaign was Dr Emil Herfurth, a member of the National People's Party who, in a pamphlet published in February 1920,[6] emphasized the weakness of the Bauhaus programme: 'Parallels to past ages, much as they flatter the ear, always bear many a concealed flaw.' He accused Gropius of 'artistic dictator-ship' and asserted that, 'in a state institution for the fine arts complete freedom for artistic work must be guaranteed. . . . At Weimar, Expressionism is the apparently solid but single brace which holds the new "building" together.' Moreover, 'the "cheerful ceremonial" which according to the programme of the Bauhaus determines the conduct of its students, has nothing in common with youthful freshness and healthy vigour.'

The need to counter these accusations of anachronism, dictatorship and decadence became even more urgent after the Kapp Putsch, when Weimar became the capital of Thuringia. Gropius needed credibility as well as funds to further his programme, and in order to achieve this he persuaded his Werkbund associates to oppose suggestions for his dismissal, so that a petition signed, among others, by Peter Behrens, Theodor Fischer, Richard Riemerschmid and Fritz Schumacher, all pillars of the art and architectural establishment, was sent to the authorities urging that Gropius be given the time to establish his ideas.[7] Again, when he spoke in defence of the school's programme at the Thuringian assembly in July 1920, Gropius stressed that his ideas were in no way original. The majority of the leading art, design and architectural schools in Germany had similar ideals and they had the funds to implement them. A comparison of their grants with the financial support he had requested would prove that Gropius's demands were extremely modest, particularly since there was no equipment in the school when he arrived there.[8]

Gropius, therefore, was able to speak the language of the visionary as well as the bureaucrat, and it was his ability to inspire, provoke and, where necessary, conciliate that ensured the school's survival during the first year in Weimar.

The survival of the school, of course, depended on the revival of the workshops, and this was complicated by the fact that under van de Velde's leadership they combined both state and private enterprise. There were workshops for book-binding and metal work within the school, but van de Velde owned the printing workshops, and the weaving, carpet and gold and enamel workshops were also privately owned. In spite of van de Velde's complaints about lack of interest in his activities (see p. 50), these were undoubtedly lucrative. Van de Velde's salary, as head of the *Kunstgewerbeschule*, was four thousand marks, but he claimed to earn an additional eighty to one hundred thousand marks from personal commissions.[1] Gropius's statement in his 1919 memorandum that the workshops would eventually finance the school was, therefore, not mere rhetoric.

Most of Gropius's time and energy during the Weimar period, therefore, was spent on political manoeuvres, and on efforts to re-equip and finance the workshops. Printing, print-making and book-binding, which were already well established within the Fine Art Academy, presented few problems. The weaving workshops were privately owned, but Hélène Börner, who had run them in collaboration with the van de Velde school, continued to work for the Bauhaus. Sculpture and wood-carving also survived within the Fine Art Academy, but Gropius had to set up carpentry, metal and ceramics workshops, as well as facilities for mural work and glass-painting (Illus. 30–33).

The metal workshop which according to the original prospectus was intended to train 'blacksmiths, locksmiths, founders and metal-turners', as well as 'enamellers and chasers' opened at the end of 1919, with the emphasis on the skills of the goldsmith and silversmith, rather than the blacksmith. The potters had access to the kilns of a local stove manufacturer in Weimar, but this arrangement inhibited experiment and training; the craftsmen of Bürgel, a local pottery town, wanted nothing to do with the school, and it was not until October 1920 that the workshop was established in Max Krehan's pottery at Dornburg, about twenty-five kilometres outside Weimar, the stables of Dornburg Castle providing the extra space needed. The glass-painting and mural workshops were also launched in 1920, but the carpentry workshop was not established until the autumn of 1921, when the wood-carving workshop in the Academy was rebuilt. During the first two years in Weimar, therefore, it was a constant struggle to transform the ideal into reality. As Oskar Schlemmer

30–33 Workshops in the Weimar Bauhaus (*Above left*) Weaving workshop (*Right*) Metal workshop (*Opp. top*) Sculpture workshop (*Bottom*) Carpentry workshop *All pictures courtesy Hochschule für Architektur und Bauwesen, Weimar*

remarked in a letter to Otto Meyer in August 1920 (four months before he was to join the school): 'Incredibly, the workshop equipment, which was in beautiful shape before the war, was sold during the war, so that there is hardly even a planing bench left; and this is supposed to be an institute "based on craftsmanship". Building, even in the most Utopian sense, can hardly be considered.'[2]

Nevertheless Gropius continued to make appointments to the school, although their terms of reference and their relationship to the activities of the workshops were somewhat ambiguous. Neither Feininger, nor Paul Klee, who joined the staff at the same time as Schlemmer, was assigned to a workshop. Schlemmer had a similarly open brief, and

34 Earthenware tea pot and milk jug designed by Otto Lindig, *c.* 1920
35 (*Right*) Coffee pot in white porcelain, designed by Otto Lindig for the Staatliche Manufaktur,
    Berlin, 1923

hoped that he would 'not have to be a real teacher'.[3] Georg Muche, who arrived in 1921,
went there, he said 'not because of the programme, but because of the people'. He made it
clear to Gropius that 'the art of handwork was not my thing. The ideas of Ruskin, Morris
and the German Werkbund were not for me. . . . I wanted to remain a painter, and not
become involved in polemics about the social significance of art.'[4] He was, however,
appointed *Formmeister*, first in the woodwork shop and then in the weaving workshop,
where he guarded his independence: 'I promised myself never in my life to weave a
thread, tie a knot, or make a textile design with my own hand. I have kept that promise.'[5]
It was only Gerhard Marcks, therefore, who had already worked in ceramics, who was
able to adapt to the ideal of workshop production. The location of the Dornburg pottery

70

isolated its masters and apprentices from the day-to-day pressures on the Bauhaus. Its original owner, Max Krehan, a master-potter, came from a family of potters, and, according to Scheidig, 'worked in the traditional, almost folk-art manner, supplying the needs of the little rural town and countryside around, unaffected by designers or reformers of the late nineteenth or early twentieth century'.[6] At first the pottery workshops continued to produce these traditional designs in earthenware that was thrown or moulded and then painted or glazed – Gerhard Marcks in some cases decorating the traditional shapes with abstract patterns as well as figurative designs (Pl. 2). The contribution of Otto Lindig (Illus. 34) to the workshops was perhaps just as important as that of Marcks and Krehan. Lindig had worked for a Thuringian porcelain manufacturer before he joined the van de Velde school in 1913; he transferred to the sculpture department in the Fine Art Academy when the *Kunstgewerbeschule* closed, and had his own studio there. Nevertheless, he elected to work in Dornburg, and together with Theo Bogler, an apprentice potter, transformed the regional designs, first by experimenting with shapes and forms within the craft tradition, and then by producing prototypes for mass production. In their 'craft' designs Lindig and Bogler were obviously experimenting with a range of techniques to demonstrate both formal and practical innovation. In some of the work, the accentuation of the handles, lids, spouts and bases is almost grotesque. In others pure form predominates, and new production processes enabled them to achieve the sharp rims and conical lids that were to become a hallmark of twentieth-century production in Scandinavia as well as Germany. By 1923 a range of kitchenware and a porcelain coffee set by Theo Bogler were in production, as well as a range in white porcelain by Otto Lindig (Illus. 35). The success of this workshop demonstrated the feasibility of the Bauhaus ideal; nevertheless its situation, and its students and staff, were unique in that most had some experience of working with the medium before they joined a well-established workshop, and they obviously relied on collaboration rather than conflict (however creative) to achieve their goals.

In Weimar, however, there was confusion and a multitude of convictions: '. . . the Bauhaus programme has attracted a fearless band of young people (we have a crazy sampling of modern youth),' wrote Schlemmer. 'All this means that the Bauhaus is "building" something quite different from what was planned – human beings. Gropius seemed very aware of this; to his mind the academies made a grave mistake by neglecting the formation of the human being. He wants an artist to have character, and this should come first, not later. Yet at times he appears alarmed at the outcome: no work gets done, but there is a great, great deal of talk . . . the young men express their inner confusion by throwing aside conventions and inhibitions and sliding into the Great Indolence.'[7] This letter was written in February 1921, a month after Gropius had formalized the school's statutes and teaching programme. The *Statutes of the Staatliches Bauhaus in Weimar*[8] confirm and extend the foundation document of 1919, and some of the regulations reflect the problems associated with 'fearless bands of young people'. Attendance was compulsory, materials and equipment had to be treated with care; the students were liable for any damage they caused within the school and all work produced within the Bauhaus was to remain the property of the school. Major decisions were made by a Council of Masters who were responsible to the Ministry of Culture, and student representatives were able to submit recommendations to the Council. The curriculum, admissions policy and examinations policy were clearly set out and Regulation 6, dealing with examinations, reads: 'Apprentices who have joined a workshop after their successful completion of the six-month probationary period, conclude an apprenticeship agreement with the Apprenticeship Board. At the end of the legally set duration of their apprenticeship and after fulfilment of the legal requirements, apprentices may enrol for their journeyman's and journeymen for their master's examination. The examinations are taken before the Apprenticeship Board, and the Council of Masters respectively.' The traditional guild system of training and examination was, therefore, maintained, but this document introduced the now familiar concepts on which the training in Weimar was based: first that there should be a six-months' probationary period, and second that the workshop training was by a 'master of craft' and a 'master of form' – 'both masters [working] in close collaboration with each other' (Illus. 36).

The celebration of painters as form-givers was fundamental to early twentieth-century design theory. Le Corbusier evoked the aid of 'painters and sculptors, champions of the art

36 Plan of the training programme in Weimar

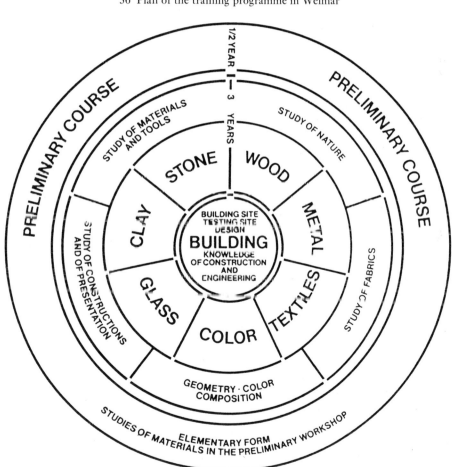

of today' in formulating the new architecture[9] and De Stijl philosophy, as interpreted by van Doesburg (see pages 93–96) was based on the assumption that abstract painting demonstrates universal laws of form. Gropius, however, believed that the skill and vision of the painter could be directly related to industrial production. 'Modern painting,' he wrote, in *Idee und Aufbau des Staatlichen Bauhauses Weimar (The Theory and Organization of the Bauhaus)*[10] 'breaking through old conventions, has released countless suggestions which are still waiting to be used by the practical world. But when, in the future, artists who sense new creative values have practical training in the industrial world, they will themselves possess the means for realizing those values immediately. They will compel industry to serve their ideas and industry will seek out and use their comprehensive training.'

This optimistic statement was written in 1923, when the school put on its first major exhibition, which could be (and was) interpreted as a vindication of Gropius's policies. Admittedly *Idee und Aufbau* presents an idealized and edited account of the first years at the school, but the conviction that the students should be taught by artists as well as craftsmen was fundamental to Gropius's theories of education. He saw the methods of the *Kunstgewerbeschule* as élitist and outdated, and he strove towards a synthesis of the arts – the ideal of the collective as formulated in the *Arbeitsrat für Kunst*. That most of his first appointments to the staff were drawn from *Arbeitsrat* or *Novembergruppe* circles indicates that he was trying not only to attract artists of 'character', but artists who were sympathetic to ideals. Again the fact that neither Feininger, nor Schlemmer, nor Klee professed any interest in 'formal' teaching was immaterial: they were there to provide the leaven. Confusions about their role, however, led to confusions within the school. The majority of the students in the early years, attracted by the charisma of the Bauhaus and its staff, went there to be 'modern' painters, rather than practical craftsmen, and in any case the state of the craft workshops did not encourage practical work. 'One may say with some justification,' wrote Schlemmer in 1921, 'that the Bauhaus is a beautiful façade, a concept, an idea for Germany, shored up by the names of a few artists and a programme.'[11] Gropius, however, had other ideas for the school, and his tenacious belief in the validity of his programme and his subsequent campaign to spread its gospel throughout Western Europe led to a canonization of the ideal (rather than the reality) of its teaching methods especially in the early years. For Gropius claimed to be training the 'architects of a new civilization'. 'That was why we made it a rule in the Bauhaus that every pupil and apprentice had to be taught throughout by two masters working in the closest collaboration with each other; and that no pupil or apprentice could be excused from attending the classes of either. The Practical Instruction was the most important part of our preparation for collective work, and also the most effective way of combating arty-crafty tendencies.'[12]

This was Gropius speaking with hindsight: the rules, the certainties and his description of the steady and inevitable progress towards 'collective' work were certainly not reflected in the day-to-day life of the school in Weimar. The promotion of the ideal of the 'collective' implied a rejection of individualism in both the product and the producer: an idea that was resisted by most of the students and the staff. It also implied a redefinition of the relationship of 'art' to industry. The Weimar Bauhaus, therefore, was not a 'beautiful façade', it was a battle ground where concepts of 'progress' and universality were demonstrated in conflicting theories and a variety of forms.

Ironically, it was Johannes Itten, the only new appointment to the staff with any consistent experience of teaching, who was to present the greatest challenge to Gropius's ideals for the school. Itten arrived in Weimar in the summer of 1919; he left the school four years later, but during those four years his approach to teaching and his conception of creativity reinforced the ambiguities of the school's programme, challenging Gropius's attempts both to clarify his own priorities, and, at the most basic level, to establish some semblance of the order and direction required by the bureaucrats.

In 1919, however, Johannes Itten seemed an ideal candidate for the Bauhaus; he was a teacher and a painter, and he had rejected academic traditions in both professions. Itten was born in Switzerland, trained as an elementary school teacher in Berne, and began teaching children in 1908, attempting to 'respect and guard the indescribable wonder of humanity in every child of man'.[1] He taught children for a year, studied painting in Geneva, and after vacillating for some time about whether he would continue painting or become a school teacher, he went to the Stuttgart Academy which was then run by Adolf Hölzel, 'a man,' according to Oskar Schlemmer, 'the likes of whom cannot be found at any of Germany's academies of art'.[2]

Itten met Schlemmer at Stuttgart, and Ida Kerkovius, who was his tutor there (and who came, at the age of forty, to Weimar to study at the Bauhaus). It was Hölzel, however, who determined Itten's teaching methods, and his approach to painting, both as a teacher and a practitioner. ('As a teacher,' wrote Itten, 'he was receptive to everything new.'[3]) Hölzel is chiefly remembered today for his work on colour theory, and his investigations into the relationship between colour and sound. Hölzel also initiated studies of 'old master' paintings, not within the context of art historical or academic analysis, but as expressions of form, as well as emotion, demonstrated through light and shade. He encouraged his students to experiment with collage, and began each session with 'eurhythmic' exercises.

Itten remained in Stuttgart for three years (from 1913–16) before moving to Vienna to set up a private school there. Little is known about his time in Vienna. He described it as a 'city . . . full of sombre tensions',[4] and himself as 'totally isolated'.[5] He met Schönberg, Berg and Adolf Loos there, however (as well as Alma Mahler). Loos, who through his friendship with Kokoschka, had been associated with the *Sturm* circle before the war, organized an exhibition of Itten's paintings in 1919. Although there seem to be no records of his meeting Franz Cizek, Itten knew his work and some of his students.[6] By 1913, when Itten arrived in Vienna, Cizek was head of the department of education in the *Kunstgewer-beschule* there, and had established an international reputation for his encouragement of freedom and spontaneity in children's art, and for the extension of these methods to the training of art and design students. Cizek's work with children was well known in Germany before the war (there had been an exhibition of his pupils' work in Dresden in 1912) and it was no doubt the success of these methods, and Itten's association with them, together with his growing reputation as a teacher and a painter, that encouraged Gropius to invite him to Weimar.

The Preliminary Course (which Itten always referred to as the Basic Course) was officially 'announced' in the January 1921 statutes, which state that: 'Every applicant will at first be admitted only for a trial period of six months. This probationary period can be suspended only in exceptional cases of special talent, artistic maturity and personal know-ledge. During this period the preliminary course is obligatory. This course consists of elementary instruction in form, in conjunction with studies of materials (in the experi-mental craft workshops).'[7]

Itten (who had brought with him fourteen of his students from Vienna) began the course in the autumn of 1919. 'Walter Gropius,' he wrote, 'generally gave me complete freedom with the structure and theme of the course.' During the first winter, when the students had 'neither chairs nor tables', and 'worked squatting on the floor',[8] they would come into the school for one day a week. Since 'self-discovery' was one of the basic aims of the teaching, Itten did not find this a major drawback. The course, however, was carefully structured. 'Three tasks,' writes Itten, 'were set for me in the Basic Course:

1. To free the creative powers and thereby the art talents of the students. Their own experiences and perceptions were to lead to genuine work. The students were to free themselves gradually from dead conventions and to take courage for work of their own.

2. To make the students' choice of career easier. Here the exercises with materials and textures proved a valuable aid. In a short time each student found out which materials appealed most to him; whether wood, metal, glass, stone, clay or yarn best stimulated him to creative activity. Unfortunately, at that time we lacked a workshop for the Basic Course in which all fundamental skills, such as planing, filing, sawing, bending, glueing and soldering, could be practised.

3. To convey to the students the fundamental principles of design for their future careers. The laws of form and colour opened the objective world to the students. In the course of the work the objective and subjective problems of form and colour were integrated in many ways.'[9]

These aims and intentions have been quoted in full, since they not only sum up Itten's (and presumably Gropius's) ideals for the Basic Course, but they also indicate its ambi-guities, which anticipate several of the issues that were to divide the school. Itten's pro-gramme, for example, presents certain assumptions about the nature of 'art', and its relationship to 'design' that the school was never able to resolve. Creativity, experiment and the rejection of 'dead conventions' were essential – empty studios and workshops, therefore, were welcomed 'so that the new could be built without much tearing down of the old'. At the same time, however, the 'fundamental' craft skills – planing, filing, sawing – were also necessary for the expression of the 'new', creativity being related to the 'fundamental principles of design' which the students would discover, both intuitively and intellectually, thus reconciling the rival claims of subjectivity and objectivity, and making 'new ideas take the shape of art'.

THE TEACHER AS 'MAGUS'

In order to achieve these aims, therefore, Itten was attempting to transform rather than reject certain assumptions about the nature of art and design that were already inherent in nineteenth-century theory. The recognition of the unique qualities of the individual, with its stress on self-expression and self-discovery, had been acknowledged in ideals for child-education throughout the nineteenth century, and these ideals were already being associated with the 'liberation' of the artist before the First World War. The need to demonstrate and express the nature and qualities of materials in design and architecture were fundamental to arts and crafts philosophies, and the concept of some kind of 'preliminary' course in art and design education that would both 'liberate' the student, and direct him or her towards an appropriate specialization was, as we have seen, not a new one. The conviction that there were certain definable 'principles of design' and 'laws of form and colour' was also fundamental to nineteenth-century design theory. Itten, however, believed that these laws could be interpreted and understood both intuitively and objectively, and it was his method of achieving and demonstrating this fusion that led to the confrontations that forced him to leave the school. For Itten's semi-mystic, semi-didactic conception of the teacher as 'magus' who would guide his disciples through personal experience to a personal expression of the material world, ran counter to the guild system of instruction that the school was pledged to follow.

In its methods and its structure, the course was in many ways based on the ideas that Itten had gained from Hölzel's teaching. The study of contrasts, the analyses of 'old master' paintings, the colour theory and the breathing and concentration exercises were all part of the training in Stuttgart. What made Itten's course seem so radical were his stress on the achievement of objectivity through empathy or personal experience, and his cult of Mazdaznan, which reinforced the mystical dimension of Hölzel's teaching. In his book *Design and Form: The Basic Course at the Bauhaus*, first published in 1963, Itten makes very few references to Mazdaznan. 'I studied oriental philosophy,' he writes, 'and concerned myself with Persian Mazdaism and Early Christianity. Thus I realized that our outward-directed scientific research and technology must be balanced by inward-directed thought and forces of the soul.'[10]

At its most basic level, Itten's philosophy was an extension of nineteenth-century Romanticism and pre-war Expressionism, in that it demanded a fusion between experience and expression. In order to achieve this fusion, however, Itten's students had to relate spiritual to physical experience. Before they drew a circle, for example, the students had to *experience* a circle, swinging their arms 'first simply, then together, in the same and opposite directions';[11] before drawing tigers they roared like tigers; before expressing the weeping Mary Magdalen in Grünewald's crucifixion, they were meant to break down and weep. A similar approach was adopted in the study of materials and texture. The students absorbed the qualities of materials by touching, handling, blending, contrasting and drawing from memory. They used 'found' materials to create montages, collages and bizarre structures. 'A whole new world was discovered,' Itten wrote, '. . . Manual abilities were discovered and new textures invented. They started a mad tinkering, and their awakened instincts discovered the inexhaustible wealth of textures and their combinations. The students discovered that wood could be fibrous, dry, rough, smooth or furrowed; that iron could be hard, heavy, shiny or dull. Finally they investigated how these textural qualities could be represented.'[12] The results of these experiments have a Dada-like quality (Illus. 37, 38 and 39). The students' exercises, however, were not intended to demonstrate a random combination of forms and textures, and their 'mad tinkering' was not play, nor an anarchic gesture against the assumed conventions of design, but, as Itten insisted, it was meant to provide a 'sensuous' appreciation of the qualities of materials that would lead to an understanding, on both an intellectual and emotional level, of their potential for design in various media. Studies of form and three-dimensional design were similarly structured. The 'three basic forms' – the square, the triangle and the circle – were first experienced through gesture and motion; they were then modelled in clay so that the student 'could feel these forms three-dimensionally',[13] and then the forms were represented graphically, as pattern, as studies in proportion, or as attempts to convey, through light and shade, the third dimension on a two-dimensional plane.

Given the meagre resources of the Bauhaus at this time, and the lack of workshop facilities, Itten's basic course could simply be seen as a triumph of ingenuity. The students took what was available to them, and made something out of nothing. Itten's teaching, however, obviously encouraged creativity, analysis and invention, and at the same time transcended the dogmas of abstraction and representation. Felix Klee, who joined the course (as its youngest member) when he was fourteen, was 'fascinated by his personality, his teaching ability, and his overwhelming imagination',[14] and describes Itten's lectures – the analyses of Old Masters, the commentaries on the materials studies and the introduction to life drawing – as 'eye-opening'. 'Itten was often merciless and unbending in his judgements, but never unfair.'[15]

MAZDAZNAN

The course, however, was far from undogmatic. It was dominated by Itten's philosophy and personality, and as he became more deeply involved with Mazdaznan, Itten assumed, among the students, the character of a saint, a tyrant or a clown. Paul Citroen, who joined the course soon after Itten was introduced to the doctrines of Mazdaznan, wrote: 'There was something demonic about Itten. As a master he was either ardently admired, or just as ardently hated by his opponents, of whom there were many. At all events, it was impossible to ignore him. For those of us who belonged to the Mazdaznan group – a unique community within the student body – Itten exuded a special radiance. One could almost call it holiness. We were inclined to approach him only in whispers; our reverence was overwhelming, and we were completely enchanted and happy when he associated with us pleasantly and without restraint.'[16] In the cause of Mazdaznan Citroen fasted, purged himself, 'communed with nature, took hot baths, read spiritual works, sang, and communicated only with understanding friends'.[17] He also underwent some form of acupuncture:

37 Three-dimensional montage by M. Bronstein, 1921 *Bauhaus-Archiv*

'. . . There was, among other things, a little needle machine with which we were meant to puncture our skins.' The intention was to release 'wastes and impurities', but the result was 'months of torment and itching'. Citroen recognized that these cults could lead to 'sectarianism' – 'These tricks we played had dangerous repercussions: they made us arrogant and made us despise the uninitiated.'[18] They also contributed to the bewilderment of the authorities, since Itten and his disciples were unorthodox in their appearance, as well as in their achievements. The men shaved their heads (hair, according to Mazdaznan doctrine, being associated with sin) and they wore special clothes – monk-like garments for the masters, and baggy shirts and trousers (ex Russian prisoner of war stock) dyed in various colours for the students. The girls had short hair and short skirts, and if they followed

Mazdaznan 'radiated true serenity'. (In some cases this serenity must have been difficult to maintain: Lothar Schreyer, who had joined the school in 1921, described a journey undertaken by Itten and Georg Muche to Berlin to consult the 'Ministerium'. Itten, wearing a habit of 'costly purple-violet cloth', looked like an archbishop, and Muche, tall and thin, was cloaked in mouse-grey. Both had shaven heads, and attracted so much attention that they were unable to get through the streets, and had to take a taxi back to the station and refuge in Weimar.)[19]

During his first year at the Bauhaus, Itten was obviously the most dominant, charismatic, and to some, the most subversive figure in the school, Gropius being too involved with administration (and private commissions) to supervise its day-to-day activities. Early in 1921 Schlemmer was describing Itten as a 'dictator' – 'exhibiting such ruthlessness and schoolmasterly pedantry that the students finally cried "coercion".' 'I am amazed,' he also wrote, 'at the bad will towards Gropius among the students I know. . . . They say he has changed greatly, that it even shows in the expression of his eyes and the expression round his mouth; and the present programme of the Bauhaus contains no trace of the inspiring original programme . . . what the students actually produce in the way of art or handcrafted objects can only be called meagre. Almost shockingly so.'[20]

Schlemmer's letters were written in February and March 1921, when, as well as running the Basic Course, Itten was involved with the sculpture, glass-painting and metal-workshops. By this time Klee and Schlemmer had joined the staff, and Lothar Schreyer had arrived in 1921. The new appointments, however, did not diminish Itten's responsibilities, or his influence, and it was a confrontation with Gropius over Itten's involvement (or interference) in the wood-working shop (the only workshop at that time officially under Gropius's direction) that precipitated Itten's resignation. The crucial 'incident' occurred in December 1922, when Gropius discovered that Itten and Josef Zachmann (then *Lehrmeister* in the wood-working shop) were taking an unauthorized trip to Leipzig to buy wood for 'extensive commissions' proposed by Itten. A few days earlier Gropius had informed the workshop that it would be involved in at least six months' work for the theatre that he was redesigning in Jena, and he obviously saw Itten's gesture as a deliberate affront both to his policies and his authority. Itten, for his part, was deeply offended by Gropius's interference in his own plans for the workshop. He had, he said, spent months laying the foundations for a programme of work there, and now these efforts were being sabotaged. He detailed his responsibilities throughout the school, his struggle to establish the various workshops, and declared that in future, he, like the other 'masters', would do no teaching, and would also relinquish his responsibility for the Basic Course. He had, he said, no more interest in the school. Gropius, while expressing pain at Itten's antagonism, which he interpreted as personal hatred of himself and his work, attempted to diffuse the tension by reallocating responsibilities in the workshops. Schlemmer was to take charge of the sculpture workshops; Klee the book-binding workshop; Muche (who had been helping Itten on the Basic Course) was to run the weaving workshop and Feininger the print workshop, leaving Itten responsible for the metal and glass-painting workshops. Itten,

38 Wood drawn from memory, L. Leudesdorff, 1922 *Bauhaus-Archiv*
39 *The Big City*, collage, Paul Citroen, 1921 *Bauhaus-Archiv*

however, was not pacified by these arrangements (which were obviously designed to restrict his influence), and in October 1922 he finally handed in his notice.[21]

There were, of course, many factors that led to Itten's 'expulsion' from his dubious Eden in Weimar, not least among them his threat to Gropius's authority. His conviction that his was the one true path to self-knowledge and self-fulfilment could have been a challenge rather than a crusade had the school been able to develop alternative attitudes to design and architectural education. For two years, however, Itten's philosophies and his personality had dominated the school; his teaching was obviously stimulating, but since it was directed towards expressive rather than practical achievements, it presented the perennial challenge: should design education be concerned with the exploration and demonstration of theory, with knowledge through self-knowledge, or with the demands of commerce? Gropius proposed compromise, which Itten despised and rejected. The inevitable confrontation with Itten, however, forced Gropius to redefine his aims, which he outlined in a memorandum to the Bauhaus masters in February 1922.[22] 'Recently,' he wrote, 'Master Itten demanded from us a decision either to produce individual pieces of work in complete contrast to the economically oriented outside world or to seek contact with industry. It is here, in this method of formulating the question, I believe, that the big unknown that needs to be solved is hidden. Let me at once clarify this: I seek unity in the *fusion*, not in the separation of these ways of life.' The document is revealing, however, in that Gropius, in refuting Itten's 'either . . . or' demands, begins to redevelop the ideals for the school that he had outlined in his memorandum of 1915 (see page 53). 'The Bauhaus could become a haven for eccentrics if it were to lose contact with the work and working methods of the outside world. Its responsibility consists in educating people to recognize the basic nature of the world *in which they live*, and in combining their knowledge with their imagination so as to be able to create typical forms that symbolize that world.' He goes on to say that the school should be concerned with the creation of 'prototypes' which would serve as 'guides to craftsmen and industry', and that the school should produce designers capable of working in both areas. 'If the words "art" and "religion" were answered with silence, then they might be able to regain their substance,' he concluded.

With this statement Gropius was not only repudiating the cults of 'art' and 'religion' that Itten had introduced into the school, he was also demanding a new role for art both in society and in the training of the craftsman/designer. Itten, after declaring that he intended to 'cling to his romantic island', left to open a private school in Berlin. Before he left, however, his attitude to the nature of the work in the school was re-emphasized in a pamphlet that was published on the occasion of the first public exhibition of the students' work in April and May 1922:

> 'The exhibition has on display apprentice work from the weaving, pottery, metal, and cabinetmakers' workshops. It is a general principle that students in the workshops do not work from outside designs, nor from designs supplied by the Bauhaus masters. Instead, every apprentice must design and execute his own work. Only when form and material are brought into intimate fusion through an independent mind can creative work be achieved. Only in this way is it possible to come nearer the objective that craft is not only a prerequisite for a work of art but that in a work of art spiritual work and manual work form a single entity.'[23]

1   KANDINSKY AND KLEE

'All of us are fully aware,' Gropius wrote in his memorandum of 1922, 'that the old attitude of *l'art pour l'art* is obsolete, and that things that concern us today cannot exist in isolation, but [must] be rooted in our developing attitudes. Thus the basis upon which our work is built cannot be broad enough. Today this basis is too small rather than too large. This is made clear by news of Russian experiments, similar to ours, which have incorporated music, literature and science as coming from *one* source. . . .'[1]

In this early attempt to reorientate and redefine the aims of the school, Gropius was once again evoking the concept of the *Gesamtkunstwerk* – the total work of art. Instead, however, of presenting the guild-inspired image of the Gothic cathedral as a demonstration of this ideal, Gropius's conception of collective endeavour was now based on the assumption that new developments in the arts, as well as in science, shared a common impulse that would be revealed in what he described as a 'big transformation from analytic to synthetic work'. In this transformation, the primacy of the crafts, implicit in the foundation manifesto, was replaced by what Gropius described as 'the creative process of design', and following Itten's resignation, it was the artists at the Bauhaus – Klee and Kandinsky, as well as the artist/designers – van Doesburg and Moholy-Nagy – who were most concerned with the redefinition of the creative process, and its ambiguous relation to design.

It is important to establish the chronology of events in 1922–3, since the various crises, internal and external, that confronted the school during this period, as well as the staff's interpretation of their role there, were to influence its subsequent policies. Itten handed in his resignation in October 1922 (he left for Berlin early in 1923); Paul Klee and Oskar Schlemmer had been teaching at the school since January 1921, and Kandinsky joined the staff in the summer of 1922. All three were to develop their ideas and their priorities for art in a school of design and architecture over a long period in Weimar and Dessau. (Schlemmer left the Bauhaus in 1929, Klee in 1931, and Kandinsky in 1933.) Itten's departure, however, coincided with, or confirmed a practical and ideological 'call to order' in the school. On the practical level Weimar, now the capital of Thuringia, could no longer be considered a citadel of the crafts, for although it had absorbed more craft-based enterprises with the expansion of its territory, the industries of Erfurt, Mülhausen and Nordhausen were also within its province, and both craft and industrial activities, threatened by post-war economic crises, needed to consolidate, expand and export.[2] Gropius's original proposals for the school, therefore, with their stress on industrial as well as craft production, were obviously appropriate to the post-war realities of Weimar. Definitions of 'reality' in Weimar, however, were determined by a right-wing and reactionary bureaucracy, increasingly irritated by the Bauhaus and its activities, and in the autumn of 1922 the school was asked to prepare a major exhibition to justify its work, to be held in the summer of 1923.

In the autumn of 1922, however, the school was far from united about the nature of its activities. Kandinsky and Klee were initiating courses structured around their individual interpretations of what Gropius described as 'the developing attitudes' within the school. Yet neither of them had, or wished to acquire, the 'decided talent for leadership' that Schlemmer ascribed to Itten. Kandinsky was the more experienced as a teacher, having taught briefly in Munich and in Moscow, and although, like Klee, he was primarily concerned with the *Formlehre* – studies in what is now called 'basic design' – he was obviously considered as a prestigious 'antidote' to Itten, since by then he had established his reputation as a theorist, as well as a painter.

KANDINSKY: MUNICH AND MOSCOW

Kandinsky, who was fifty-six when he came to the Bauhaus, was born in Moscow in 1866, and had studied law before he became a painter – an experience, he maintained, which helped him to 'acquire the capacity for abstract thought'.[3] His formative years as an artist, however, were spent in Munich. He arrived there in 1896 when the town's *Secession* movements in both art and design made it a centre of the avant-garde. It was the fairy-tale quality of the place, as much as its artistic activities, that made the greatest impression on him at first: 'The German fairy tales I had heard so often as a child came to life. The tall, narrow roofs of the Promenadenplatz and the Maximilianplatz, which have now disappeared . . . turned those fairy tales into reality. The blue trains threaded their way through the streets like the incarnation of the air of a fairy story, which one inhales with delightful ease. The yellow mailboxes sang their shrill canary-yellow song from the street-corners. I welcomed the label "art-mill", and I felt I was in the city of art, which for me was the same as being in fairyland.'[4]

Kandinsky was preoccupied with this 'fairyland' of colour and sound and folk architecture during his early years in Munich. He studied for two years at Anton Ažbè's private academy where, he wrote, 'I . . . forced myself to study the organic side of drawing, which I found uncongenial.'[5] As Peg Weiss has pointed out, however, Ažbè's teaching stressed the use of pure colour, as well as the development of individual talent,[6] so that Kandinsky was able to follow his personal preoccupations at that time – the transformation, or translation, through his own work, of the memories and obsessions of his early life in Russia – the 'magical' wooden houses he had seen on his journeys through Vologda, their rooms crammed with ornaments, 'folk-pictures' and colour. 'They taught me to move within the picture, to live in the picture.' Scientific discoveries also confirmed Kandinsky's questioning of the nature of the reality depicted by painting: 'The collapse of the atom was equated in my soul with the collapse of the whole world. Suddenly the stoutest walls would crumble. Everything became precarious and insubstantial.'[7]

During the years in Munich, therefore, Kandinsky's evocation of fairy tales, his pre-

84

occupation with colour, with the relationships between music, sound and colour, were reflected in paintings which evolved from symbolic interpretations of myth and landscape towards pure abstraction. His activities in Munich obviously stimulated him to clarify as well as promote his own ideas and his work. In 1900 he organized the Phalanx group, an exhibiting society, with an associated art school and gallery. In 1903 Peter Behrens invited him to teach decorative painting in the *Kunstgewerbeschule* in Düsseldorf; Kandinsky declined, and spent some time travelling in Russia, Holland, Italy, France and North Africa. In 1911 he heard Schönberg's music for the first time in a concert in Munich, founded the *Blaue Reiter* group of painters, and completed his seminal book *Über das geistige in der Kunst (Concerning the Spiritual in Art)*.

Kandinsky was also involved in design reform movements in Munich. He was associated with the activities of the *Vereinigung für angewandte Kunst (Society for Applied Art)*; he knew Obrist and the work of the Debschitz School, and he produced designs for jewellery, embroidery, book covers, ceramics and furniture, as well as dresses for Gabrièle Münter. Before his return to Russia at the outbreak of the First World War, however, these activities remained peripheral, and although he was concerned, in his theoretical writing, with the relationship between the 'ornamental' in decorative art and in painting, he could never consider himself as a 'designer', either in Munich, or later in Moscow and at the Bauhaus. His primary concern was with art, and with the role of the artist in 'conscious creation'. Throughout his period in Munich, Kandinsky had been formulating his theories of art in articles and exhibition catalogues. *Concerning the Spiritual in Art*, published in December 1911 to coincide with the first *Blaue Reiter* exhibition, was his first major polemical statement. In it Kandinsky condemns the 'materialism' both of contemporary society, and of those periods 'when art possesses no outstanding representative. . . . At such blind, dumb times men place exclusive value upon outward success, concern themselves only with material goods, and hail technical progress, which serves, and can only serve the body, as a great achievement.'[8] Art, at such times, is 'without a soul'.

The true artist, however, is driven by 'inner necessity', and like the musician and the writer, can be an agent of spiritual change. Kandinsky draws analogies between art and music throughout the essay: music, he writes, is the art which 'is completely emancipated from nature, [and] does not need to borrow external forms from anywhere in order to create its language'.[9] The painter who does not wish merely to imitate 'natural appearances' envies the musician: 'Hence the current search for rhythm in painting, for mathematical, abstract construction, the value placed today upon the repetition of colour-tones, the way colours are set in motion, etc.'[10] These experiments are only viable, however, in so far as they respond to the laws of 'inner need' and to 'inner nature', expressed through form and colour which are subject to their own laws. Music, like art, has its own evolving laws and grammar, and even Schönberg whose 'music leads us into a new realm, where musical experiences are no longer acoustic, but purely spiritual' recognized that there was no such thing as absolute freedom.[11] The new 'grammar of painting' still had to be defined, but it would be 'constructed not so much on the basis of physical laws . . . but rather upon the laws of internal necessity'.[12] Without the recognition of these spiritual laws, an exclusive preoccupation with 'pure colour and independent form' would lead to the creation of 'works having the appearance of geometrical ornament, which would – to put it crudely – be like a tie or a carpet'.[13] (Ironically one critic of the second *Neue-Künstler Vereinigung* exhibition in Munich in 1910 wrote: 'A colourful hodge-podge of Kandinsky's is called, significantly, *Composition 2*; presumably the artist himself was unable to think of a title for this involuntary conglomeration of colours. I would have few objections if it said underneath "Colour sketch for Modern Carpet". But far from it! These people who are exhibiting here are too good to let themselves be put on a par with "designers".')[14]

Until 1933, however, when Kandinsky left the Bauhaus, he was working almost exclusively with designers and architects, so that in Moscow, Weimar and Dessau he was attempting to construct and justify methods of teaching that would relate the 'ideal' and the 'material' in the 'creation of a new spiritual realm'.[15] The conclusion of *Concerning the Spiritual in Art* anticipates the advent of the 'epoch of the great spiritual'. In 1914, however, just before a fourth edition was due to be published in Germany, the war broke out, and Kandinsky left Germany, first for Switzerland and then for Moscow.

Kandinsky's work and theories were well known in the cosmopolitan and avant-garde circles of Moscow and St Petersburg. His paintings had been included in Russian exhibitions, and a version of *Concerning the Spiritual in Art* had been read at the Pan-Russian Congress of Artists in December 1911. When he returned to Moscow, he taught at the Moscow Academy, and then became involved with the politics of revolutionary art. Politics, however, did not interest him, although he claimed that the Revolution itself had a liberating effect on his painting. His ideal since 1900, he told Charles-André Julien,[16] had been to paint a 'tragic' picture. 'During October I saw the revolution from my windows. Then I painted in a totally different manner. I felt within myself a great peace of soul. Instead of tragic, something peaceful and organized. The colours of my work became brighter and more attractive.'

Kandinsky had little time to paint, however. He was appointed commissar of Russian Museums, 'spent three years organizing over thirty museums in the provinces',[17] and in May 1920 initiated and was appointed the first Director of Inkhuk (Institute of Artistic Culture). Inkhuk, as Kandinsky conceived it, was to be devoted to theory and to an ambitious programme of research into what he described as 'the effect of the means of expression on the inner experience of man'.[18] Kandinsky was proposing a 'scientific', or what he called 'purely schematic' analysis of the spiritual in art – art encompassing painting, sculpture, music, dance and poetry. The programme, therefore, was an attempt to establish a rational or analytical basis for the theories he had put forward in *Concerning the Spiritual in Art*. The 'physiological and psychological' effects of line, form, colour, sound and movement were to be investigated. Sculptors and architects would be involved with the 'elaboration of specific methods for the investigation of volumetric and volumetric-planar forms', and the 'positive sciences' – botany, biology, chemistry, engineering, etc. – might also provide 'useful pointers, or at least inferences for the work of the Institute'.

This programme, however, with its stress on the psychological, and therefore personal or individual interpretation of the processes of art, was rejected by other members of Inkhuk, and Kandinsky was forced to resign from the organization. The reasons for this rejection were most clearly stated by Nikolai Tarabukin, who wrote: 'The form of the work and its elements are the material for analysis, and not the psychology of the creation, nor the psychology of aesthetic perception, nor the historical, cultural, sociological or other problems of art.'[19] Tarabukin elaborated these ideas in his seminal essay *From the Easel to the Machine*,[20] published in 1923, which demanded 'production skills' from the artist, and 'works which are socially justified in form and purpose'. It was this stress on the social rather than the spiritual role of art which drove Kandinsky from Russia. He had, as he pointed out in his interview with Charles-André Julien, been one of the first artists in Russia to design cups; at the same time, however, he had little sympathy for the 'Constructivist' ideals of the Vkhutemas, the 'Art-Technical Studio' which had been established within the Moscow Academy, and in December 1921 he left Russia with a three-month exit permit and never returned.

KANDINSKY'S BASIC COURSE

When he invited him to join the staff of the Bauhaus, Gropius was aware of Kandinsky's ideals for Inkhuk, and the reference in Gropius's statement of 1922 to 'Russian experiments, similar to ours, which have incorporated music, literature and science as coming from *one* source' obviously related to Kandinsky's rather than to the Russian Constructivists' priorities. Kandinsky's brief in Weimar was to contribute (together with Paul Klee) to the *Formlehre* – the studies of form that complemented the Basic Course – and he was also appointed master of the mural workshops. Kandinsky ran two of the 'basic' courses that every student was required to attend in Weimar – one on the *Basic Elements of Form (Grundelemente der Form)*, and a colour course and seminar more specifically related to the experiments in the mural workshop.

Kandinsky's programmes for these two courses in Weimar read like an abstract of his Inkhuk proposals.[21] There are no references to the 'spiritual', to intuition, or to inner experiences, and the emphasis is on methods of progressing from analysis to synthesis in the study of the 'science of art'. Again 'art' is not considered as an end in itself (neither Klee nor Kandinsky gave painting classes in Weimar), but as part of that triumvirate of art, science and industry that the Bauhaus was trying to unite. Since research of this kind was unprecedented, attempts to achieve a 'synthetic method' of design had to proceed from analysis of the simplest shapes and 'systematically progress towards more complicated ones'. Investigations of form, therefore, were initially confined to the 'three basic elements – triangle, square and circle', and volume 'to the basic solids deriving from them – pyramid, cube and square'. Colour was also to be examined objectively, its use and application related to 'the aims of the different workshops', and its study based on 'co-operation between teachers and students on basic course material'.

These tersely written and carefully organized programmes give the impression that Kandinsky had absorbed the criticisms of his former compatriots, and was proceeding with some caution to establish a method of teaching and research that was appropriate to the aims of the school. In 1919, in an essay entitled *Little Articles on Big Questions*[22] he had referred to 'geometrical figures – the circle, the triangle, the square, the rhomboid, the trapezoid, etc.', as 'forms belonging to the first sphere of graphic language'. 'This sphere of draftsmanship,' he wrote, 'with its limited means of expression, is akin to a language without declensions, conjugations, prepositions, or prefixes'; it was this sphere of draftsmanship, however, that he was to transform in his own painting into complex compositions with their own inner language of colour, form and line (Pl. 3). In his teaching at Weimar, Kandinsky used these 'geometrical figures' to establish a basic language of form that he would elaborate later at Dessau, and which he used in the mural workshop to reinterpret his Munich ideal of 'living within the picture'.[23]

KLEE: ART AND PERCEPTION

When Kandinsky arrived at the Bauhaus, Paul Klee had been teaching there for more than a year. Klee and Kandinsky had already met in Munich where both had been pupils of Franz Stuck at the Munich Academy, and Paul Klee had also been associated with the *Blaue Reiter* group. 'In those days,' wrote Kandinsky, 'he was very small fry.' (Klee was thirteen years younger than Kandinsky.) 'I can claim with justifiable pride, however, that I was able to detect in his little drawings . . . the great Klee of later years.'[24] For his part, Klee was fascinated by Kandinsky's 'strange pictures without object',[25] and at the same time he was attempting to create a visual language that would express his own perceptions of nature and the structures of nature. In order to do this he felt that he needed to identify himself with the natural world at every level, understanding not only the processes of growth and movement, but the relationship and reaction of every kind of organism to these processes. He wanted to be 'as though new-born, knowing nothing about Europe, nothing, knowing no pictures, entirely without impulses, almost in an original state'.[26] Klee's early work, therefore, his 'little drawings' were seemingly naïve, linear and graphic: they were, however, totally 'knowing' in their demonstration of the use of line. In the early years at Munich Klee remained a peripheral figure; he admired the work of his *Blaue Reiter* colleagues, Franz Marc and August Macke, as well as that of Kandinsky, but he could not, at that time, evoke the sense and sensations of nature as they did with an exuberant and iconoclastic use of colour. 'In Marc,' he wrote, 'the bond with the earth takes precedence over the bond with the universe . . . my fire is more like that of the dead or the unborn. . . . I place myself at a remote starting point of creation.'[27] And from that 'remote starting point' he wished to investigate 'the powers that do the forming', rather than the 'final forms'.[28] The processes of these investigations are analysed in his diaries, and in the notes he made for his courses at the Bauhaus. The interaction of analysis and synthesis, a *leitmotif* of Kandinsky's theory, is implicit rather than stressed in Klee's writing, and his concept of form was based on theories of perception as much as on a preoccupation with the elements of form. What is interesting about Klee's development as a painter (and of course relevant to his teaching at the Bauhaus) is his gradual discovery of the relationship between line and plane, colour and form through the medium of architecture, and what he called 'architectonic form'. Before the war he had travelled in France, Italy and Tunisia, and after his visit to Italy (in 1902) he wrote: 'wherever I look I see only architecture, linear rhythm, rhythm of planes.'[29] It was his experience of North Africa, however, in April 1914, that brought the revelation of colour. 'Colour has taken possession of me,' he wrote '. . . colour and I are one. I am a painter.'[30]

During the war Klee, who was called up in 1916, was on the staff of a Bavarian Flying School; at the same time, however, his reputation was growing. 'Klee is the finest of the better known moderns,' Oskar Schlemmer wrote in his diary in 1916. '. . . He can reveal his entire wisdom in the barest of lines . . . that is the way a Buddha draws.'[31] Schlemmer, who returned as a student to the Stuttgart Academy after the war, campaigned for the appointment of Klee as a teacher there, to replace Hölzel, who had resigned. The campaign was unsuccessful because, as Schlemmer explained, the authorities considered Klee an 'unworldly visionary' and 'hardly to be the teacher to advocate modern style with the vigour necessary in a city like Stuttgart.'[32] And again, early in 1921, soon after Klee arrived in Weimar, Schlemmer was writing to his wife: 'Klee's appointment seems to

40 *Magnetic apparatus for plant cultivation* watercolour, Paul Klee, 1921 *Busch-Reisinger Museum, Harvard University*

provoke the greatest head-shaking, for he is considered a *l'art pour l'art* type, with no conceivable practical contribution to make.'[33]

Nevertheless, Klee obviously wanted to teach, not only for the money, which was important to him, but because he needed to communicate his ideas both through his work, and through the elaboration of the theory and philosophy that sustained it. At the end of the war he was concerned, like many of his contemporaries, with the 'relevance' of art, and in 1919, in a letter to Alfred Kubin (which indicates that he might have known about Gropius's plans for Weimar), he put forward the idea of a new kind of art school that would further the ideals of a 'communist community'. The art of the individual, he wrote, is capitalist luxury, and the artist should do more than provide 'curiosities for rich snobs'.

The initiatives and the innovations of the artist should be more broadly based in order to reach the masses. 'This new art would then be absorbed into handwork, where it would blossom freely. For there are no more academies, only art schools for handworkers.'[34]

Like Kandinsky, however, Klee was not interested in social and political issues in the 1920s, nor did he make any significant contribution to debates within the school, or to the activities in the workshops. After Itten left Weimar he became *Formmeister* in the bookbinding and glass painting workshops – both established in the van de Velde era – and some of the designs in the weaving workshops show his influence, as well as that of Georg Muche. His main contribution was in the teaching of 'basic design', which he shared with Kandinsky, and like Kandinsky he aimed to investigate methods of teaching based on the analysis of the creative process. He did not wish to teach his students how or what to draw and paint, but he encouraged these activities because they demanded 'theoretical principles'. Implicit in his teaching was the conviction that the artist must 'place himself at the starting point in creation'. 'You will never achieve anything unless you work upwards towards it,' he told his students. 'You can't break in halfway through the process, and least of all can you start with a result. You must start at the beginning. Then you will avoid all trace of artificiality, and the creative process will function without interruption.'[35] (Pl. 4 and Illus. 40 and 41.)

In his lecture *On Modern Art*, which he gave at Jena in 1924, Klee used the simile of the growth of a tree to describe the artist's role in the creative process: 'The artist has studied this world of variety and has, we may suppose, unobtrusively found his way in it. His sense of direction has brought order into the passing stream of image and experience. This sense of direction in nature and life, this branching and spreading array, I shall compare to the root of the tree. From the root the sap flows to the artist, flows to his eye. Thus he stands as the trunk of the tree, he does nothing other than gather and pass on what comes to him from the depths. He neither serves nor rules – he transmits. His position is humble. And the beauty at the crown is not his own. He is merely a channel.'[36]

This identification of creativity in art with the processes of natural growth is romantic in its conception and rhetoric. At the same time, however, Klee's analogy reveals the complexity of his theory; he is not looking *at* nature for inspiration, nor is he considering its evolutionary processes in order to establish laws of form and growth. The artist, for Klee, like the trunk of the tree, has 'direction' and 'order'; his vision is moulded, and he can transmit this vision through his eye. What the eye sees, however, is the totality of the experience of growth and of existence. As Klee wrote in *The Thinking Eye*: 'His (the artist's) growth in the vision and contemplation of nature enables him to rise towards a metaphysical view of the world and to form free, abstract structures which surpass schematic intention and achieve a new naturalness – the naturalness of work. Then he creates a work, or participates in the creation of works that are images of God's work.'[37]

Klee's interpretation of the creative process, therefore, implied that the artist should work without historical precedent or any preconceived conception of the phenomenal world in order to express its essence. 'Art does not reproduce the visible, but makes visible,'[38] he wrote; and again: 'The object is surely dead. The *sensation* of the object is of first importance.'[39] These preoccupations with 'sensation' and 'making visible' that Klee shared with Kandinsky, and which formed the basis of their courses at the Weimar Bauhaus, had a common source in studies that were taking place in Munich prior to the war. The philos-

41 *Perception of an animal* ink, Paul Klee, 1925 *Busch-Reisinger Museum, Harvard University*

opher and psychologist Theodor Lipps was lecturing in Munich from 1894–1913; his book on the nature of perception (*Raumaesthetik und geometrische-optische Täuschungen: The Aesthetics of Space and Geometrical Optical Illusions*) was published in 1897 and his two-volume *Aesthetik: Psychologie der Schönen und der Kunst (Aesthetics: the psychology of beauty and art)* appeared in 1903 and 1906. These two books were major influences on theories of perception, as well as on concepts of abstraction and expressionism in early twentieth-century art theory and Klee and Kandinsky were influenced by them. The concept of 'inner necessity' is discussed in Lipps's writing, as well as the tendency towards 'empathy' or 'abstraction' inherent in works of art and their interpretation. Wilhelm Worringer, who was Lipps's pupil and associated with the *Blaue Reiter* group elaborated this aspect of Lipps's theory in *Abstraction and Empathy*, published in Munich in 1908. Worringer described 'the precondition for the urge to empathy' as 'a happy pantheistic relationship of confidence between man and the phenomena of the external world', while 'the urge to abstraction' is 'the outcome of a great inner unrest inspired in man by the phenomena of the outside world'.[40] It is not surprising, therefore, that Klee describes himself in his diary during the war as 'abstract with memories'.[41]

For Klee's paintings are rarely totally abstract: they evoke landscapes, plant forms, the sea, sky and stars, buildings and the structure of buildings as well as the human condition. Again, the paintings are named; they are not 'Compositions', but *Forest, Architecture, Fire in the Evening, Possibilities at Sea*, etc., so that the 'sensations' that inspired them are evoked. The 'sensations', however, are expressed in lines, forms and colours that demonstrate Klee's preoccupation with perception – 'making visible'. Marianne Teuber has traced the origins of these theories in the works of Lipps and Hermann von Helmholtz.[42] In a lecture in 1870, Helmholtz had described 'how a moving point produced a line, a moving line a plane, and a moving plane a volume'. Lipps related these theories to aesthetics, and both Klee and Kandinsky reconstructed them in their teaching at the Bauhaus.

The transformation of these theories based on scientific research through aesthetics to the courses taught at Weimar is a complex one. Klee and Kandinsky shared the experience of pre-war Munich; Klee was a musician and Kandinsky, like Klee, constantly referred to analogies with music in the development of his theories. Both were concerned with colour theory, and with the relationship of colour to form. Yet in spite of these shared interests, their courses, like their paintings, were totally different, and their students would have been presented with different responses to similar phenomena.

Klee's *Paedagogical Sketchbook*, first published as the second of the fourteen Bauhaus Books in 1925, is based on the notes he made for his lectures in Weimar. A facsimile of the courses for 1921–1922 has also been produced – an exercise book in his handwriting with numbered sketches.[43] At the most basic level they show how carefully he prepared these seminars, which he called 'Contributions towards creative studies of form' (*Beiträge zur Bildnerischen Formen*). They reveal Klee's preoccupation with the *genesis* of form, with concepts of unity in plurality, with organic growth, and with the structural as well as cosmic analogies that can be created through the manipulation of point, line and plane. The *Paedagogical Sketchbook*, an abstract of these and later notes, is more terse, but both deal with the interaction of the physical and the metaphysical in the creation of form.

Kandinsky's *Point and Line to Plane*, also published as a Bauhaus Book in 1926, is an elaboration and extension of his 'science of art' proposals for Inkhuk; the text moves from analysis to synthesis in its discussion of the basic elements of art, and its underlying theme is the need for a theory to replace intuition in the creation or interpretation of art. 'The progress achieved by systematic research,' writes Kandinsky, 'will give birth to a dictionary of elements that, developed further, will lead to a "grammar" and finally to a theory of composition that will overstep the boundaries of the individual arts and refer to "Art" in general.'[44] By 'art in general' Kandinsky is referring, as in *Concerning the Spiritual*, to music, poetry and architecture, as well as to the fine arts. *Point and Line*, however, abandons the mysticism of the earlier work and stresses the demonstration of 'mathematical expression' which is common to all these arts. 'Interest in mathematical expression,' he maintains, 'tends in two directions – the theoretical and the practical. In the former, it is the logical that plays the more important role; in the latter the purposive. Here, logic is subordinated to purpose, so that the work attains the highest quality – that of naturalness.'[45]

Thus Kandinsky, like Klee, is evoking the concept of 'naturalness' as a determinant for form. The nature of nature, or 'naturalness' however, could be interpreted in many different ways. Itten had demanded an empathy with materials as essential to the process of design. Klee and Kandinsky, however, were not discussing the nature of wood, fibres, metal or clay; they were demanding a more scientific and at the same time a more transcendent experience of form, which they expressed through painting. The challenge and dilemma, therefore, lay in debates about the relevance of applying these ideas to design for craft and industrial production.

2   VAN DOESBURG AND MOHOLY-NAGY

Criticisms of the relevance of the work and ideologies of the school in Weimar came not only from local bureaucracy, but from European protagonists of the 'new spirit' in design and architecture such as Le Corbusier and Theo van Doesburg. In the December 1923 issue of *L'Esprit Nouveau* Corbusier wrote a brief review, '*Pédagogie*',[1] of Gropius's publication *Idee und Aufbau*. In it Corbusier criticized the school for aiming to create and promote standards for industry; standards, he maintained, emerge from the masses ('*le standard surgit de la masse profonde*'); they are determined by processes of production, as well as by social, economic and technical forces, and they cannot be taught or imposed. The school at Weimar, therefore, could contribute nothing to industry; it was merely a school of decorative arts, and consequently anachronistic. Architecture, however, Corbusier maintained, being based on technique, could be taught. Gropius, therefore, should be concentrating on the urgent problems of architecture, rather than wasting the time of his young students on problems of decorative design.

What is interesting about this article apart from its demonstration of the author's priorities, is Corbusier's reference to Theo van Doesburg. Gropius, according to Corbusier, 'gathers around him all the most active elements of young Germany, and has formed an alliance with the ideas of the Amsterdam *De Stijl* group, represented by the painter Theo van Doesburg, theoretician of a young architecture whose aesthetic is based upon a few brutally simple principles (interesting, nevertheless, because it demonstrates the power of *systems*, whatever form they take)'.

Neither Gropius nor van Doesburg could have been particularly encouraged by this assessment of their aims and alleged allegiance. Van Doesburg, who was born in Holland in 1883, had emerged after the war as an entrepreneur in international ideologies. He was a painter and an art critic, and in 1917 had founded the magazine *De Stijl* with a group of contributors who included the painters Mondrian, Bart van der Leck and Vilmos Huszar, the Belgian sculptor Georges Vantongerloo, the architects J. J. P. Oud and Jan Wils, and the poet Anthony Kok. Their aim was the promotion of a 'universal language' which would 'manifest itself in all objects as a style, born from a new relationship between the artist and society'.[2] Van Doesburg's initial conception of 'the new relationship between the artist and society' owed a great deal to Kandinsky's *Concerning the Spiritual in Art*, as well as to his interpretation of Mondrian's abstract paintings as a demonstration of 'the internal structure of the real'. However, unlike Kandinsky (and Mondrian, who was always uneasy about the reinterpretation of his paintings into three-dimensional design), van Doesburg saw this relationship as active rather than passive, and the artist as a mediator in practical as well as spiritual change. In his lecture *The Will to Style*, which he gave in Berlin, Jena and Weimar in 1922, van Doesburg maintained that 'the struggle for a solution to the problem of art' was not being 'waged in art, science, philosophy and religion alone, but in our daily life where it takes the form of the struggle for spiritual and material existence'.[3] Material existence, of course, was supported by methods of production, so that, according to van Doesburg, in present society 'the machine takes pride of place in the concept of cultural style'. Van Doesburg, therefore, saw the machine as 'the only means of bringing about . . . social liberation'. 'This is by no means to say,' he continues, 'that mechanical production is the only requirement for creative perfection. A prerequisite for the correct use of machines is not quantity alone, but above all, quality. To serve these ends the use of machines must be governed by artistic consciousness.'

Gropius, of course, could hardly quarrel with these ideas, since they related to his initial ideals for the school. Van Doesburg's attitude to the Bauhaus in Weimar, however, was distinctly critical, and the extent of his influence there is difficult to evaluate, mainly because of conflicting accounts of his activities in 1921 and 1922. He gave his own account in *De Stijl* in 1927. 'At the house of Expressionist architect Bruno Taut, the editor gets to know Walter Gropius, his assistants Meyer and Forbat, and several Bauhaus students. Here the editor shows an extensive collection of photographs of work by the De Stijl group. . . . Invitation by Gropius to visit the Bauhaus, January 1921 . . . where, in addition to Expressionist degeneration, so-called "root-compositions" in the manner of Vantongerloo, produced by the students, are found. . . . A correspondence between the editor of *De Stijl* and the Bauhaus develops. Gropius and Meyer express the wish to stay in contact with *De Stijl*. In April (1921) the editor of *De Stijl* is installed at Weimar by Meyer and De Stijl adherents.'[4] What is significant about this account is the fact that, according to van Doesburg, it was Adolf Meyer, and not Gropius, who 'installed' him in Weimar. Gropius was subsequently to reject any suggestion that he had invited van Doesburg to the school. In a letter to Bruno Zevi he wrote, '. . . I have never invited van Doesburg to the Bauhaus. He came there on his own initiative because he was attracted by our courses. He hoped to become a professor at the Bauhaus, but I did not give him a position, because I judged him aggressive and fanatic and considered that he possessed such a narrow, theoretical view that he would not tolerate any diversity of opinion.'[5]

Obviously Gropius could not countenance the presence of two 'fanatics' – Itten and van Doesburg – in the school. At the same time van Doesburg's philosophy, if not his personality, evoked some positive response from both staff and students, especially among those who were disenchanted with Itten. The prestige of Dutch architecture and design at that time could also have contributed to the initial enthusiasm for van Doesburg. Adolf Behne and Bruno Taut had both visited Holland in 1920, and Behne had published articles on Dutch architecture and architectural theory in the early twenties. In his book *Der Moderne Zweckbau*, which was written in 1923,[6] and which is a pioneering survey of work by the European as well as the American avant-garde, Behne included illustrations of designs by Berlage, Stam and J. J. P. Oud as well as van Doesburg. Behne also comments on the consistent development of Dutch theory and practice, and, quoting Oud and van Doesburg, approves their promotion of an aesthetic that combines form and function.[7]

Adolf Meyer who, according to van Docsburg, offered him a studio in Weimar, would have been anxious to encourage the Dutch connection – not only to strengthen the role of architecture and architectural theory in the school, but also because he had been taught by the Dutchman, J. L. Lauweriks, in Behrens's school in Düsseldorf. Lauweriks's stress in his teaching on the social responsibility of the architect, and on the demonstration, through the geometry of structure, of universal harmony, had obvious equivalents in van Doesburg's thinking. Van Doesburg's concern for universality and harmony, however, did not extend to his relationships with his colleagues and collaborators. While he was in Weimar, he was working on colour schemes for housing by Oud, which Oud proposed to modify. 'Now according to your latest letter – you want to change the whole thing and murder one of my most successful solutions,' he wrote '. . . given the fact that the execution of the work was assured; given the fact that I am no house-painter but take these things seriously; given the fact that I am van Doesburg, *I have, I seize* the right to cry: No – No – No. *Entweder so – oder Nichts.*'[8]

This 'those who are not with me are against me' approach obviously soured his relationship with the Bauhaus, and it is clear that he moved into the offensive immediately after his arrival in Weimar. Writing to Anthony Kok in January 1921 he reports, 'At Weimar I have turned everything radically upside down. This is supposed to be the most famous Academy with the most modern teachers! Every evening I have talked to the students and spread the vermin of the new spirit. Within a short time De Stijl will reappear in a more radical way. I have tremendous energy and know now that our views will achieve victory over anyone and anything.'[9]

THE DE STIJL AESTHETIC

Van Doesburg's evangelism, like that of Itten, obviously gained him some supporters, and several Bauhaus students worked with him while more attended his lectures. In 1922, as part of his De Stijl course in Weimar, he designed two model houses, or what he called 'architectonic sculptures', and one of the models for these was made by Hans Vogel, a student at the Bauhaus. Unlike the prototypes for 'serial houses' that Gropius had produced in 1921, which were formed from six basic blocks or units which could be combined in various ways (a refinement of his proposals for standardized housing for AEG), van Doesburg's designs are concerned with the articulation of space through the interpenetration of squares and cubes. They demonstrate 'the will to materialize in architecture the ideal aesthetics established by the "liberal" arts'. For according to van Doesburg, painting had 'first created an ideal aesthetic' by rejecting 'the world of duality . . . the common concept of an imaginary world of the mind which is superior and opposed to the concrete world of matter'. Moreover, traditional concepts of matter had been challenged by modern physics: 'Because of the advance of physics in our own times, the concept of matter as solid substance was changed, and, as in the field of art, came to be seen as a *unit of energy*.' This unity of the spiritual and the material could not be demonstrated by 'the placing of boxes or cells of a predetermined or standard type side by side or on top of each other', nor by the 'mere exhibition of columns and joints from the building's structural skeleton (criticism of Gropius and the Constructivists is implied here), but by the organization of 'various materials (light included) . . . into a unity which expressed the maximum energy'.[10]

The use of colour was, of course, integral to the expression of energy. 'Colour is of extreme importance to the new architecture,' he wrote in 1923. 'It represents an intrinsic part of the material of expression. Colour renders *visible* the spatial effect for which the architect strives.' Colour, therefore, could be used to define or dematerialize space and form, and to 'visualize relationships' within an interior, so that 'space and the objects contained within it are perceived as a unity'.[11] Van Doesburg, therefore, like Kandinsky, wanted to 'live within the painting'; again like Kandinsky, he believed that scientific research had not only challenged traditional concepts of the nature of reality, but could also be used to establish what he described as a 'methodology' or 'objective system' of reconstruction. For Kandinsky, however, this reconstruction was to be demonstrated through the analysis of the processes and powers of perception, whereas van Doesburg believed, in the early twenties at least, that 'painting has no reason to exist separately from architectural construction (that is, easel painting)'.[12]

Van Doesburg continued to work as an 'easel painter', but his paintings, unlike those of Klee and Kandinsky, were programmatic, a demonstration in two dimensions of his ideals for three-dimensional form: 'art as the collective expression of a nation, of a style'.[13] The Bauhaus, of course, was dedicated to the unity of painting, sculpture and architecture in the creation of 'the new building of the future', but neither van Doesburg nor his colleagues could see any evidence of this unity when they arrived at the school. Vilmos Huszar, reviewing an exhibition in Weimar which included work by members of the Bauhaus staff, described Klee's work as 'morbid dreams', Kandinsky's as 'intermingled decorations', and Itten's as 'empty, gorgeous daubings'. 'Faced with the predominance of a crass individualism, in which each works according to his mood, can the desired goals be reached? . . . In a country which is torn politically and economically, can one justify the spending of large sums of money on an institute such as the Bauhaus is today? My answer is: No.'[14]

Criticisms such as these, of course, did not improve van Doesburg's relationship with the school, particularly since they had some validity. When he arrived at the school, he wrote to Gropius later, he had found only tenuous links between theory and practice, no discipline, no organization, and no evidence of a common objective within the individual workshops, or in the school as a whole.[15]

The problem, of course, lay in conflicting interpretations of the creative process, and its relationship as well as its relevance to design. Gropius, bound by the dedication to craftsmanship which had justified his appointment to the school, had attempted to revitalize the crafts by involving fine artists with the forms, if not the techniques, of production. The courses given by Klee and Kandinsky were presented as objective analyses of visual experience; they were obviously intellectually stimulating, and it is significant that both claimed a basis in scientific research. Although the Bauhaus in Weimar lacked a consistent theory of design, the 'crass individualism' that Huszar condemned had produced interesting and in some cases innovatory work within an existing tradition. Obviously the school had set out to do more than this; the ideal of universality was a potent one, but not as presented either by van Doesburg or Corbusier. Van Doesburg's theories, despite his claims to the contrary, involved the imposition of an ideology, rather than the interpretation of 'the will to style', while Corbusier's evolutionary concepts, however realistic and respectable their pedigree, ran counter to the idealism that demanded a role for the designer in industry. The Bauhaus needed a positive philosophy: instead it found a slogan – 'Art and Technology: a new unity' – Gropius's persuasive, if ambiguous, prescription for the future of design.

THE APPOINTMENT OF MOHOLY-NAGY

Several factors were involved in the school's seeming change of direction in 1922–3, and van Doesburg's presence in Weimar was undoubtedly one of them. 'Tell me, honestly,' wrote Feininger to his wife in September 1922, 'how many are there in the Bauhaus who really know what they want to achieve, or who are strong enough to make something of themselves through painstaking work? For most of them the unsentimental – if also completely uninspired – Doesburg is something of a pillar among all the heated and conflicting points of view, something definite and clear, which they can hold on to. . . .'[16] Feininger wrote this in September 1922, when it was rumoured that van Doesburg was leaving Weimar; in October 1922, however, he was presiding over a Constructivist Congress that he had organized in the town, with Lucia and Laszlo Moholy-Nagy, El Lissitzky, Hans Richter, Hans Arp and Tristan Tzara in attendance. This influx of European avant-garde representatives of Constructivism and Dada was not primarily designed to challenge the Bauhaus; van Doesburg was now campaigning on a wider front, and the Weimar meeting was a gathering of dissidents from the Congress of International Progressive Artists that had been held in Düsseldorf earlier that year. The Congress had marked the renewal of contacts with Russia, and its aim, as its title suggests, was to establish a union or mutual support system for 'progressive' artists throughout Europe. Its proceedings, however, according to van Doesburg's account in *De Stijl*,[17] were confused and ill-defined, so that van Doesburg, Lissitzky and Hans Richter had formed a splinter group – The International Faction of Constructivists – with their own definition of the role of the artist: 'We define this progressive artist as one who fights and rejects the tyranny of the subjective in art, as one whose work is not based on lyrical arbitrariness, as one who accepts the new principles of artistic creation – the systematization of the means of expression to produce results that are universally comprehensible.'[18]

This substitution of the subjective for the systematic was implicit in the group's definition of 'constructive', and it was reiterated in Lissitzky's statement to the Congress. 'The new art is formed, not on a subjective, but on an objective basis. This, like science, can be described with precision and is by nature constructive. It unites not only pure art, but all those who stand at the frontier of the new culture. The artist is companion to the scholar, the engineer and the worker.'[19]

Given these clearly defined convictions, it is difficult to explain the presence of Hans Arp and Tristan Tzara, then associated with Dada, at the conference. For van Doesburg, however, who contributed to Dada manifestations under the pseudonyms of I. K. Bonset and Aldo Camini, Dada was Constructivism's *alter ego* – Dadaists were 'destructive constructivists', attacking current complacency in order to 'annul the divorce of transcendental and everyday reality'.[20]

More significant for the future of the Bauhaus, however, was the presence of Laszlo Moholy-Nagy (Illus. 42) and his wife Lucia at the conference. Moholy-Nagy was born in Hungary in 1895, and had studied law before he joined the army. He began to draw during the war and continued when he returned to Hungary. Apart from a few evening classes, however, he was largely self-taught, learning through the experience of looking at and reading about paintings. His approach then, he wrote 'was more that of "hearing" the picture's literary significance than seeing form and visual elements'. Significantly enough, in view of Kandinsky's, and more particularly Klee's, experience, Moholy's first attempts 'to express three-dimensional plastic quality' was through the use of line: 'I tried to analyze bodies, faces, landscapes with my "line", but the results slipped out of my hands. The drawings became a rhythmically articulated network of lines, *showing not so much objects, as my excitement about them*.' These experiments, however, enabled him to 'decipher' the work of Munch, Kokoschka, Schiele and Marc, and to 'dare to examine' the Cubists, Futurists and Expressionists, since the use of line in their paintings 'was part of their language, based on visual fundamentals'.[21]

His experience during the war (when he was badly wounded), and his social commitment, however, had forced him to question the relevance of art. 'Can I assume the privilege of becoming an artist for myself, when everybody is needed to solve the problems of simply managing to survive?' he wrote in his diary in May 1919. 'During the past hundred years art and life have had nothing in common. The personal indulgence of creating art has contributed nothing to the masses.'[22] The Russian-inspired Hungarian 'art-activists' associated with the *MA (Today)* group convinced him that art had a role to play in a revolutionary society, especially when several of them were forced to leave Hungary after the counter-revolution in 1919. In December 1919, after his first exhibition, Moholy also left Hungary, first for Vienna, where Kassak, the editor of *MA* magazine was in exile, and then for Berlin, where he was to become *MA*'s German correspondent.

In Vienna he had felt 'lost among the depressed conformists of the post-war period', and he went to Germany because he was 'intrigued with the highly-developed technology of industrial Germany'. 'Many of my paintings of that period,' he wrote, 'show the influence of the "industrial landscape" of Berlin. They were not projections of reality rendered with photographic eyes, but rather new structures, built up as my own version of machine technology, reassembled from the dismantled parts. . . . On my walks I found scrap machine parts, screws, bolts, mechanical devices. I fastened, glued and nailed them on wooden boards, combined with drawings and painting.'[23] Moholy, therefore, had outgrown his use of line to express his emotions and reactions, and was now 'constructing' his work, preoccupied not only with machine analogies, but also with 'the spatial articulation' that could be achieved through the manipulation of two- and three-dimensional form, and the effect of light and transparency in the painting.

Once in Berlin he rapidly became involved with the avant-garde culture and counter-culture. In October 1921, he was a co-signator, together with the Dadaists Raoul Hausmann and Hans Arp, and the Russian Constructivist Ivan Puni of 'A Call for Elementarist Art', which was published in *De Stijl* in 1922;[24] he met Lissitzky when he came to Berlin in 1921; the 15 September issue of *MA* was devoted to Moholy's work, and in May 1922 he had a one-man exhibition in Herwarth Walden's *Sturm* gallery. Adolf Behne, who had introduced van Doesburg to Gropius, also took Gropius to see this exhibition, and it was there that negotiations began to appoint Moholy to the staff of the Bauhaus.

It is not easy to understand why Gropius should invite this relatively unknown painter, who had no experience of teaching, or of designing, and who spoke German with difficulty, to teach at the school. In the introduction to *The New Vision*, Gropius writes that at

42 Moholy-Nagy, *c.*1919 *Bauhaus-Archiv*

that first meeting he was 'impressed by the character and direction of his work'. He obviously felt that Moholy was one of those 'young artists' who were 'beginning to face up to the phenomena of industry and the machine'.[25] Unfortunately the experimental reliefs that Moholy wrote about in *Abstract of an Artist* are lost or destroyed, but in some of the paintings that do survive from 1921 22 there are cogs, wheels, and gears, as well as numbers and letters (Pl. 5), clearly organized in geometric configurations. He also began to paint what he called his 'transparent' pictures at this time 'completely freed of elements reminiscent of nature'. 'I wanted to eliminate all factors which might disturb their clarity in contrast, for example, with Kandinsky's paintings, which reminded me sometimes of an undersea world. My desire was to work with the peculiar characteristics of colours, with their pure relationships. I chose simple geometric forms as a step towards such objectivity.'[26] This emphasis on clarity, objectivity and abstraction, the antithesis of Itten's approach, obviously appealed to Gropius, and Moholy's theories, published in various manifestoes, also stressed the democracy of art. In May 1922 he had written in *MA*: '. . . this reality of our century is *technology* – the invention, construction and maintenance of the machine. . . . There is no tradition in technology, no consciousness of class or standing. Everyone can be the machine's master or its slave.' It was, however, art – Constructivism – 'the art of our century, its mirror and its voice' – that could determine whether society

99

would be destroyed by the machine. 'Constructivism is not confined to the picture frame and the pedestal. It expands into industrial designs, into houses, objects, forms. It is the socialism of vision – the common property of all men.'[27]

MOHOLY–NAGY, ALBERS AND THE BASIC COURSE

When Moholy-Nagy returned to Weimar as a teacher in the spring of 1923 he was faced with opposition and incomprehension. Paul Citroen describes him as 'bursting into the Bauhaus circle like a strong, eager dog . . . sniffing out with unfailing scent the still unsolved, tradition-bound problems in order to attack them. The most conspicuous difference between him and the older teachers was a lack of typically German dignity and remoteness among the older Masters.'[28] This lack was compounded by his bad German, his extrovert enthusiasms and his impatience with mysticism and cults. According to Lothar Schreyer, he brought 'a new and totally alien world into the Bauhaus'; 'You are all sick romantics,' Schreyer reports him as saying, and after an exchange about ideas for the Bauhaus theatre: 'Forgive me if I have perhaps sinned against the Holy Ghost of the Bauhaus. But how could I know that the Bauhaus was some kind of monastic order?'[29]

It was obvious that Moholy-Nagy was to be no 'corridor master'[30] and that he was not going to bring a weight of theory to his experiments. According to his first wife Lucia 'Moholy-Nagy was, in those days, mainly concerned with unequivocal statements, not with the intricacies of a philosophical approach.' This was partly due, she wrote, 'to his inadequate command of German'; but in spite of this he managed to communicate 'and spread a notion of the world as he then saw it. He always had the present and future in mind, hardly ever looking back to the historical past.'[31]

His initial brief was to take charge of the metal workshop and to direct the preliminary course, both formerly Itten's domains. Since the beginning of 1923, however, Josef Albers, a newly-qualified 'master' at the school, had been running a component of the course, and Albers continued to do this, although Moholy-Nagy was in charge of the programme as a whole. Both Albers's and Itten's experience, before joining the school, had been similar. Albers had been trained as an art teacher, and had taught in schools before attending the School of Arts and Crafts in Essen, and the Munich Academy. He was thirty-two (the same age as Itten) when he came to Weimar; he went there on the strength of the manifesto, and the preliminary course with its stress on self-discovery through empathy with materials was a revelation to him. It confirmed all his theories as to how art should be taught to school children, but at the same time, unlike Itten, Albers did not believe that the course should be an end in itself, but should prepare for, rather an inspire, the workshop production. The aim of his course, he wrote in *Bauhaus 1919–1928*[32] was 'to prepare the first semester students . . . for the later craft studies in the various Bauhaus workshops. The students were introduced to a simple, elementary, but appropriate use of the more important craft materials, such as wood, metal, glass, stone, textiles, and paint, and to an understanding of their relationships as well as the differences between them. In this way we tried, without anticipating later workshop practice, and without workshop equipment, to develop an understanding of the fundamental properties of materials and of the principles of construction.' The stress on manual work and craft materials, therefore, remained unchanged, but according to Lux Feininger, 'The concept of the course itself, however, was so drastically changed by Albers that nothing but the name remained.'

'Expendable materials of ordinary everyday life were favoured; I remember a most impressive structure composed of nothing but used safety razor blades (which are slotted and punched by the manufacturers) and burnt-up wooden matches.' Lux Feininger also remembers Albers introducing a stapler 'and demonstrating its possibilities with great inward satisfaction'; he also led them round a cardboard box factory 'pointing out the manufacturing particulars, both good and bad (i.e. capable of improvement) with the kind of religious concentration one would expect from a lecturer in the Louvre'.[33]

Albers, therefore, was responsible for the materials or workshop component of the preliminary course, while Moholy-Nagy directed experiments in form. This demarcation, however, was obviously theoretical rather than practical, and the two courses complemented each other in various ways. The emphasis in both courses (which lasted two terms under Moholy-Nagy's direction rather than one) was on economy of materials and means. 'The principal emphasis of the course was on economy,' wrote Otto Stelzer, 'with a minimum of effort, a maximum of effect was to be achieved.'[34] The 'free association' of materials, characteristic of the Itten courses, the experiments with textures, collages, the 'light-dark' studies, and the analyses of old masters were replaced by exercises which demonstrated the structural, kinetic, and spatial articulation of materials. The forms which were created out of paper, metal, wire, fabric, glass and wood were minimal, tensile, suspended in space and abstract; they were self-referential and defined by light and shadow. Albers defined the aims of the Preliminary Course in a letter to George Rickey: 'If a general denominator could be found for all three *Vorkurs* teachings – Itten taught four years, Moholy for five years, I for ten years – all three aimed at the development of a new, contemporary visual idiom. And this, with time, led from an emphasis on personal expression and individualistic graphic and pictorial representation of material, to a more rational, economic and structural use of the material itself. It led to the recognition of, beside its outer appearance (*matière*), its inner capacities or practical potentialities; and so, to a more impersonal presentation. Or, in pictorial terms, from collage to montage.'[35]

This change of emphasis from a subjective to an objective approach to materials obviously challenged the 'aura' of the crafts in Weimar. At the same time, however, it also challenged the autonomy of fine art; Klee and Kandinsky, as well as the Constructivist painters, had attempted to establish a theory, or 'science' of art in such a way as to express universal experience through their work. Painting, however, as Walter Benjamin was to point out in his essay 'The Work of Art in the Age of Mechanical Reproduction'[36] 'simply is in no position to present an object for simultaneous collective experience, as it was possible for architecture at all times'. The 'montages' produced by Albers and Moholy-Nagy were primarily a demonstration of the architectonic, rather than the expressive potential of material, and this was emphasized through photography, which presented them in abstract space, light and shadow being essential components in their composition.

Photography, significantly enough, was to play an important part in the work of the school following the appointment of Moholy-Nagy. Both he and his wife had been experimenting with photograms and photomontage in Berlin, and Moholy found in photography an extension of his ideals for art. It enabled him 'to paint with light', and to investigate the possibilities of 'light-composition'; and as far as he was concerned there was a positive interaction between his work in both media. 'I myself have learned from my photographic work much that is of use in my painting and conversely problems posed by my paintings have often provided hints for my photographic experiments.' At the same time, however, he maintained that 'traditional painting has become a historical relic and is finished with'.[37]

The work of all the painters at the Bauhaus, of course, was based on the assumption that the academic or historicist approach to painting was 'finished with'; the conviction that art still had a direct and creative role to play in the regeneration of the crafts, however, was implicit in the direction of the workshops, where the painter, as *Formmeister*, assumed a more prestigious role than the *Lehrmeister*, craftsman or technician. Moholy, therefore, with his alien enthusiasms and reinterpretation of construction, represented a threat to the values of the school, so that the formerly avant-garde assumed defensive positions. 'Only optics, mechanics and the desire to put the old static painting out of action,' wrote Feininger: 'There is incessant talk of cinema, optics, mechanics, projection and continuous motion and even of mechanically-produced optical transparencies, multi-coloured, in the finest colours of the spectrum, which can be stored in the same way as gramophone records. . . . Is this the atmosphere in which painters like Klee and some others of us can go on developing? Klee was quite depressed yesterday when talking about Moholy.'[38] By equating painting with photography and film, Moholy was challenging traditional as well as avant-garde attitudes to art. In his interpretation, photography had the potential to transform rather than destroy art; at the same time, however, it had the potential to destroy what he described as ' "the personal touch" so highly valued in previous painting'. In order to achieve 'machine-like perfection' he used air-brushes and spray guns; he gave up signing his paintings, and put numbers and letters with the necessary data on the back of the canvas, as if they were cars, airplanes or other industrial products.[39] As early as 1922 he had produced his famous 'telephone' abstract enamels, ordering the panels and the colours by telephone to the factory. He described them, when they were exhibited in the *Sturm* gallery in 1924 as 'enamel pictures executed by industrial methods'.[40]

The search for 'machine precision' rather than the spiritual in art reversed the role of the fine artist in Weimar. Klee and Kandinsky had developed and demonstrated techniques of visual analysis derived from their own experience and painting on the assumption that they would contribute to workshop practice.

Moholy, on the other hand, with his belief in the 'socialism of vision' maintained that: 'In our industrial age, the distinction between art and non-art, between manual craftsmanship and mechanical technology is no longer an absolute one.'[41] By redefining the boundaries of art, and relating art to technology, Moholy was introducing one of the most persistent twentieth-century concepts of the designer. Just as Moholy produced 'art' without applying paint to canvas, so the designer could conceptualize his work without necessarily becoming involved with the processes of making a product. This shift from the demonstration of art through craft to the demonstration of art through technology confirmed Gropius's aims for the school, so that when he began to write its history, the workshops became 'laboratories', 'manual instruction' . . . 'a practical first step in mastering industrial processes', and 'handicrafts' valuable as a preparatory stage in 'evolving new type-forms for mass production'.[42]

The transformation of the Bauhaus from a 'cathedral of socialism' into a 'laboratory' for the production of prototypes for industry was, however, prompted by expediency as well as ideology, since the school was funded by, and accountable to, local government, which obviously influenced, and ultimately ratified its policies.

In March 1923, two months after French and Belgian troops had occupied the Ruhr, intensifying Germany's economic crisis, Gropius was involved in a major debate in the Thuringian *Landtag* about the financing and policies of the Bauhaus. The arguments for and against its programme reflect the debates within the school, and demonstrate how far its activities, and Gropius's priorities, were influenced by political and financial pressures. Dr Emil Herfurth, one of the bitterest opponents of the 'Cathedral of Socialism' in Weimar, accused the school of extravagance (two masters for every workshop, prestigious painters, and a theatre) and, with reference to Vilmos Huszar's *De Stijl* review of 1922, mismanagement. Other speakers in support of Herfurth stressed the fact that the school had established few links with either craft or industrial production: the textile industry, for example, had no use for the experiments in the weaving workshop. Tenner, the representative of the Communist party, rejected the right-wing move to destroy the school before it had time to develop. Although the concept of 'art in handwork' was essentially *petit bourgeois*, art had a major role to play in a socialist society. He therefore welcomed the change of emphasis in the school's programme from crafts to industrial production and recommended that Gropius should have time to put his theories into practice.

Gropius, for his part, also pleaded for time and for money. The school had its own allotments, grew its own vegetables, but it could not make bread out of a stone. The students needed funds for survival, and the school needed money for development. It could have become self-sufficient if the state had given it commissions: the various commissions the school had been involved in were due to his own and the staff's initiatives. Rejecting suggestions that he despised traditional Thuringian craftsmanship, he maintained that, for his part, he considered 'handwork' within the school should concentrate on the development of prototypes for industry. Since it took three years to train a student, the school had scarcely had time to demonstrate its professionalism. In spite of this, however, the Bauhaus 'idea' had achieved world recognition; the work of its painters had been exhibited in Zurich, New York, Calcutta, Sweden and Berlin, and the forthcoming exhibition, given adequate funding, would demonstrate the school's potential for establishing links with industry.

Fortunately for Gropius, the Bauhaus had the total support of Dr Max Greil, the

Thuringian minister for education. He acknowledged the experimental nature of the school, but agreed with Gropius about its reputation and potential. He welcomed its proposal to establish 'norms' that could be adopted or adapted by industry. 'Considering that the experiment has been under way for three years, it would be the greatest folly to break up its development and to abandon the incomplete experiment at the moment when the Bauhaus is able to demonstrate what it is capable of achieving. One first has to give the Bauhaus an opportunity, through an exhibition, to present a complete picture of what it is able to do. . . .'[1] What is significant about this debate is the shift of emphasis, in Gropius's speech, from art and craftsmanship to industrial production. The painters were seen to contribute to the fame of the school because of their reputation as *artists*, not because of their involvement with workshop production, and it was left to Tenner, the Communist representative, to repeat the *Arbeitsrat* (and Constructivist) ideal of art transforming industrial production. Greil's contribution is also interesting, not only because he wished to see the school working towards 'norms' that could be taken up by industry (the Muthesian theory), but because he acknowledged the Bauhaus as the most radical art school in Germany, *educating* its students rather than providing them with a vocational training.

Because of the opposition within the *Landtag*, it was obviously vital that the exhibition planned for the summer of 1923 should be a success, but it was also obvious to many of the staff that the issues involved were political rather than educational. Feininger wrote to his wife in October 1922: '. . . we are making a great and weighty concession in the Bauhaus by going ahead with the planned exhibition. We are all reluctant inside to abide by such "art politics". . . . But this much is sure – if we cannot show "results" to the outside world and win "industrialists" to our side, then the prospects for the future existence of the Bauhaus are very dim indeed. We have to steer towards profitable undertakings, towards mass-production! That goes decidedly against our grain. . . .'[2] Schlemmer wrote in his diary in November 1922: 'I do not believe that craftsmanship as practised at the Bauhaus can transcend the aesthetic and fulfil more serious social functions. "Getting in touch with industry" will not do the trick; we would have to commit ourselves and merge completely with industry. But we cannot make that our goal; it would mean turning our backs on the Bauhaus.'[3] Significantly enough, he also expressed some dismay that 'Marcel Breuer (voluntarily and certainly at a cost) abjures painting, at which he would be talented, and does cabinet-making instead'.[4]

THE SOMMERFELD HOUSE

By the beginning of 1923, however, the workshops were overcoming their initial problems, and designs were being produced by the 'apprentices' that demonstrated formal as well as practical competence. Some of the workshops had already had experience of working in collaboration in the commission for the Sommerfeld House (Illus. 43), which was designed by Gropius and Meyer in 1921 and completed in 1922. Adolf Sommerfeld, one of the first patrons of the school (he was to put up the money for the Haus am Horn, the major 'exhibit' in the 1923 exhibition) was a timber merchant, and the house was built mainly from teak he had acquired from a dismantled ship. The house provided Josef Albers, Marcel Breuer and Joost Schmidt, three of the students who were to teach at the school, and, of course, to become important as designers in their own right, with the opportunity

43 The Sommerfeld house, designed by Walter Gropius and Adolf Meyer, 1921 *Bauhaus-Archiv*

to carry out commissioned rather than experimental work. Obviously the nature of this work was largely determined by the facilities in the workshops, and the most ambitious contributions to the Sommerfeld House were the carvings on the doors and staircases by Joost Schmidt, and the stained-glass windows by Albers – both produced in workshops that were already established in the school. Schmidt, who had arrived in Weimar to study sculpture, first with Max Thedy from the former academy, and then with Schlemmer, designed and carved complex reliefs on the staircases, which although basically abstract and geometric, symbolized the activities of the timber industry, Albers's windows combine abstract patterns which demonstrate the influence of Klee as well as his own preoccupation with the juxtaposition of squares of colour. The windows, the carving, and the panelling of the interior all relate to that unity of form, expression and decoration that Adolf Meyer, trained by Lauweriks, would wish to achieve. Only Marcel Breuer's furniture, with its weight and over-emphatic geometry strikes a discordant note,[5] and this may be due in part to the organization of the carpentry workshop, as well as to Breuer's development as a 'cabinet-maker'.

The carpentry workshop, as distinct from the wood-carving workshop, was new to Weimar, and it was first set up in 1921, with Gropius as *Formmeister* and Josef Zachmann as *Lehrmeister*. At that time, however, Itten was closely involved with both workshops, and the 'African' chair, Breuer's first experimental work as a student, with its folk-art,

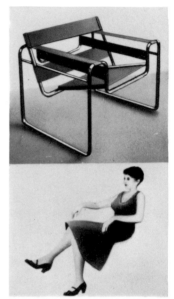

44 Photographs of Marcel Breuer's chairs in the *Bauhaus Journal* No. 1 1926, captioned 'Every day we are getting better and better . . . in the end we will sit on resilient air columns' *Bauhaus-Archiv*

totem-like quality, might have been inspired by Itten's teaching. Breuer, however, was obviously preoccupied, as early as 1921, with the simple and direct expression of form, and van Doesburg no doubt considered him as one of the 'young artists' he had brought back to 'order and discipline'.[6] It is obvious that Gerrit Rietveld's Red/Blue chair, designed in 1917, and illustrated in the *De Stijl* magazine of 1922, impressed him, since he produced his own version of the design in 1922 (Pl. 6). It is also obvious, comparing the two chairs, that the similarities are superficial, and that if Breuer were attempting to produce a 'De Stijl' chair, he had misinterpreted the philosophy of De Stijl (Pl. 7). The Rietveld chair is a statement about the relationship of form to space, made to demonstrate 'that a thing of beauty, e.g. a spatial object, could be made of nothing but straight machined materials'.[7] Its components are designed to a module, and are joined together in such a way that they explore rather than define space. Breuer's version on the other hand, in spite of its attempt at formal innovation, is contrived and clumsy, and the use of fabrics (from the weaving workshop) as a structural component on the seat and back emphasizes its inconsistencies.

Breuer's later furniture at Weimar, the children's chairs and tables, for example, also designed in 1922, is far more confident. The De Stijl influence is still there, but Breuer was now producing furniture that had no obvious precedent in Germany. The designs could not be considered as 'typeforms', however, and are in no way related to the pre-war work of Riemerschmid or Bruno Paul; they represent the search for a simplicity and clarity of form which is evident in the work of other designers in the workshop, including Erich Dieckmann, Josef Albers, and Alma Buscher. What is interesting about their work at this period is its technical competence and the pluralistic approach to the constraints imposed either by ideology or by the lack of facilities in the workshop. Reinhold Weidensee, who took over as *Lehrmeister* when Zachmann left in 1922, was a master cabinet-maker, and his skills are evident in much of the work. Erich Dieckmann, for example, was obviously the most competent craftsman among them in this early period. The angularity of the frames of his chairs is justified by construction, rather than Constructivism, and his cabinet furniture – a desk, wardrobe and bookcase – are remarkable in this context for their formal understatement; their emphasis on the qualities of the various woods used – oak, walnut and beech – belongs to the tradition of cabinet-making. (Dieckmann remained in Weimar when the school moved to Dessau, and his work in the late twenties and early thirties is interesting for the consistency of its development. By 1926, when the Bauhaus designers were experimenting with tubular steel, he was designing ranges he described as *Typenmöbel* – type-furniture – that demonstrate that quality of *Sachlichkeit* – sobriety and order – which was the ideal of the rationalists in the pre-war Werkbund. At the same time, however, before 1930, he was also undertaking ergonomic research into table heights and chair dimensions, and in the 1930s, when he was working as a freelance designer and teaching at an applied art school in Halle, he began to use tubular steel for tables and chairs that were mass-produced by Thonet, and Cebaso, a Thuringian company. Dieckmann, therefore, concentrating on furniture design, was able to work within an established tradition to produce innovations within that tradition, and when new materials were introduced, to produce designs that were acceptable in traditional as well as avant-garde markets.)[8]

In the Weimar period, however, Josef Albers and Alma Buscher used wood and the techniques of cabinet-making to create experimental and innovative work. Albers, one of the most eclectic of the Bauhaus designers, produced furniture both in Weimar and Dessau, and his interest in it seems to have developed out of his involvement with the Preliminary Course. His work in the early years shows technical competence (he designed a range of chairs with tilting seats for use in church which were exhibited in the 1923 exhibition), as well as Constructivist-inspired experiments with elementary forms (an asymmetric bookcase, a table with an asymmetric base, and a glass display case with adjustable shelves of different sizes designed to emphasize the transparency and the prismatic qualities of glass). It was Alma Buscher (Illus. 45), however, who produced the most interesting experimental work in this period with her toys and children's furniture – a play cupboard built up from brightly-coloured boxes that could be sat on or in, wheeled around, as well as used for storage. These and her wooden toys – a set of coloured wooden shapes that could be built into ships, and a range of circles, spheres, hemispheres and cones that could be slotted together in various ways – were based on her research into children's play. 'Work and play are interchangeable,' she wrote, 'as at the Bauhaus.' The

45 Toy cabinet in lacquered wood. The units can be dismantled. Alma Buscher, 1924 *Bauhaus-Archiv*

toy-shop should be the children's workshop, where children learn to build, understand form and proportion, respond to colour. . . . 'Fairy tales or reality: created only by the child.'[9] According to Wingler,[10] Alma Buscher's children's furniture was 'among the first of the Bauhaus products to be well-received by the public', and it was illustrated, together with work by Dieckmann, Breuer and Albers, in *Neue Arbeiten der Bauhaus-Werkstätten* (New Work from the Bauhaus Workshops), which was published as a Bauhaus book in 1925. A significant omission from this book, however, is Peter Keler's cradle of 1922 (Pl. 11). Based on Kandinsky's theories of the relationship of primary forms to colour, it is composed of a circle (blue), triangle (yellow) and square (red). It is a literal (and perhaps ironic) translation of theories related to art into three-dimensional design: basic design at its most basic, and, although it is heavily weighted at the bottom, a challenge to siblings who might be tempted to bowl it around, admiring the effect of form, colour and baby in motion.

THE WEAVING WORKSHOP

Alma Buscher was the only woman working in the carpentry workshop in Weimar. After the Preliminary Course, the majority of the women gravitated to the weaving workshop, which was in adequate order, since Hélène Börner, who had worked with van de Velde, owned the looms. Gunta Stölzl, who was to be in charge of weaving at Dessau has

108

described their early experiences at Weimar.[11] The *Bauhausmädchen*, she said, 'experimented in each workshop, but the heavy planes, hard metals and the physical strain of mural painting inhibited their work'. They had, nevertheless, to find some outlet for their creativity. 'Nearly all of us came from academies or schools of applied art, and we wanted to be rid of the dry exercises in drawing and painting. We wanted to make living things, with contemporary relevance.' They formed a 'women's class' and made toys – fantastic objects fabricated out of anything they could find and they sold them cheaply at the Weimar Christmas market. These experiments, however, were valuable to their conception of creative work in the weaving workshop at Weimar, for they wanted to declare independence and start again from the beginning, forgetting the past, learning or re-learning the techniques for themselves. 'They began amateurishly and playfully,' wrote Anni Albers, who joined the weaving workshop as a student in 1922, 'but gradually something grew out of their play, which looked like a new and independent trend. . . . Unburdened by any practical considerations, this play with materials produced amazing results, textiles striking in their novelty, their fullness of colour and texture, and possessing quite often a quite barbaric beauty.'[12] The tapestries and weaves produced in the workshops in Weimar as well as in Dessau are among the most remarkable achievements of the Bauhaus, since the designers not only revitalized the art of tapestry but they also realized the design potential in hand- and machine-weaving. In the nineteenth century William Morris had fought his own battles to revive 'the noblest of the weaving arts'; his concern was with colour and with the regeneration of the pictorial tradition that had inspired pre-Renaissance work. By the 1920s, however, that tradition was defunct, and the literal transformation of a figurative painting into a tapestry diminished both arts. The work of the painters in the Bauhaus obviously influenced some of the tapestries produced in Weimar; there are similarities, for example, between the work of Hedwig Jungnik (Pl. 9) and Georg Muche's paintings, although Muche himself, of course, agreed to act as *Formmeister* on the understanding that he was a painter, with no interest in craftsmanship. The apprentices in this workshop, however, also referred to earlier, non-figurative traditions for complex pattern-making, as well as designing tapestries based on the simple relationships of geometric forms; and they obviously drew on the courses on colour theory for the imagination, as well as control, they demonstrate in the use of colour. Gunta Stölzl describes these tapestries as 'the most ingratiating articles of those wildly revolutionary Bauhaus products'; by 1931, however, she is condemning them for their 'individuality' and impracticality, since they could not, in her opinion, be related to a clearly definable design ethic. 'We noticed how pretentious these independent single pieces were: cloth, curtain, wall-hanging. The richness of colour began to look much too autocratic to us, it did not subordinate itself to the home. We made an effort to become simpler, to discipline our means and to achieve a greater unity between material and function.'[13]

The unity between material and process is essential to hand- and machine-weaving, and the experiments in hand-weaving at the Weimar Bauhaus were to influence the machine work in Dessau, since they involved qualities common to both methods of production: an understanding of structure and texture, as well as the interaction of colour. At Weimar, according to Gunta Stölzl, they learned to understand the limitations and potential of different materials – wool, silk, linen, etc., and they also realized how the same colour assumed 'a life of its own' in different materials (they experimented with dyes at both

46 Fabric: cotton, synthetic wool and artificial silk; white warp, stripes of black, white, yellow and pink, 1923/4. Designer unknown *Kunstsammlungen, Weimar*

Weimar and Dessau) (Illus. 46). Towards the end of the period in Weimar, therefore, the workshop was producing hand-woven fabrics in a limited range of patterns and colours that were applicable to machine techniques – valuable apprenticeship work, which the workshop was to retain in Dessau, as a preliminary to mass production.

THE METAL WORKSHOP

From 1919 to 1923, the metal workshop had three *Lehrmeister*, with Schlemmer and Klee as well as Itten involved as *Formmeister*. During this early period, according to Wingler, 'the domain of each artist was revised repeatedly, so that not even the master-craftsmen always knew with which form master they were supposed to work'.[14] According to one student they turned out 'spiritual samovars and intellectual door-knobs'.[15] (The door furniture for the Sommerfeld House was designed by metal workshop students, Illus. 47). In 1922, however, Christian Dell, who had worked with van de Velde, was appointed craft master. Dell was an experienced silversmith, and according to Gyula Pap, he was also a patient and gifted teacher, demonstrating how different forms could be created out of flat sheets of metal and how to combine various materials.[16]

At that time Dell worked within the avant-garde and élitist traditions of the Vienna Workshops, using silver, silver-plate and ebony, and many of the early Bauhaus designs for silverware seem to relate to this tradition. As far as the apprentices were concerned, however, their work developed out of their experiments on the Preliminary Course, and then from their experience of working with metal. Pap, for example, who was impressed by Itten's teaching methods on the Preliminary Course (he taught in the Itten school in Berlin from 1926–1933) claims that he decided to work with metal in Weimar because of his fascination with geometric form. Originally trained as a painter and illustrator, he felt that the 'reduction of painting to geometry was too narrow', but that the complex forms that could be created out of metal were a challenge to him. Marianne Brandt, the only

47 Sommerfeld House; detail of door; the lock is by Naum Slutzky, 1921 *Bauhaus-Archiv*

woman in the metal workshop, also used geometric shapes for her designs which have become icons of the Weimar Bauhaus (Pl. 8). 'We wanted to return to the simplest forms', she wrote. Equally important, however, was practicality: nothing was allowed to leave the workshop without being tested – tea and coffee pots had to be well balanced, pour properly and not drip. 'We didn't think we were doing anything remarkable working this way – it just seemed obvious to us.'[17] It was Moholy-Nagy, who took over as *Formmeister* in 1923, who recommended that Marianne Brandt should transfer to the metal workshop. 'At first I was not accepted with pleasure,' she wrote: '. . . there was no place for a woman in a metal workshop. They felt . . . and expressed their displeasure by giving me all sorts of dull, dreary work. How many little hemispheres did I most patiently hammer out of brittle new silver, thinking that was the way it had to be and all beginnings are hard. Later things settled down, and we got along well together.'[18]

Moholy-Nagy obviously galvanized the metal workshop in his attempt to respond to Gropius's brief to 'reorganize it as a workshop for industrial design'. 'Changing the policy of this workshop involved a revolution,' he wrote, 'for in their pride the goldsmiths and silversmiths avoided the use of ferrous metals, nickel and chromium plating and abhorred the idea of making models for electrical appliances or lighting fixtures.'[19] When the workshop was founded, the 'craft' approach to designs in precious or semi-precious metals seemed a logical one, not only because of the pre-war demand for wine-jugs and samovars, but also because this was the tradition in which Christian Dell had worked. After Dell's appointment, innovations involved concentration on the geometry, rather than the decoration of form. In these early years Moholy, with no experience of designing for industry, could only encourage innovatory work that extended this tradition, or experiments with designs that assumed the appearance rather than the practicality of industrial production (Pl. 10). Preoccupied as an artist with light, Moholy encouraged experiments with light-fittings. 'I remember the first lighting fixture by K. Jucker, done before 1923, with devices for pushing and pulling, heavy strips and rods of iron and brass, looking more like a dinosaur than a functional object. But even this was a great victory, for it meant a new beginning.'[20] It was, however, not until the school had moved to Dessau that this 'new beginning' could be related to industrial production. Wilhelm Wagenfeld, for example, has described how Moholy's paintings, and the experiments in the Preliminary Course were a direct inspiration for the table lamp that he designed in collaboration with Karl Jucker in 1924; both Gropius and Moholy were convinced that this could be offered as a 'prototype' for industry, and a series was produced (with some difficulty because of the limited techniques available in the workshop), for exhibition at the Leipzig Fair of 1924. 'But,' wrote Wagenfeld, 'without success. Retailers and manufacturers laughed at our efforts. These designs which looked as though they could be made inexpensively by machine techniques were, in fact, extremely costly craft designs.' It was only later, according to Wagenfeld, that he realized that his lamp was a 'crippled, bloodless picture in glass and metal'[21] (Illus. 48).

48 Electric table lamp: glass base and tube; opalescent glass shade. Designed by K. J. Jucker and Wilhelm Wagenfeld, 1923–4 *Kunstsammlungen, Weimar*

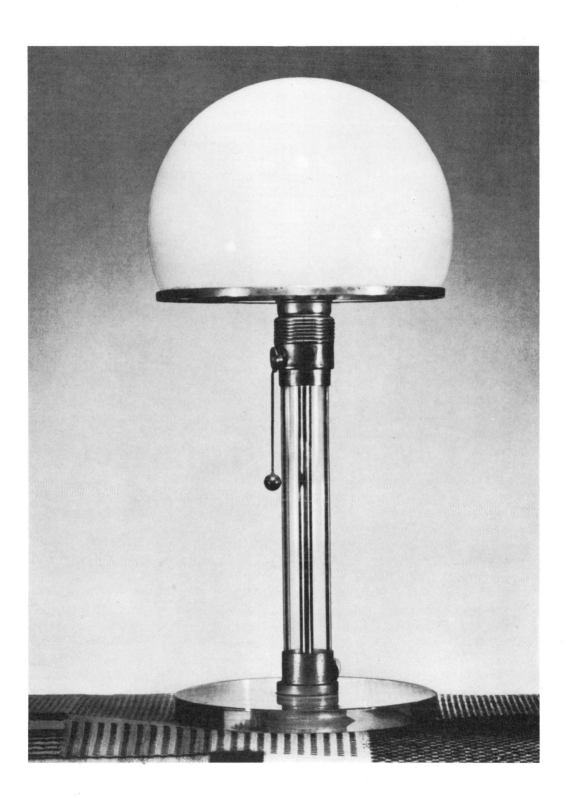

THE HAUS AM HORN

In spite of the lack of any direct liaison with industry, the output of the workshops was directed towards a more specific goal in the period leading up to the exhibition. They had, of course, to demonstrate their capabilities in order to ensure the survival of the school, and at the same time they had a brief to furnish a prototype house that was to be built on the Am Horn road, on a site selected for a Bauhaus 'settlement'. However acrimony and inflation held up this project. There was, of course, no architecture department in the school at that time, although students had worked with Gropius and Meyer on private commissions. The design for the experimental house was chosen democratically, by staff and students, and the one selected was not by Gropius, but by Georg Muche, the painter who had no time for handicraft.

Since joining the school in 1920, Muche had become involved in its practical and polemical crises. It was Itten who had introduced him to Weimar, and he was to join Itten's school in Berlin in 1927. During his period at the Bauhaus, however, Muche was an acute observer of the school's ideological dilemmas, and his article on 'Fine Art and Industrial Form' (see page 127) which was published in the first issue of the Bauhaus magazine in Dessau in 1926, is one of the most cogent critiques of the 'Art and Industry' debates.

His decision to enter a 'project' for the prototype house was personal rather than ideological. He was about to get married, and had planned a 'dream-house' for himself and his wife. There was to be 'a large central living-room, and around it, in contrast, low, small and very practical rooms. In the kitchen everything that was needed was to be within easy reach.'[22] Muche stressed that this was a practical and 'human' approach to a design problem, and that although the solution was related to the personal ideal of a small self-contained house that was inexpensive and easy to run, the house as planned could relate to universal human needs, the balance between 'communal' and 'private space' being carefully preserved. Once the design had been chosen, Gropius, who must have been somewhat deflated by the fact that his own work for the site was not considered, approved the project, and Adolf Meyer worked with Muche to translate his 'dream' into reality.

To the residents of Weimar, however, this white, single-storey house, with its central living-room lit by clerestory windows (Illus. 49), and its doors and windows cut flush into the walls, seemed unconventional, and to some completely alien to the 'culture' of Weimar, expressed by the large and opulent residences on the Am Horn site. Some newspaper critics shared their reservations: one compared it to a public lavatory; another thought it an ideal setting for Strindberg's *Totentanz*, while a middle-class matron complained that its ease of maintenance marked the eclipse of the German *Hausfrau*.[23]

There were, of course, defenders of the experimental house; Dr Edwin Redslob, the Administrator of Federal Art Institutions, believed that the house would have 'far-reaching cultural and economic consequences', since it demonstrated economy of construction, as well as a realistic approach to the one-family dwelling. 'There is evidence,' he wrote, 'that a type of design is developing which organically unites several small rooms around a large one, thus bringing about a complete change in form as well as in manner of living. Of all the plans I have seen, none appears to me so apt to clarify and solve the problem as the one submitted by the Bauhaus. The plight in which we find ourselves as a nation necessitates our being the first of all nations to solve the new problem of building. These plans clearly go far towards blazing a new trail.'[24]

49 Haus am Horn (*Top*) 1923 *Bauhaus Archiv*; (*Bottom*) 1982 *Photograph Gillian Naylor*

The nation's plight which he referred to was, of course, inflation. At the beginning of 1923, the dollar was worth 18,000 marks; in August, when the exhibition was due to open, it was worth 4,600,000 marks and by November four billion marks. The exhibition, therefore, could not have been held at a worse time, and attempts to build, equip and furnish the house, as well as organize displays of student work and supporting exhibitions, were hampered by this disastrous financial situation. The fact that the house could be built at all was due to the generosity of Adolf Sommerfeld, who loaned most of the money for its construction, and sold it later at a loss. Several firms also contributed materials and services either free of charge or at a minimal cost. Where possible these were industrially produced; the house was built from 'Jurko-stone' concrete blocks, with white rendering, and insulated throughout with Torfoleum panels. The rubber and linoleum for the floors, the central heating system, the plate glass, as well as door and window furniture (no 'intellectual door-knobs') were also provided by industry. The furniture and furnishings for the house, however, were designed and made in the school's workshops: furniture by Breuer, Albers, Dieckmann and Alma Buscher (Illus. 50 and 51); ceramics from the Dornburg pottery, lights and light-fittings by the metal workshop, and textiles from the weaving workshop. Muche's determination to give each room a separate identity, however, inhibited the production of 'unit' furniture in the Bruno Paul and Riemerschmid tradition.

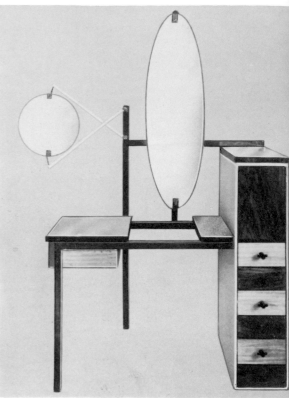

50 View into the central room, Haus am Horn *Hochschule für Architektur und Bauwesen, Weimar*
51 Dressing table for the Haus am Horn, designed by Marcel Breuer, 1923 *Bauhaus-Archiv*

Each piece of furniture can be identified through the priorities and skills of its designer. Erich Dieckmann produced solid furniture within the cabinet-maker's tradition, while Alma Buscher and Marcel Breuer introduced their more experimental designs. It was the kitchen, however, designed by Benita Otte and Ernst Gebhard, that was considered the most functional, and therefore the most innovatory room in the house. It was a 'space for cooking in', and not, as in most small one-family houses, a kitchen/dining room. All the surfaces were easy to clean; there was a large window behind the main work surface, built-in cupboards, a gas water heater, and storage jars, etc., produced from Bauhaus designs by Velten-Vordamm (ceramics) and Jena Glass. According to Albers, 'economy of space, time and energy' determined its design, as well as hygiene, and the whole house demonstrated an approach to building and design that was appropriate in a crippled economy.[25]

Ironically, however, although the house may have looked as though it had been blown to Weimar 'by the Sirocco from a North African oasis', Georg Muche's design was far from radical. It was, as one writer has pointed out, a miniaturized Palladian villa; its dimensions were based on the Golden Section, its façades have a classical symmetry, and although industrialized building techniques were used, the house could just as easily have been built by traditional methods.[26] There were, of course, several critics who recognized this, and whose commentaries went beyond banal praise or condemnation. The most cogent appraisal of the house, however, was by Adolf Behne, whose article in *Die Bauwelt* was a perceptive analysis of its ambiguities.[27] Among the displays in the main Bauhaus building was an international exhibition of modern architecture, with work by Corbusier, Oud, Wils and Gropius. Muche's house, according to Behne, was the complete antithesis of this dynamic or functional architecture. Compared with Corbusier's 'machine for living in', Muche's solutions were rigid and formalistic; industrialization implied a liberation from the conventional house plan, but Muche's design was locked within its rigid symmetry: 'without scale, alien, self-referential – there stands the Haus am Horn.' Behne was equally critical of the furniture and furnishing: 'it flirts with the machine', he wrote, 'but it is all art, and a debasement of art – pseudo-constructivism'.

THE WALL-PAINTING WORKSHOP

Behne also commented on the fact that there were no paintings hanging on the walls of the living-room. 'There is', he wrote, 'no longer any need for "salon" art, but this room is a traditional "salon"; and because it is traditional, its walls cry out for paintings.' Paradoxically, however, although the wall-painting workshops had provided colour schemes for the house, it was their work in the van de Velde building that achieved Muche's ideal of the synthesis of humanism and abstraction. Gropius's original conception of a scheme to remodel the vestibule of the Art School building was pragmatic: 'Here, for the want of bigger tasks, painting and sculpture have an opportunity to display themselves and to work in collaboration with each other.' He saw the exercise as informative and educational, as a 'visual demonstration of general elementary laws and art forms'.[28] Although Kandinsky was in charge of the wall-painting workshop, Schlemmer was asked to co-ordinate the scheme. By then one of the 'old masters', Schlemmer had been at the school since 1920 and his interests went far beyond 'general elementary laws and art forms'. In June 1920 (before he joined the Bauhaus) he was writing to Otto Meyer: 'I have moved from the geometry of the one-dimensional surface to the half-plastic (relief), and thence to the fully plastic art of the human body. . . . There is also a geometry that applies to the surface of the dance floor, though only as part of and a projection of spatial solid geometry. I am working out a similar geometry of the fingers and the keys on the piano, in an effort to achieve identity (or unity of movement and bodily form) and music'.[29]

Klee and Kandinsky were also concerned with music, geometry, space and with the relationship of forms to space; Schlemmer, however, focused these concerns on 'the fully plastic art of the human body'. 'The portrayal of man will always remain the great symbol for the artist,'[30] he had written in 1919, when he was already establishing his reputation as a painter and a choreographer. Schlemmer had been interested in dance since his student days in Stuttgart, and parts of the *Triadic Ballet* were performed there, during the war, in 1916. The exhibition of 1923 gave him the opportunity to stage the *Triadic Ballet* again (it had had its first full performance in Stuttgart a year earlier), and it also allowed him to explore his theories of the relationship of painting and sculpture to architectural space. 'The vestibule cries out for creative shaping', he wrote in his diary. 'It could become the trademark of the Bauhaus; within the space created by van de Velde we shall combine

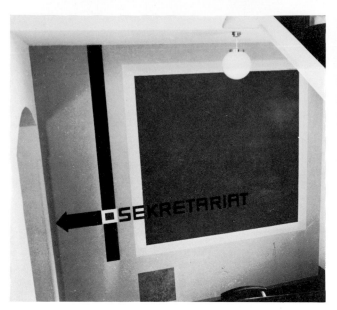
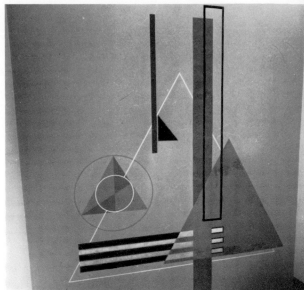

52, 53 Wall paintings in the Weimar Bauhaus by Herbert Bayer, 1923. (Restored in 1976 by Werner Claus) *Hochschule für Architektur und Bauwesen, Weimar*

wall-painting with sculpture, displaying them in a context which normally seldom presents itself.'[31] In his scheme for the vestibule of the workshop building, Schlemmer used what he described as 'earth' colours – brown, ochre and various tones of blue and pink – to delineate and transform the space. There were murals and reliefs on the walls and ceilings, and at the head of the stairwell. In contrast to the hierarchical, semi–abstract and sentinel-like figures in the vestibule, those on the stairwell appear, from reproductions of the work, like a giant shadow play of dancing figures. Joost Schmidt also designed abstract reliefs for the vestibule of the main building, and Walter Passarge, a contemporary critic, wrote: 'Special emphasis is given to the design of space. The most significant achievement in this area is by Oskar Schlemmer in the decoration of the vestibule and staircase in the workshop building. His work is most convincing in his paintings: giant figures of marionette-like ornamentality, their sensitive contours placed against a light coloured background, enlivening and intensifying the form of each corresponding wall surface to perfection. . . . The abstract architectural sculpture in the vestibule by Joost Schmidt is an attempt to derive sculptural effects from complex stereometric forms.'[32] Until the 1970s, descriptions such as these, and contemporary photographs, were the only record of this work in the van de Velde buildings. At the scheme's conception, Gropius had to have van de Velde's permission before the authorities would allow him to 'deface' the space, and in 1930 Paul Schultze-Naumburg, the Nazi director of the school, had the work painted over or removed. Restoration began in 1976, and visitors to the school now can gain some idea of its impact and originality.

First to be restored were three murals by Herbert Bayer, then an 'apprentice' in the wall-painting workshop. Totally different in conception from Schlemmer's use of muted colours and abstract human form in architectural space, Bayer's designs (he was then twenty-three) were a demonstration of Kandinsky's theories on the relationship of colour to basic form. The murals are at the head of each staircase in the three-storey building

(Illus. 52 and 53). The mural on the first floor is dominated by a blue circle (blue, according to Bayer, symbolized eternity and mystery); there is a large red (powerful and aggressive) square on the second floor, with a direction sign to the secretariat, while the third-floor mural, with its yellow triangles, is lighter and less static.

GRAPHIC WORK

This approach to colour and form, although based on Kandinsky's theories, bears no relationship to his painting; the geometry is that of Moholy-Nagy and the Constructivists, and the graphic work at the Bauhaus in 1923 demonstrates the pluralistic concepts of 'communication' in the various graphic media. In 1919, the printing workshop, which had survived from the van de Velde era, was not reorganized under the apprenticeship system, but trained 'Bauhaus members, on request, in all the techniques of print processing'.[33] Its most ambitious project in the early years was the publication of a series of portfolios of prints by, or from the work of, international artists. The production of the 'New European Graphics' portfolios (Illus. 54) was shared between the printing and book-binding workshops, but technical as well as economic problems prevented the publication of the whole series as planned. Those that were produced have covers by Paul Klee, Feininger, and Ludwig Hirschfeld-Mack, with title pages in hand-lettering by Feininger. The contents, were, of course, 'fine art' graphics but the creative use of hand-lettering in much of the Bauhaus 'printed ephemera' in the early years – posters and post-cards, for example, produced to advertise the various events and festivities – was obviously related to work done for these projects.

By 1923, however, the approach to letter-forms, typography and layout had changed radically. Through van Doesburg and Moholy-Nagy, the students were obviously aware of Futurist, De Stijl and Constructivist graphics, and their attempts to 'break the conventions of content and the customary form of typography, and with it, symbolically, the content and form of society which applied its great rules of the past only mechanically'[34] were supported by the enthusiasms of Moholy-Nagy. There were, nevertheless, few experiments with the Futurist *Mots en Liberté* (Liberation of Words) at the Bauhaus; the hand-lettering of Feininger, for example, was individualistic rather than anarchic – an extension of the art of calligraphy. Moholy-Nagy considered typography and page layout as an art as well as a science, developing from the potential of printing techniques as a factor in communication. 'The nature and purpose of the communication (leaflet or poster) determine the manner and use of the typographic material,' he wrote. 'In contrast to the centuries-old static concentric equilibrium, one seeks today to produce a dynamic-eccentric equilibrium.'[35] The now-familiar 'composition' of page layout, with type set vertically and diagonally as well as horizontally, and equal weight given to the 'design' of space as well as print, was introduced into Bauhaus graphics in 1923. Herbert Bayer and Joost Schmidt were both obviously influenced by Moholy's experiments at the time, and the work done in connection with the promotion of the 1923 exhibition (as well as the launching of the Bauhaus book series in 1924) justified the establishment of a Printing Workshop in Dessau. The main concerns of the Dessau workshops (run by Bayer from 1925–28) were typography and 'commercial art'; in Dessau, therefore, the emphasis was on advertising rather than 'fine art' graphics (Pl. 12), economic viability being a decisive factor in the survival of the school.

VOM HERGESTELLT UND HERAUSGEGEBEN
STAATLICHEN BAUHAUS IN WEIMAR
IM JAHRE
1921
ZU BEZIEHEN DURCH
MÜLLER & Co VERLAG
POTSDAM

THE 1923 EXHIBITION

As far as Gropius, the students and the staff were concerned, the 1923 exhibition was a success in that it provided a focus for their activities. Although it certainly did not represent a 'collective' approach to design and architecture, production from each workshop did achieve a specific identity and there was a modest increase in sales and orders, especially from the ceramics and weaving workshops. The promotion of the exhibition demonstrated Gropius's skill as a publicist (Illus. 55). Fifteen thousand people visited the exhibition; during the 'Bauhaus week' there were lectures by Gropius, Kandinsky and Oud, a performance of Schlemmer's *Triadic Ballet*, concerts with music by Hindemith, Busoni and Stravinsky, as well as performances by the legendary Bauhaus jazz band. Weimar, therefore, became the focus of the avant-garde; there were few local converts, however, and when the Nationalists gained the majority in the Thuringian Parliament early in 1924, it was obvious that the school would not survive in Weimar. In May 1924 Schlemmer was writing to Otto Meyer, 'The rightist government of Thuringia, the bourgeois circles, the master craftsmen, the local artists, who claim to be fighting "with their backs against the wall" are all raising a hullabaloo and slinging slogans about. . . . Gropius circulates a summary of the favourable press opinions; a counter-brochure appears, then a pamphlet, a newspaper campaign. . . .'[36]

54 Title page for the first Bauhaus portfolio. Lithograph by Lyonel Feininger, 1922/23 *Kunstsammlungen, Weimar*
55 Postcard advertising the Bauhaus exhibition in Weimar. Lyonel Feininger, 1923 *Busch-Reisinger Museum, Harvard University*

During this 'hullabaloo' Gropius, as well as orchestrating a pro-Bauhaus campaign (he organized an association of 'The Friends of the Bauhaus' which included, as well as Peter Behrens and Joseph Hoffmann, Einstein, Schönberg and Berlage), was attempting to sort out the complex finances of the school. A corporation had been formed for the sale of workshop products, but although sales did increase, any profit was eroded by inflation. The idea, therefore, that the 'productive' workshops might contribute to the support of the experimental ones – wall-painting and stage workshop, for example – proved totally unrealistic; to sacrifice the experimental work, however, would have destroyed the Bauhaus ideal, as well as the school's originality. Workshop production in Weimar was in many ways unique in its attempts to extend traditional concepts of craftsmanship; and no other art school in Europe (apart, of course, from those in Russia which were fighting a different battle for the avant-garde) could have contemplated incorporating experimental theatre, 'light-plays' and mural design, as conceived by Kandinsky, Schlemmer and Moholy-Nagy in their programme. It was these activities, as well as Gropius's tenacious promotion of the school, that established its reputation in the early twenties.

In December 1924, however, the new Thuringian government cut the school's grant, and limited staff contracts to a six-monthly renewal, making it impossible for work to continue there. There were several issues involved in this attack on the school: it threatened the livelihood of local craftsmen; it violated the academic traditions of the town's artists, and in spite of Gropius's attempts to maintain an a-political stance, it was compromised politically as a 'Cathedral of Socialism'. The vendetta was, indeed, first and foremost political, the accusations and manoeuvres anticipating the events that were to lead to the closure of the Bauhaus by the Nazis in 1933. For it was the school's alleged association with Bolshevism, rather than its economic or practical viability, that was under attack. The right-wing faction had gained power in Thuringia after the former Socialist government had joined forces with the Communists during the social and political unrest in 1923. This coalition survived for a month before the Reichswehr – troops of the central government – moved in and deposed it. During this period Gropius's house was searched, and the students were denounced as political activists, and therefore enemies of the state.[37] Obviously the school could not survive political sabotage as well as financial restraint; in December 1924, Gropius and the masters announced that the school would be dissolved when their contracts expired in March 1925, and the majority of the students also declared that they would leave Weimar with the staff.

Several towns, including Darmstadt and Frankfurt, offered to take over the school. Frankfurt's invitation seemed to be the most promising, in view of the town's progressive housing programme and the growing prestige of its art school. In 1923 the Institute of Social Research, then an obscure organization, had been founded in Frankfurt, and although the significance of the Institute's theories, and its social and philosophical methods of enquiry are associated with the radicalism of the 1960s, the existence of such an organization in the town might well have influenced theoretical attitudes in the Bauhaus.

Negotiations with Frankfurt, however, were frustrated by the fact that the art school was more interested in Bauhaus painting than Bauhaus design, and in April 1925, the Bauhaus moved to Dessau, with the promise of funding and architectural commissions, including the design of a new school purpose-built to demonstrate the new Bauhaus credo – Art and Technology: a new unity.

PART III   THE BAUHAUS IN DESSAU

1 DESSAU: THE GREAT TRANSFORMATION

'Dessau. Mentioned for the first time in 1213. Since 1603 the seat of a line of the House of Anhalt. Important industrial town and transportation centre: Junkers Works (all-metal airplanes), chemical industry, manufacture of machinery, railroad cars, wooden articles, chocolate, sugar. Renaissance palace, residence of the Dukes of Anhalt; small palaces and town houses in baroque and neo-classic styles. Near the town, at Wörlitz, are large eighteenth-century parks in the English "Romantic" style.'

This is the description of the town in *Bauhaus 1919–1928*.[1] Dessau, like Weimar, was a provincial 'capital', and had enjoyed the privileges of Ducal patronage. Unlike Weimar, however, it was not a citadel of traditional culture, and by the 1920s it was first and foremost an industrial city, its parks and palaces recalling, rather than as in Weimar, representing, the values of the past. Today it is difficult to visualize the Dessau of the twenties, since much of the town centre was destroyed during the war. According to Feininger, 'Mrs Kandinsky and Mrs Muche,' who were 'delegated to look around the town' were not favourably impressed. The 'workers' quarters' then, as now, were in the centre of the town (now tower blocks, public gardens, sculptures and playgrounds predominate), but then, as now, the outskirts were devoted to recreation as well as industry: 'Water everywhere,' wrote Feininger, 'the Mulde meets the Elbe, water-sports, sailing, fishing, motor-boating.'[2] Moreover Berlin was only two hours away by train, so that Dessau was a more realistic location for a school that aimed to work directly with industry in the design and marketing of its products. There was some local opposition to the move at that time, more on grounds of cost than ideology, but the mayor of Dessau, Fritz Hesse, was a shrewd politician; he was determined to re-establish the school in Dessau, and protect its independence without antagonizing the rate payers. In March 1925, therefore, the Bauhaus was incorporated into the local trade-school, with Gropius (on a five-year contract) in charge of both establishments. Ironically, the courses in the trade school, with their emphasis on mechanical engineering and the building trades, were to continue independently, and as in Weimar the proposed fusion of the old and new establishments did not take place. The Bauhaus, however, was to have a new building, with student accommodation; houses were to be built for Bauhaus masters, and the school was also commissioned to design a Labour Exchange, as well as a *Siedlung* (housing estate).

The move to Dessau provided Gropius with the opportunity to redefine the aims of the school. The Preliminary Course (lasting two terms and run by Albers and Moholy-Nagy) remained. Moholy was also in charge of the metal workshop; Marcel Breuer ran the furniture workshop, Herbert Bayer the printing workshop, Hinnerk Scheper, who had left the Weimar Bauhaus in 1922 after studying in the wall-painting workshop, was appointed head of that workshop in Dessau; Joost Schmidt was head of the sculpture workshop; Georg Muche ran the weaving workshop, and Gunta Stölzl, who had left Weimar to work in Zurich, returned to Dessau as his 'technical' assistant. The ceramics workshops were not moved to Dessau, and Otto Lindig took over their direction in Weimar. (The Weimar School was then directed by Otto Bartning; Gerhard Marcks went to teach at Giebichenstein, and Adolf Meyer became director of the municipal building council at Frankfurt, and taught architecture there. Christian Dell also went to Frankfurt to take charge of the metalwork department in the art school.)

This meant, of course, that the workshops in Dessau were run by Bauhaus-trained designers, who were, for the most part, sympathetic to Gropius's ideals, which were to be demonstrated in the design of the school itself, as well as in its programme and production. According to Tut Schlemmer: 'This was the beginning of the great transformation. The workshops became model workshops and the heart of the Bauhaus. The machine was accepted.'[3] Obviously this 'great transformation' had been implicit in Gropius's attempts to shift the stress from craft to 'prototype' production when the school was in Weimar. Ironically, however, when defining and justifying this 'transformation', Gropius uses the arguments and analogies that Muthesius had put forward in the Werkbund in 1914. 'The creation of types for useful objects of everyday use is a social necessity', Gropius wrote in 1925. Modern man, he argued, who wears modern clothes, needs an equivalent modernity in housing and household equipment; it was the aim of the school, therefore, to undertake systematic research in order to establish the appropriate formal, technical and economic requirements for design. The workshops became 'laboratories' in which 'a new kind of collaborator' was trained to acquire 'an exact knowledge of the design elements of form and mechanics and their underlying laws'.[4]

Gropius's theories echo those of Muthesius when he refers to concepts of 'the type', and 'type-forms', and the need for 'standards' as well as 'standardization' in industry. Gropius's interpretation of 'the design elements of form and mechanics and their underlying laws' is very different from that of Muthesius, however; for whereas Muthesius tended to turn to classical referents in his attempts to define 'the norm', Gropius is concerned with contemporary analogies with art as well as with science and 'mechanics'. Gropius, therefore, in relating the processes of analysis and synthesis to these analogies, could not, in theory, anticipate the formal solution of any given design problem. For the designer, part artist, part technician/craftsman (the dual role having been established in Weimar) would combine his understanding of the laws of form with his knowledge of the nature of materials and the processes of manufacture so that his work (in architecture as well as design) would be 'the inevitable logical product of the intellectual, social and technical conditions of our age'.[5] At this stage, therefore, Gropius believed that the designer could be trained to interpret 'the will to form', and that 'the design elements of form' were demonstrated by art as well as science. It was important, therefore, that the school should retain its 'resident artists', and that the courses given by Klee and Kandinsky, as well as the work in the Preliminary Course, should continue. For these studies, according to Gropius, provided the student with an objective theory of form. 'What is called "the freedom of the artist" does not imply the unlimited command of a wide variety of different techniques and media,' he wrote in *The New Architecture and the Bauhaus*, 'but simply his ability to design freely within the preordained limits imposed by any one of them. Even today a knowledge of counterpoint is essential for a musical composer. That is now the solitary example of the theoretic basis every one of the arts formerly possessed but all the others have lost: something, in fact, which the designer must rediscover for himself. But though theory is in no sense a ready-made formula for a work of art it certainly remains the most important prerequisite of collective design.'[6]

This is a revealing statement: it implies that nineteenth-century expectations for craft and design, because of their stress on individualism, historicism and associationism, did not have a viable theoretical base, and that the social and redemptive roles attributed to the crafts did not constitute a 'theory'. Theory, according to Gropius, was related to objective laws rather than personal convictions; these laws, like counterpoint, provided a structure or base for determining design solutions which bore no relation to tradition or to past achievements. As far as Gropius was concerned, there were no precedents or models for contemporary design and architecture. New materials, new production methods and the emergence of a new social order demanded a new approach to the ideal of the 'collective'. 'The revolution in aesthetics', he wrote, 'has given us fresh insight into the meaning of design, just as the mechanization of industry has provided new tools for its realization.'[7]

In Dessau both Klee and Kandinsky, representatives of 'the revolution in aesthetics', taught painting (to students who volunteered to work with them) as well as continuing their theoretical courses. Kandinsky's *Point and Line to Plane*, a summary of his convictions as well as an analysis of his teaching methods, was published as a Bauhaus Book in 1926, and in that same year he contributed an article on *The Value of Theoretical Instruction in Painting* to the first issue of the Bauhaus magazine.[8] In this he reaffirms his conviction that the 'young artist . . . must from the outset accustom himself to objective, i.e. to scientific, thought' – to what he called 'the building blocks of art' in order to achieve the transition from analysis to synthesis in all branches of design. He also taught analytical drawing on the Preliminary Course – analytical drawing being the equivalent of Gropius's 'counterpoint': 'The teaching of drawing at the Bauhaus is an education in looking, precise observation, and the precise representation not of the external appearance of an object, but of constructive elements, the laws that govern the forces (= tensions) that can be discovered in given objects, and of their logical construction – an education in clearly observing and clearly reproducing relationships, where two-dimensional phenomena are an introductory step leading to the three-dimensional.'[9]

Kandinsky, the painter, clearly believed that the 'building blocks' of art could and should be related to the 'building blocks' of design, and that both activities were determined by objective laws. Klee's courses, as in Weimar, were intended to complement those of Kandinsky; the preoccupation with the nature of perception, with the need 'to look behind the façade to grasp the roots of things' remains, but at the same time Klee gives the impression that these concerns could lead to subversion rather than construction. 'One learns about the things that form a connection along the way between cause and reality. Learns to digest. . . . Learns logic. Learns organism. . . . All this is fine, yet it leaves a void: intuition, after all, cannot be entirely replaced. One proves, explains, justifies, one constructs, one organizes: these are good things, but one does not arrive at "totalization".'[10]

Klee wrote this article 'Exact Experiments in the Realm of Art' for the *Bauhaus Journal* in 1928, soon after Hannes Meyer had been appointed director of the school. In spite, however, of the tensions that this appointment created, it is clear that Klee, during the Dessau period, was more concerned with his painting and with the theories that sustained it, than with any relationship his work might have with design and architecture. Gropius's clarion call for Dessau – 'Art and Technology: a new unity' may have been based on the conviction that 'the revolution in aesthetics' which had been instigated by painters could contribute to 'meaning in design', but as the work of the school developed, it became obvious that the designers were formulating their own laws, their own aesthetic, and their own interpretation of 'meaning'.

The conviction that there could and should be a relationship between 'art' and 'industry' was a potent one in the 1920s and '30s, especially in Britain, where Sir Herbert Read was to champion his own version of Gropius's cause. 'In every practical activity', Read wrote, 'the artist is necessary to give form to material. An artist must plan the distribution of buildings within a city; an artist must plan the houses themselves, the halls and factories and all that makes up the city; an artist must plan the interiors of such buildings – the shapes of the rooms and their lighting and colour; an artist must plan the furniture of these rooms, down to the smallest detail, the knives and forks, the cups and saucers and the door-handles. And at every stage we need the abstract artist, the artist who orders materials till they combine the highest degree of practical economy with the greatest measure of spiritual freedom.'[11]

This redefinition of the role of the artist had, of course, been debated in De Stijl and Constructivist as well as Bauhaus polemics. The practical implications of the concept of the 'practical artist' had driven Kandinsky from Russia, and alienated Mondrian from the De Stijl group. In Gropius's Bauhaus Klee and Kandinsky continued to work as artists (painters), their *theory* rather than their practice contributing to a theory of design or form. Nevertheless in the ideals for the school, theory and practice were generally conflated, and in Read's interpretation of these ideals the artist is presented as a designer. The fact that 'art' and 'technique' might be subject to different and not necessarily compatible laws tended to become submerged in the general euphoria associated with Gropius's slogan. In 1926, however, Georg Muche had published one of the most cogent statements on the fallacies as well as the implications of these assumptions. His article 'Fine Art and Industrial Form' was first published in the *Bauhaus Journal* in 1926, and was generally overlooked until it was republished in Wingler's documentation of the Bauhaus, and in *Form and Function*, edited by Tim and Charlotte Benton.[12] 'The illusion that fine art must be absorbed in the creative types of industrial design is destroyed as soon as it comes face to face with concrete reality. Abstract painting, which has been led with convincingly unambiguous intentions from its artistic Utopia into the promising field of industrial design, seems quite suddenly to lose its predicted significance as a form-determining element, since the formal design of industrial products that are manufactured by mechanical means follows laws that cannot be derived from the fine arts.'

This statement is convincing in its self-evidence, as are Muche's analyses of the consequences of an illusion of unity between fine art and industrial form; as far as Muche is concerned, any attempt at such a unity destroys the validity of both 'fine art' and 'industrial form'. For the artist 'disproves his own existence', while 'industrial form' becomes a surrogate for art – in other words – style. 'The forms of industrial products, in contrast to the forms of art, are super-individual in that they come about as a result of an objective investigation into a problem. Functional considerations and those of technological, economic, and organizational feasibility, become factors determining the forms of a concept of beauty that in this matter is unprecedented. . . . Art and technology are not a new unity: their creative values are different by nature. The limits of technology are determined by reality, but art can only attain heights if it sets its aims in the realms of the ideal.' Although disillusioned with the activities of the school, Georg Muche remained in Dessau until 1927. As in Weimar, he had a triple role: he was a painter; he was responsible, with Gunta Stölzl, for the weaving workshop, and he continued to work as an architect, designing projects for apartment blocks in 1924, and an experimental metal house for the Dessau-Törten Siedlung in 1925. As far as he was concerned, however, these activities were totally separate, and his ideals for architecture were in no way related to his personal development as a painter. At the same time the new buildings were going up in Dessau, the laboratory, rather than the cathedral, now being the 'crystal symbol of a new faith'.

The new buildings in Dessau (Illus. 56, Pl. 14) were designed as an architectural manifesto, and the school itself (described by Gropius as an 'anti-academy') was intended to demonstrate Gropius's 'conception of design as one great cognate whole'. 'The band of fellow-workers inspired by a common will had become a reality,' he wrote in *The New Architecture and the Bauhaus*.[1] Ironically, however, the school still had no architecture department. An architectural 'group' had been established in Weimar on the insistence of Georg Muche, Farkas Molnar and Marcel Breuer; they were advised by Adolf Meyer and Ernst Neufert, from Gropius's private office, but they had no official status, and were not involved in the architectural design of the new school. This was undertaken in Gropius's private office: a fact which Gropius acknowledges in *Bauhausbauten Dessau*, and justifies by maintaining that the school virtually 'designed itself', since its planning was based on the requirements of the workshops and the spiritual life of the school.[2]

In designing the school Gropius had to incorporate workshops, administrative offices, a lecture theatre and stage, as well as small work-rooms, a canteen, separate premises for the technical school, and student accommodation. His aims, he wrote in *Bauhausbauten*, in his organization of the plan, were: orientation to achieve maximum natural light; easy and quick access from one area to another; a clear separation of the various 'components' of the building, and the ability to change or adapt the spaces for possible variations in use.[3] There were no restrictions on the site in 1925, so that the plan of the buildings was in no way determined by available space, or by the presence of other buildings. Nevertheless, in spite of its seeming simplicity in plan (two L-shaped blocks in counter-composition), the layout and the linking of the various components is complex, and as Gropius pointed out: 'One must walk round this building in order to understand its form and the function of its components.'[4] Approaching the building from Dessau town centre, one passes the student block on the left (Illus. 57), with its cantilevered balconies. From this a single storey link block (housing the canteen and the lecture theatre) runs through to the main building; to reach the entrance (Illus. 59), one walks under another link block (with Gropius's office and administrative offices) which is built over the road, and which links the premises of the technical school on the right with the main building on the left. This is the workshop wing (Illus. 58), the most important area of the school, with its curtain wall of glass, its

56 The Bauhaus in Dessau, 1926; restored 1976 *Dessau City Archive*
57 (*Below left*) The student block in Dessau, in process of restoration 1982 *Photograph Gillian Naylor*
58 (*Below right*) The workshop wing in Dessau, as restored in 1982 *Photograph Gillian Naylor*

59 The entrance of the Bauhaus in Dessau *Dessau City Archive*
60 The entrance hall in the Dessau Bauhaus *Dessau City Archive*

metal framed windows, and its corners defined by glass. As in the Fagus factory, the transparent wall reveals the structure of the building as well as the activities going on inside. The structure was partly experimental, partly traditional: brick masonry was used throughout the building, coated with cement stucco and painted white; the workshop wing had a reinforced concrete frame, with mushroom columns and hollow-tile floors supported by beams. Drainage was by cast-iron pipes inside the building, and the flat roofs, as in the Haus am Horn, were laid on insulation boards of 'torfoleum' – compressed peat moss – which caused many problems.

The building, nevertheless, was a 'statement of intent', and it demonstrated, as far as Gropius was concerned, the variety and clarity as well as the unity of the activities that went on inside it. 'A modern building', he wrote in the *New Architecture and the Bauhaus*, 'should derive its architectural significance solely from the vigour and consequence of its own organic proportions. It must be true to itself, logically transparent and virginal of lies or trivialities, as befits a direct affirmation of our contemporary world of mechanization and rapid transit.'[5] The building, therefore, rejected historicism and tradition. It was devoid of overt and decorative symbolism, but it could not reject associationism: it represented, in Gropius's terms, the vitality of the present, as well as the purity of its intentions; it was a 'spiritual centre' created for 'our young people, the creatively talented young people who some day will mould the face of our new world . . .'.[6]

Subsequent events were to prove the pathos of such idealism; in December 1926, however, the future seemed reasonably secure, and the new building was formally opened with lectures, exhibitions and festivities to celebrate the occasion. At the same time as the new school was being built, a 'housing colony' for Bauhaus masters was also planned and completed. Designed by Gropius and equipped by the workshops, this was also program-matic; Gropius's aim was to achieve the 'smooth and sensible functioning of daily life . . .' in order to provide 'a maximum of personal freedom and independence'. This involved the rejection of the 'false sentimentality' demonstrated in the yearning for traditional solutions in design as well as architecture, and the conviction that the 'age of the car and the railway' demanded new forms.[7] Four houses were built (Illus. 61–73) – three 'double houses' for Klee and Kandinsky, Muche and Schlemmer, Moholy-Nagy and Feininger, and a single house for Gropius. They were (and are) located about ten minutes' walk from the school, screened from a quiet suburban road by trees and surrounded by lawns rather than separate gardens. Their foundations were concrete, and they were built from cement-based blocks. They also had flat roofs, large windows, and terraces or balconies at each level (formed by cantilevering the ceiling slabs), and the double houses had studios. In *Bauhausbauten Dessau*, Gropius's own house is copiously illustrated: this, obviously, was his ideal home, and it was also the 'show-house' for the work and philosophy of the school. 'The house', wrote Feininger to his wife, 'is fabulously furnished and of course has been designed to be incomparably more spacious and much more for representational purposes. I can't give you a detailed account of all the time-saving appliances now – you will see

61, 62 Walter Gropius's house in Dessau, designed 1925, completed 1926 *Private collection*

63 Desk in the Gropius house, designed by Marcel Breuer *Private collection*
64 Bathroom in the Gropius house *Private collection*

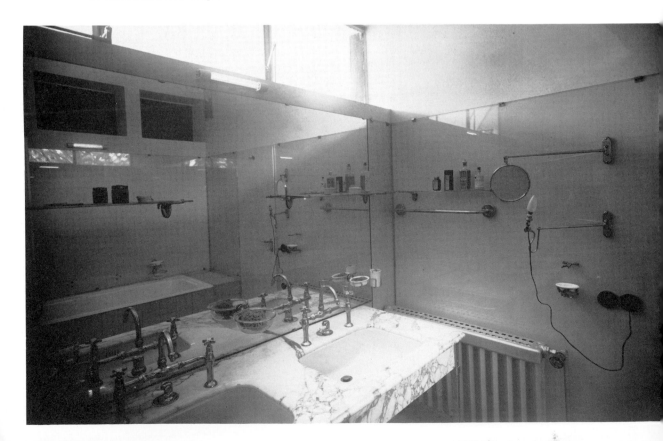

65, 66 Kitchen and pantry in the Gropius house *Private collection*
  67 Bedroom in the Gropius house *Private collection*

68, 70 (*Opposite*) The masters' 'double' houses in Dessau *Private collection*
69 (*Below*) Gropius's house in 1982 *Photograph Gillian Naylor*
71 (*Opposite below*) The masters' houses in 1982 *Photograph Gillian Naylor*

them and be enchanted. Altogether one can honestly speak of a creation, of a new achievement in building. . . .'[8] Feininger furnished his own house with antique and wicker furniture; Kandinsky brought Russian furniture, commissioned a set of dining-room furniture from Breuer, 'with as many circular elements as possible' and painted the glass wall in the entrance area white, to prevent the curious from gazing in. He also designed the colour scheme for his living room – pink and grey, with gold leaf on one of the walls. 'The individual inhabitant is not forced into anything. Even though the halves of each of the twin houses for the six Masters are almost identical, they all look different.'[9] Subsequent 'individual inhabitants', however, altered the houses in the thirties; they also suffered from damage during the war, and neglect in the post-war period, so are no longer representative of Gropius's ideals for domestic architecture.

THE DESSAU-TÖRTEN ESTATE

The Dessau-Törten estate, planned as an ideal community for local workers, and intended to demonstrate the potential as well as the efficiency of new construction techniques, was, from its inception, a flawed Utopia, although the success of the scheme was important for Gropius's long-term plans for the school. Whereas money for the construction of the Bauhaus and the masters' houses came from the local authority in Dessau, the Dessau-Törten estate was largely state-financed, and in theory the scheme should have marked the realization of Gropius's pre-war plans for the rationalization and standardization of building components. For whereas in 1910 Gropius was virtually alone in recommending the mass-production of housing components, research in this area had become a matter of national concern by the 1920s, when the *Reichs-Wohnungstypen-Ausschuss* (State Commission for Housing Types), and the *Reichskuratorium für Wirtschaftlichkeit* (State Efficiency Board) had been established to research and recommend practical solutions to Germany's production and housing problems. Developments in Frankfurt under the direction of the city architect, Ernst May, were the most positive response to this research, but Gropius obviously needed to make his own contribution to low-cost housing, and he also obviously wanted to establish Dessau and the Bauhaus as a centre for research.

'The time of the manifestoes on the new architecture, which helped to clarify the theoretical foundations, has passed,' he wrote in the *Bauhaus Journal* in 1927. 'It is high time for us to progress to the stage of sober calculation and accurate analysis. . . .' In order to do this, the programmes of the various organizations already involved in this analysis needed to be co-ordinated, and 'centres of research – theoretical and practical' were essential, as 'permanent places for experimentation, which are best established in conjunction with housing development projects'. Gropius then went on to elaborate the priorities for such research, under twenty-one headings. These included: the setting up of a national housing finance plan; a study of methods for the industrial production and storage of housing units; a study of new space and material-saving techniques, and investi-

72 Dining room in Kandinsky's house, with furniture by Marcel Breuer *Private collection*
73 Living room of Georg Muche's house *Private collection*

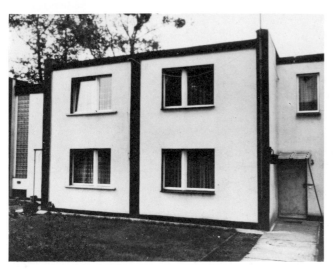 

74, 75 Houses on the Dessau-Törten Estate in 1982 *Photo Gillian Naylor*

gation of new materials; official standardization of building components and household appliances, as well as the establishment of 'suitable building methods that eliminate chance and the elements of surprise that used to be part of the old methods'.[10]

Unfortunately the Bauhaus, with its embryonic architecture department, was incapable at that time of undertaking such research, and the problems of the estate indicated that the 'new methods' could be as subject to 'elements of surprise' as the old ones. The brief involved the construction of 316 one-family dwelling houses; the houses were to be rented, the rents being kept to a minimum through the rationalization of the building programme and the economical use of building materials and techniques. The houses went up in three stages: 60 were completed in 1926; 100 in 1927, and 156 in 1928. The majority had three bedrooms, a kitchen/dining room, and a living room, and since the scheme was part rural, part urban, each house had its own plot of land for growing vegetables and outbuildings for storage or for animals. All had central heating, double glazing, and built-in cupboards. The wall slabs and the concrete wall units were made on the site, and the construction, including the installation of gas, water, light and heating, was carefully programmed to avoid delays: 'an accurate time-table was worked out,' wrote Gropius 'similar to the construction programme for railways.'[11] The estate went up according to schedule, and work was completed in 1928. In 1929, however, it was obvious that there would be problems: there were cracks in the façades of some of the houses, the central heating systems did not work, and most of the windows had to be replaced. Wingler attributes these problems to 'technical shortcomings, caused by pilferage, unauthorized use of poor materials, and . . . acts of sabotage by contractors.'[12] These problems could be considered characteristic of the building trade, especially in times of economic depression. From its inception, however, the scheme was attacked by right-wing critics in Dessau, partly because it did not conform to their concepts of 'nationalism' in architecture, and partly because it was seen to threaten the livelihood of craft-based organizations – still a powerful lobby in

Dessau, in spite of its industries. The houses were described as 'dog-kennels', 'concrete stables' and 'prison cells' in the local right-wing press, and in spite of the enthusiasm of some of the tenants, the estate was condemned as a social and practical failure.[13] Prior to 1939, much remedial work had to be done, and parts of the *Siedlung* were damaged during the war. Sufficient numbers of houses remain, however, to indicate the ideals that inspired them, and several have been restored (Illus. 74 and 75).

The estate also provided the opportunity to test work of an even more experimental nature. In 1926 Georg Muche and Richard Paulick, from Gropius's architectural office (Paulick had been a student of Hans Poelzig), designed a house that was to be constructed from steel plate. This method of 'prefabrication' had preoccupied Muche since the completion of the Haus am Horn. The plan of the Haus am Horn was classical in conception, and although Muche claimed that it could be adapted to meet the needs of a growing family, it was obvious that *ad hoc* changes would destroy its symmetry. (This has subsequently happened, and the house no longer looks like a Palladian villa in miniature.) Muche, therefore, rejected the tyranny of the plan, and attempted to design a 'house-type' with built-in flexibility. 'The residence which can be added on to, and which has a flexible floor plan is a requisite of our era,' he wrote in the *Bauhaus Journal* in 1927 (a year after he had published *Fine Art and Industrial Form*). The steel house (Illus. 76) was built with the co-

76 Steel house in Dessau, designed by Georg Muche and Richard Paulick, 1926 *Dessau City Archive*

operation of Carl Kästner AG, a Leipzig firm, which then went on to advertise the potential of construction from a material that could be used for houses, hotels, and '*Week-end Häuser*' – buildings that could take days, rather than weeks or months, to construct. The Dessau steel house has survived, and has also been restored. This was Muche's last experiment with architecture, however, and he left the Bauhaus in 1927 to teach in Itten's school in Berlin.

HANNES MEYER AND THE NEW WORLD

In 1927 the school's architectural department was formally established, and Gropius invited the Swiss architect, Hannes Meyer, to direct it. Meyer was then virtually unknown in Bauhaus circles; but although he was only thirty-eight when he arrived in Dessau, Meyer had more professional and practical experience than the 'young masters' who had been trained in the school. Meyer was born in Basle in 1889; his family was of Huguenot descent and, like that of Gropius, had been associated with architecture for several generations. Meyer, therefore, had a traditional architectural apprenticeship; he studied at the *Kunstgewerbeschule* in Basle, and had worked as a stonemason and carpenter before he was twenty. He then worked and studied in Berlin, where he became interested in the social implications of town-planning through the activities of Adolf Damaschke and the *Bund Deutscher Bodenreformer* (Organization for German Land Reform). He spent a year in England (1912–13), visiting Bath, Birmingham and London, as well as the new garden cities, and studying the country's 'social structure, the co-operative movement, theatres, cinemas and music-halls'.[14] After military service in Switzerland, he returned to Germany in 1916 to work for Georg Metzendorf who, as architect for Krupps, was involved in the design and planning of the *Margaretenhöhe* – the garden city for Krupps' workers in Essen. According to his biographer, Claude Schnaidt, Meyer rejected 'the paternalism and pseudo-romantic conception of these housing schemes, which were intended to perpetuate the *petit bourgeois* way of life . . .';[15] nevertheless during his time at Essen, Meyer began to consider concepts of standardization of housing 'types', as well as the sociological problems associated with the Krupps' ideal of 'community'. In 1918 he went back to Switzerland to set up his own architectural practice, and to work on the Freidorf Siedlung near Basle, which was sponsored by the Swiss Co-operative Union, and which also involved the application of social and sociological research to community living. He then spent three years travelling in Germany, France, Scandinavia and Belgium studying co-operative movements, as well as experimental theatre, and in 1926, just before he was invited to Dessau, he formed a partnership with Hans Wittwer.

In 1926 he also published his social and architectural manifesto, 'The New World' in the Zurich magazine *Das Werk*.[16] Part Futurist, part Constructivist in tone, the article defines the nature of the new world according to Meyer. It is a world transformed by technology: 'Fordson tractors and von Meyenburg cultivators have resulted in a shift of emphasis in land development and speeded up the tilling of the earth and the intensive cultivation of crops. Burrough's calculating machine sets free our brain, the dictaphone our hand, Ford's motor our place-bound senses, and Handley Page our earthbound spirits.' It is a world of mass, rather than élitist culture: 'The stadium has carried the day against the art museum, and physical reality has taken the place of the beautiful illusion. Sport merges the individual into the mass. . . . The standardization of our requirements is shown by: the bowler hat, bobbed hair, the tango, jazz, the Co-op product, the DIN standard size and Licbig's meat extract.' Its economics are based on an international and 'communal productive system'. 'The folding chair, roll-top desk, light bulb, bath tub and portable gramophone are typical standard products manufactured internationally and showing a uniform design.' It is a world that has rejected the past: 'The unqualified affirmation of the present age presupposes the ruthless denial of the past. . . . Today is ousting yesterday in material, form and tools. Instead of the random blow with an axe, we have the chain mortiser. Instead of the scrumbled line of the charcoal pencil, we have the clean-cut line produced with the T-square; instead of easel work, we have the drafting machine. Instead of the French horn, the saxophone.' In the new world, the artist's studio becomes 'a scientific and technical laboratory', and art 'invention and controlled reality'. Building becomes a 'technical, not an aesthetic process' and 'architecture has ceased to be an agency continuing the growth of tradition or an embodiment of emotion.'

Such ideas were, of course, characteristic of the manifesto-prone avant-garde of the 1920s, and Gropius was obviously aware of Meyer's convictions, as well as his achievements, before he asked him to take over the architecture department. Meyer, on the other hand, wanted to make his position perfectly clear before he moved to Dessau. Money and security did not worry him, he wrote in a letter to Gropius in January 1927;[17] he and his family (he had a wife and two children) were used to a 'semi-nomadic' life, and as long as he could support them adequately in a healthy environment, without restrictions on his own activities, he did not mind where he lived or worked. But, he wrote, he had no idea of what sort of role he was to play in the Bauhaus; he had visited it in 1926 for the opening ceremonies, but he did not know a single student. He had had interesting and positive talks with Gropius as well as with Kandinsky, Moholy, Schlemmer and Breuer. He thought that 'things like the steel house, steel furniture, parts of Schlemmer's theatre and Kandinsky's contribution to the preliminary course had positive potential,' but a lot of what he saw reminded him of Rudolf Steiner's work in Dornach: the cult of sects and the aesthetic. Again, in a letter dated 16 February 1927 he wrote: 'the fundamental tendency of my work will be functional – collectivist and constructive – in the spirit of ABC and *The New World*'.[18] Gropius obviously approved of these clear-cut and uncompromising attitudes, and Meyer took charge of the architecture department on 1 April 1927.

Meyer had agreed, in his correspondence with Gropius, that the course should, in the early stages, be loosely structured, and that the work should be related to 'live' projects. Work continued on the Dessau-Törten estates, and further housing blocks in brick were designed by Meyer and completed in 1930. The Dessau Labour Exchange, designed by Gropius, was completed in 1929. Semi-circular in plan, with an administrative block in the rear, this was the only Bauhaus building in Dessau which was not badly damaged during the war. The 'consultation' rooms are in the semi-circular block, steel-framed and built in brick; the roof of this area is in glass, supported by the exposed steel frame, and as with so much Bauhaus architecture, the quality of the building, and the impact of light within the building cannot be conveyed by photographs.

By the time it was completed, however, Gropius had resigned from the school, and Hannes Meyer had taken over as director. With the Bauhaus building and the Labour Exchange as symbols of the ideal and the reality, the Bauhaus entered its third phase of ideological and political conflict.

143

The move from Weimar to Dessau in 1925 was symbolic as well as expedient. The school had left an 'art town' for an industrial city, so that the potential for collaboration in industrial production could, in theory, be exploited, and in an attempt to consolidate the school's finances, as well as its professional intentions, a Bauhaus Corporation was formed to deal with the marketing of Bauhaus products. (In 1926–27 the business manager was the second-highest paid member of the school's staff; he was paid RM 10,000 a year, while Gropius received RM 11,000.)

In spite of these practical measures, however, the fundamental problem remained: how was the school to identify, test and establish the 'norms' or prototypes for industrial production? The theories of standard and standardization on which the Dessau programme was based implied both an ideal and achievable concept of form: the need for standardization at various levels of production had been acknowledged throughout German industry, but the identification and definition of 'standards' remained elusive. The belief in 'art' as a determining force in establishing standards for industry, which was fundamental to Gropius's declared philosophy at this time, was not necessarily a viable one, as Georg Muche was to point out. Feininger, one of the 'old masters' who was persuaded to move to Dessau because of his conciliatory personality and his long association with the school, identified the problem at its most basic level. Describing Moholy's enthusiasm for 'movies, optics, mechanics, projections and movement' in the letter to his wife that has already been quoted (see page 102) he wrote: 'We can say to ourselves that this is terrifying and the end of all art – but actually it is a question of mass-production, technically very interesting – but why attach the name of art to this mechanization of all visual things, why call it the only art of our age and, moreover, of the future?' These were, of course, personal pre-occupations, and not, like Muche's essay, polemical in intention. Nevertheless, the Constructivist vision of the 'systemization of the means of expression to produce results that are universally comprehensible'[1] remained the goal of the Bauhaus. The role played by 'art' in the expression of this ideal was difficult to define, for art, as both Feininger and Muche realized, could no longer be autonomous if its methods as well as its values were related to objects – objects which, as far as the Bauhaus was concerned, were for the most part designed according to expectations that had been established in Weimar, and which therefore bore little or no relationship to industrial production. But as Kandinsky confidently put it, 'the obsolete word Art has been positively resurrected at the Bauhaus. And linked to the word, The Deed.'[2]

The form and nature of the 'deed', however, was determined by the Weimar-trained designer in the early years at Dessau, and work there demonstrated the personal preoccupations and convictions of the new 'Masters of Form' rather than any objective ideal of design for industry.

MOHOLY-NAGY AND THE NEW VISION

The most exuberant and perhaps the most dominant personality in the school after the move to Dessau was Moholy-Nagy – 'Gropius's faithful drummer-boy and teeth-chatterer', as Schlemmer uncharitably described him.[3] In spite of his Constructivist allegiances, however, Moholy's approach was pragmatic: he wrote copiously and enthusiastically about his discoveries and convictions, but his writing is too mercurial and derivative to constitute a consistent theory. Magpie-like, he picked up current ideas and added them to his stockpile, but two themes persist in his writing: first that design is a social process, and second that intuition has a major role to play in this process. Whether the end-product was called 'art' or 'design' was immaterial to him: 'The criterion should never be "art" or "not art", but whether the right form was given to the stated function,' he wrote in *The New Vision*, 'whether this ever will be called "art" is of secondary importance.'[4] Establishing the 'right form for the stated function' could never be predetermined. In *The New Vision* Moholy considers what he describes as 'biotechnics as a method of creativity', quoting Raoul H. Francé's *Die Pflänze als Erfinder (Plants as Inventors)*: 'All technical forms can be deduced from forms in nature. The laws of least resistance and of economy of effort make it inevitable that similar activities shall always lead to similar forms. . . . Every bush, every tree, can instruct him, advise him, and show him inventions, apparatuses, technical appliances without number.' Biological and botanical analogies alone, however, are not a sufficient basis for design since, according to Moholy, 'psychological, social and economical conditions' must be taken into account, and the results might 'even serve functions which could not be foreseen during the process of designing'.[5] Moholy's ideal was 'an organic system of production whose focal point is man, not profit', and he was, significantly, one of the few Bauhaus designers to discuss the role of the worker in the process of production. In *The New Vision* he considers that 'the Taylor system, the conveyor belt, and the like remain misinterpreted as long as they turn man into a machine'. When he wrote *Vision in Motion*, however (the book was published in Chicago in 1947), Moholy's holistic attitude to design was reinforced by his experience of the United States – a country 'rich in resources, raw materials and human ingenuity', which could 'afford to be wasteful', and where the design profession had been established to satisfy the salesman's 'desire for the sensationally new'. Such a society, according to Moholy, demanded more than skill, knowledge, and an understanding of techniques and production processes from the designer: it forced him to recognize his social obligations. 'He should make his design with the aim of eliminating fatigue from the worker's life. He must see his design through, not only in the technical but in its human effects as well. This quality of design is dependent not alone on function, science and technological processes, but also on social consciousness.'[6] Again, it is significant that Moholy predicted 'the coming of an "electronic age",' with 'the reduction of manpower and labour hours' as an 'inevitable consequence'; the dilemma of 'technological unemployment', he wrote, although essentially political, also involved 'the social obligations of the designer'.

Moholy's awareness of the social implications of design had, like that of his colleagues, been reinforced by his experiences in Germany in the 1920s and '30s, when design, as well as art and architecture, were subject to political interpretation. His aim then was to 'translate revolution into material reality', and he attempted to do this at the Bauhaus 'through form and word'.[7] Underlying these activities was the assumption that the worker would participate in this revolution through design: the tragic ideal of William Morris as well as Moholy-Nagy. The ambiguity of this idealism did not strike Moholy until Hannes Meyer took over the school, so that Moholy had three years at Dessau in which to attempt to translate his philosophies into action.

Gropius has described how Moholy approached his work with the 'attitude of an unprejudiced, happy child at play';[8] the 'play' element in his teaching, however, owed nothing to Froebel or Montessori and had more to do with his enthusiasm for the integrative ideals of the school, and the release they represented from 'the terrible great quietness of his childhood' as well as the trauma of the war.[9] 'Many of us used him for our own advantage,' wrote Paul Citroen, 'and burdened him with tasks we ourselves should have solved. But, with the smiling enthusiasm of a child, Moholy accepted all demands, and his vitality seemed unlimited.'[10]

At Dessau, Moholy continued to accept demands: he contributed to the Preliminary Course, he was also in charge of the metal workshop, and he became more involved in typography, photography and film. His work on the Preliminary Course, which, as in Weimar, complemented that of Albers and Kandinsky, extended the preoccupations he had established in Weimar. His main concern was with what he described as 'spatial design', and the demonstration of concepts of space in three- rather than two-dimensional form. The exercises – abstract constructions in wire, metal, glass and wood – were intended to demonstrate the 'interweaving of shapes' and 'the fluctuating play of tensions and forces', and to serve as an introduction to concepts of architectural space, light and shadow and transparency.[11] In the metal workshop, on the other hand, Moholy was in theory more concerned with practicality than with abstract concepts. 'Goods intended for common use', he wrote, 'are neither sacramental vessels nor objects of contemplation,'[12] and it is significant that his 'statement' about the Metal Workshop in *Bauhaus 1919–1928* is called 'From Wine Jugs to Lighting Fixtures'. The transition from the concentration on craft-based objects in precious metals to the design of 'lighting-fixtures' for mass-production was due more to developments within the German lighting industry, however, than to efforts on the part of the school to establish 'norms' or prototypes (Illus. 77). Körting and Matthiesen, the Leipzig firm that produced the Kandem range of light-fittings, worked with Christian Dell, as well as with the Bauhaus. But as John Heskett points out in *Industrial Design*, the German lighting industry in the 1920s was involved in advanced research into lighting in factories and offices, and Körting and Matthiesen produced a wide range of equipment for industrial use.[13] The introduction of commercial techniques and forms into ranges for the domestic market, therefore, was not difficult, although it may have needed designers of the calibre of Marianne Brandt and Christian Dell to demonstrate that the factory 'aesthetic' could also relate to the domestic market. Marianne

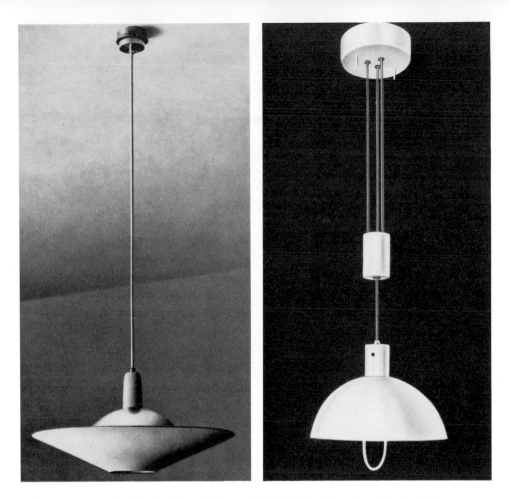

77 (*Left*) Ceiling light by Wilhelm Wagenfeld, 1927 (*Right*) Adjustable ceiling light by Marianne Brandt, 1927

Brandt, by that time well-established in the metal workshop (so much so that the Dessau metalwork designs illustrated in both Wingler and *Bauhaus 1919–28* are almost exclusively hers) has described the designers' interaction with the industry. 'Gradually, through visits to the industry and inspections and interviews on the spot, we came to our main concern – industrial design. Moholy-Nagy fostered this with stubborn energy. Two lighting firms seemed particularly interested in our aims. Körting and Matthieson (Kandem) and Leipzig Leutzsch helped us enormously with a practical introduction into the laws of lighting technique and the production methods, which not only helped us with designing, but also helped the firms.'[14] 'We also', she continues, 'tried to create a functional but aesthetic assembly line, small facilities for garbage disposal, and so forth, considerations which in retrospect seem to me no longer prerequisite for a first-class lamp.' The preoccupation with 'a functional but aesthetic assembly-line', whatever that may mean, indicates the attempts on Moholy's part to create or ape the conditions of industrial production within the laboratory/workshop. In Dessau, of course, up-to-date equipment was provided – 'presses and lathes, drills and large shears, etc.' – according to Marianne Brandt, and although the production of silverware and hollow-ware within the tradition established by Dell in Weimar did continue, there was obviously not a substantial market for avant-garde designs in this area. Lighting fittings, however, did produce royalties for the school, and between 1926 and 1928 the Bauhaus designed adjustable ceiling lamps, jointed wall-mounted fittings, and of course, the ubiquitous 'Kandem' table lamp, designed by Marianne Brandt in 1928. 'We furnished whole buildings with our industrially-produced lamps and only rarely designed and produced special pieces in our workshops for particular rooms or showrooms. At the time I was convinced that an object had to be functional and beautiful because of its material. But I later came to the conclusion that the artist provides the final effect.'[15] Such reflections highlight the dilemma of students in interpreting the philosophy of the school. Certainly in Marianne Brandt's case, there was a loss of 'artistry' in her work in the transition from Weimar to Dessau. None of her designs for lighting fittings, however commercially successful, can match the formal and iconic qualities of her work in Weimar. In this case the 'aura' of craft-based designs was replaced by the anonymity implicit in the Bauhaus ideal for mass production. It is significant, however, that in the presentation of the workshop's production in sales material and catalogues, etc., the consistency and order implicit in standardization is stressed. There is unity in the variety of the designs offered, but the light fittings are rarely presented in their 'natural' or domestic surroundings. The materials are those associated with industrial production – chrome and aluminium with combinations of clear and opaque glass, and the factory aesthetic is modified by the attention to proportion, scale and detail. They are in Marianne Brandt's terms 'functional and beautiful' in their consistency of form and their use of material, and they were no doubt commercially successful, partly because a technology existed to produce them, partly because their aesthetic was already established by commercial use, and partly because they related to national concepts of standardization.

EXPERIMENTS IN TUBULAR STEEL

There were no such precedents, however, for Marcel Breuer's attempts to produce metal furniture for the domestic market, and it is ironic that in Breuer's case, the firms which were to make such substantial profits from the use of tubular steel for furniture were at first reluctant to recognize its potential. Metal could be used for garden and café furniture, for hospital and prison beds, for children, domestics and dentists, but never in the drawing room. So that whereas with the Dessau-designed light-fittings industry had the potential as well as the techniques and incentives for their production, both the concept and the technology for mass-producing domestic furniture from metal had to be established.

As his work in Weimar had demonstrated, Breuer (Illus. 78) was a designer in search of a theory of form. In spite of his reputation (he was one of the Weimar-trained designers to become a Master in Dessau), his early wooden furniture is interesting only because of the theory that inspired it – a theory prompted by architectural or abstract concepts of the relationships between form and space. In Breuer's case, furniture made from wood, with its craft associations, could never achieve the anonymity he required for domestic design, so that the Weimar designs demonstrate a compromise with craftsmanship, complementing an as yet unrealized ideal of interior design. By 1927, however, that ideal was seemingly achievable, and Breuer wrote in *Das Neue Frankfurt*: 'The pieces of furniture and even the very walls of a room have ceased to be massive and monumental, apparently immovable and built for eternity. Instead they are more opened out, or, so to speak, drawn in space. They hinder neither the movement of the body nor of the eye. The room is no longer a

78 Marcel Breuer *Bauhaus-Archiv*

self-bounded composition, a closed box, for its dimensions and different elements can be varied in many ways.[16]

Again, in that same year he wrote: 'Our work is unrelenting and unretrospective; it despises tradition and established custom.'[17] As is now well known, Breuer's decision to experiment with tubular steel to demonstrate this relentless rejection of tradition and established custom was due to his fascination with the bicycle. He had bought his first model after the move to Dessau (the town and surrounding countryside is very flat), and was impressed by its lightness and strength, and by the fact that its handlebars could be shaped into curves. He approached the Adler Company who made the bicycle, but they were not interested in experimenting with furniture, so he bought some pre-formed steel tubing from their suppliers, the Mannesmann works in the Ruhr, and produced his first prototype, welding the pieces together with the help of a plumber. This was the first version of what is now known as the 'Wassily' chair (Illus. 79), because of Kandinsky's enthusiasm for it, but as far as Breuer was concerned, at this stage the reality fell far short of the ideal: '. . . I took the pipe dimensions (approximately 20mm in diameter) from my bicycle,' he wrote 'I didn't know where else to get it or how to figure it out.'[18] The chair, however, was too rigid and too heavy, and the nickel plating was expensive. But, as Christopher Wilk relates, Lucia Moholy-Nagy had photographed the chair (without Breuer knowing) and it was illustrated in a local newspaper, with two results: first there were enquiries from people wanting to buy it, and second, Breuer was unable to patent it, since German law forbids the patenting of a design that has been published.[19]

The public interest encouraged Breuer to continue working on the chair, and it was produced by Standard-Möbel in Berlin in 1926, and by Thonet in 1931, with various subtle variations in the design. Breuer himself was surprised by the chair's success: 'Two years ago,' he wrote in 1927, 'when I saw the finished version of my first steel club armchair, I thought that this out of all my work would bring me the most criticism. It is my most extreme work both in its outward appearance and in the use of materials; it is the least artistic, the most logical, the least "cosy" and the most mechanical.'[20] This rejection

BREUER-METALLMÖBEL

STANDARD-MÖBEL
LENGYEL & CO.
BERLIN W 62

79 'Wassily' chair designed by Marcel Breuer, 1925 *Bauhaus-Archiv*
80 Tubular steel furniture for Standard-Möbel, Marcel Breuer, 1926. Illustrated in *Bauhaus Journal*
No. 1, 1928 *Bauhaus-Archiv*

of cosiness and the artistic in favour of the logic implied by mechanization is characteristic of Breuer's work in Germany. Until he left the country at the end of 1931, most of his work is in tubular steel, ranging from the furniture he designed for the Bauhaus building in Dessau and the masters' houses, to the mass-production ranges for Standard-Möbel and Thonet.

Work of this nature, of course, altered the character of the carpentry or cabinet-making workshop, as it was called after the move to Dessau, and although Breuer had developed his first prototype independently from the school, it was obvious that the workshop would be involved in designs that epitomized Gropius's ideal of the 'type-form'. An advertisement for 'Breuer-Metallmöbel' issued by Standard-Möbel (Illus. 80) in 1928 states: 'Tubular steel furniture with fabric seat, back and armrests is as comfortable as well-upholstered furniture, without having its weight, price, unwieldiness, and unsanitary quality. One *type* has been worked out for each of the required kinds of use and improved to the point where no other variation was possible. . . . All types can be taken apart. The parts are interchangeable. . . . Due to its durability and sanitary quality Breuer metal furniture is approximately 200 per cent more economical in use than ordinary chairs.'[21]

However the percentage of this economy was worked out, and in spite of the financial problems of Standard-Möbel,[22] the use of tubular steel for furniture became the hall-mark of modernism and the avant-garde in the 1920s and 1930s, and ranges were produced

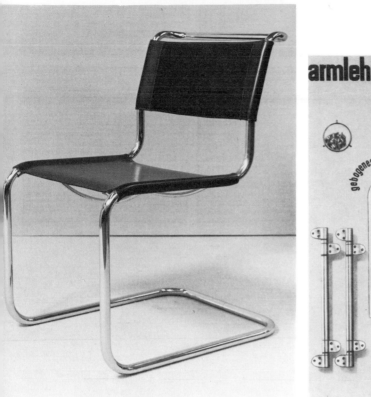
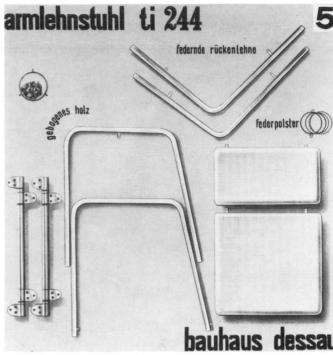

81 Variant of the cantilever tubular steel chair, Marcel Breuer, 1928 *Victoria and Albert Museum, London*
82 Dismountable chair designed by Josef Albers, 1929 *Bauhaus-Archiv*

by designers in nearly every European country. The qualities Breuer required from furniture – that it should be 'anonymous', 'drawn in space', inexpensive and simple to mass-produce – had, of course, already been achieved by Thonet in bentwood. By using what was considered an unorthodox material for furniture, Breuer was in effect transforming the uses of an already existing technology, rather than refining it, as was the case with the metal workshop. (It is ironic that he first approached Mannesmann for tubular steel when Junkers in Dessau were already using it for aircraft seats.) Breuer also defended his use of metal and his concept of furniture design on what he described as 'biological' as well as rational grounds. Like his colleagues at the Bauhaus he rejected accusations that the school was creating or conforming to a 'style'. 'Today's production of flat façades and furniture without relief or embellishment is in no way better or more lovely than the worst products of the '90s,' he said in a lecture in Delft in 1931. 'The aforementioned trademarks are not characteristic of our work. On the contrary, I consider them to be of secondary importance. We have no desire to present a purely formal point of view; instead, we see our mission in creating a home that is simpler, lighter, more comfortable in a biological sense, and independent of exterior factors.'[23] This stress on biological analogies, always latent in Bauhaus theory, was essential to counteract criticisms of formalism, and in Breuer's case the references are similar to those of Le Corbusier, whose theories were, of course, well known by 1931, and which Breuer would have encountered in 1924 when he moved to Paris before rejoining the school in 1925. 'The individual life functions', Breuer had said in the same lecture, 'must be intensively analyzed and taken into account as much as possible. The house, in other words, should be based on the body.' Corbusier had meant very much the same thing when he had written that a house should be a machine for living in; the references, however, were to a concept of efficiency rather than to the science of ergonomics, and furniture evoking that efficiency as far as Breuer was concerned, was 'furniture that is independent because it has the simplest form, furniture with no composition – neither beginning nor end –' in this case standardized units for the 'closets and all the cupboards in the house', while 'chairs, beds and tables . . . should be good, well-formed, independent models, whose main characteristics are mobility, lightness, and where possible, transparency.' (Illus. 81.)

The achievement of this 'transparency', however, was not necessarily dependent on the use of tubular steel, and the cabinet-making workshop continued to produce designs in wood while Breuer was in charge, and when Albers and then Alfred Arndt took over the workshop after Breuer left in 1928. Modular systems of cabinet furniture were produced as well as chairs combining wood, laminated ply and metal. One of the most interesting of these was a dismountable chair in laminated bentwood (Illus. 82), first developed by Josef Albers in 1926, made up of four wooden components, upholstered seat and back rest, held together by two metal bars. Ironically, this furniture, as simple, rational and anonymous as Breuer recommended, extended the craft tradition in the same way as Alvar Aalto's work in Finland. Several of these designs were awarded prizes in a Werkbund competition for the standardization of home furniture in 1931, the year that Breuer left Germany.

THE WEAVING WORKSHOP

Breuer's ideal of anonymity and 'transparency' in domestic design had, of course, implications for the weaving workshop, where the work was, by definition, craft-based, and in Weimar concentrated on the production of tapestries as an autonomous art form. Gunta Stölzl, assessing the Weimar achievement when she left the school in 1931, was to describe this work as 'pretentious' and 'autocratic' (see page 109). Already before the move to Dessau, attempts had been made to work in a more 'disciplined' way, and to consider the needs of the domestic market. In Dessau a variety of different kinds of loom could be purchased, and there were better facilities for dyeing, so the students were able to concentrate on the potential for colour, texture and structure in a variety of woven materials, rather than create, as Gunta Stölzl put it, 'pictures made of wool'. The aim in this workshop, as in the school as a whole, was to develop a 'systematic' approach to the work, and to produce prototypes (*Typen*) for industry. Weaving, of course, imposes its own discipline and order, as well as the potential for 'unity in variety'. It is essentially 'constructive' in character and its 'construction', even with mechanization, can still relate to traditional methods and materials.

Gunta Stölzl developed a consistent programme for the workshop in Dessau. Although better equipped, the work there was, of necessity, based on the potential of the hand-loom; in the initial stages the students were encouraged to exploit this potential. 'Only work at the hand loom', she wrote, 'allows the kind of latitude for an idea to be developed from experiment to experiment until it is defined and clarified to the point that sample products can be handed to industry for mechanical reproduction.'[24] In this case, therefore, it was essential to maintain the craft approach in the creation of the 'prototype' in order to influence developments in industrial production. The weaving workshop therefore, was the only department in Dessau to insist that its work must, of necessity, remain craft-based if it were to have any influence on current production. Rather than producing prototypes that acknowledged existing methods in industry (as in the metal workshop) or anticipated the potential of new materials (Breuer's use of tubular steel), the aim of the weaving workshop was to promote, through experimentation with traditional techniques, a more flexible approach from industry. This approach had to be practical, and in Bauhaus terms relevant to the needs of the market: the workshop, therefore, considered 'resistance to wear and tear, flexibility, elasticity, permeability or impermeability to light, fastness to colour and light, etc.' in its experiments. At the same time, however, it had to demonstrate an aesthetic that was appropriate to the properties of the materials used, so that the samples offered to industry concentrated on structure and texture, colour being used to emphasize these qualities. 'The vitality of the material forces people working with textiles to try out new things daily,' wrote Gunta Stölzl, 'to readjust time and again, to climb from experience to experience in order to do justice to the needs of our time.'[25] The production of wall-hangings and tapestries was still encouraged, therefore, partly because they demonstrated the full creative potential of weaving, and partly because 'free' work of this kind encouraged skills that could be related and adapted to material sold by the yard.

When the workshop moved to Dessau, Georg Muche was still nominally in charge as *Formmeister*. Relationships between Muche and the weavers had already been strained in Weimar, however; he had, of course, refused to become involved with the practicalities of weaving there, and when he did try to help equip the new workshop in Dessau, his efforts were considered far from practical. 'Muche returned Saturday evening from Berlin in a truck with seven looms which he had bought there at an outrageous price, to the horror of poor Gunda (sic),' Schlemmer wrote to his wife in 1925: 'Muche – he is tired of being a businessman.'[26]

A year later there was a fracas in the weaving workshop, again over Muche's purchase of a loom – this time a Jacquard – which implied a greater concentration on mechanization. The students refused to accept Muche as an instructor, and although Gropius and Fritz Hesse tried to persuade him to stay on, he left to join Itten's private school in Berlin, and to concentrate on painting, especially fresco painting. In 1939, however, he founded and ran a master class in 'Textile Art' in the Textile School in Krefeld, where the emphasis was on machine production, and where, in spite of his isolation during the war, he was able to put his ideals for Dessau into practice.

In Dessau, Gunta Stölzl, who took over the direction of the workshop after Muche had relinquished it, insisted that free experimentation at the most basic level as well as work on tapestries should be maintained if the workshop was to be defined as a 'laboratory' (Pls. 15 and 16). New students, who had little or no knowledge of weaving were encouraged to improvise – these 'improvisations' furnishing 'a fund of ideas from which more carefully considered compositions were later derived'. The use of materials was not confined to wool, cotton and silk, and the students experimented with cellophane, paper fibre and rayon. The transition from experimental to practical work was, according to Gunta Stölzl, 'a curious revolution'. 'Previously they had been so deeply interested in the problems of the material itself and in discovering various ways of handling it that they had taken no

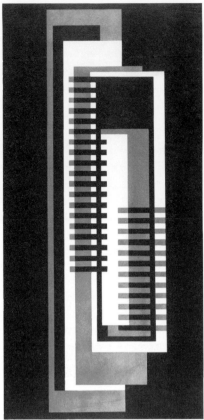

83 Tapestry in black, white and different tones of grey. Woven silk. Designed by Anni Albers, 1927
Bauhaus-Archiv

84 *Overlapping* sandblasted laminated glass by Josef Albers, 1929 *Busch-Reisinger Museum, Harvard University*

time for practical considerations. Now, however, a shift took place from free play with forms to logical composition. As a result more systematic training in the mechanics of weaving was introduced, as well as a course in the dyeing of yarns. The whole range of possibilities had been freely explored: concentration on a definite purpose now had a disciplinary effect.'[27]

As a result of this dual approach – 'free play' leading to practical work – the weaving workshop developed a good relationship with industry, the Dresden Werkstätte as well as firms in Berlin producing their designs. The workshop was also in a position to urge industry to produce more experimental work, and to anticipate the introduction of man-made fibres, which could, of course, replace traditional weaving techniques. 'Why are we still weaving fabrics, why are we not searching for entirely new materials that correspond to woven fabrics – being capable of being dyed and produced in any size, being elastic and easily divisible, being soft and, most of all, being economically advantageous, without having to be subjected to that troublesome and – despite the technical sophistication – restrictive process of weaving?' Hélène Schmidt-Nonne asked in 1926.[28] Such research, according to Schmidt-Nonne, was 'a job for the chemical industry and for university laboratories', and if it was successful 'weaving [would] be obsolete'. It is interesting, however, that Hélène Schmidt-Nonne considered that tapestries 'freed from serving practical ends' would survive as 'a purely visual experience'. 'Their special distinction, as against painting,' she wrote, 'is the wealth of possibilities they offer for varying surface effects by using different materials, such as wool, cotton, linen, silk, rayon, metal, and glass, to obtain smooth, rough, glossy, matt, coarse, fine, soft, hard, thick and thin effects.'

Tapestries, therefore, were still produced by the most accomplished designers in the weaving workshops at Dessau, including Otti Berger, Anni Albers and Gunta Stölzl. Ironically one of Gunta Stölzl's finest designs, a Gobelin produced in 1926–27, which draws on Klee's and Kandinsky's theories of colour and perception, as well as demonstrating the richness of pattern and texture which can be achieved within the constraints of the medium, has recently been produced in printed cotton, and in plastic for tote bags: both travesties of the original, of course. This mutation between 'high' and 'popular' art could not have been contemplated in the thirties. The Bauhaus tapestries, like those of William Morris some fifty years earlier, were a celebration of the 'noblest of the weaving arts'. Unlike those of Morris, however, they were not produced to recreate or preserve a lost art, but were intended partly as 'masterpieces' in the guild sense, to demonstrate confidence in skills (both aesthetic and practical) that could be utilized (but not imitated) on a less élitist level, and partly to experiment with materials and techniques that might be adapted by industry. At the same time the Dessau tapestries represent, almost literally, the 'hidden order of art' implicit in the teaching on the basic course. Anni Albers's work, for example (Illus. 83), with its graduations of colour tones, and use of squares and rectangles, not only anticipated 'Op Art', but also reflects the preoccupations of her husband, Josef Albers.

ALBERS AND THE PRELIMINARY COURSE

Josef Albers was the first of the Bauhaus students to become a 'master', and in Dessau he was in charge of the first term of the Preliminary Course, consolidating the programme he had established in Weimar. As in Weimar, his Dessau programmes involved experiments or 'constructions' with paper, 'straw, corrugated cardboard, wire mesh, cellophane, stick-on labels, newspapers, wall-paper, match-boxes, confetti, phonograph needles and razor blades'.[29] The aim, according to Albers, was to develop 'constructive thinking' and 'spatial imagination' through the transformation of material into form. This transformation, however, was intended to involve objective rather than what Albers described as 'aesthetic' considerations, since Albers at that time associated the 'aesthetic' with 'the exaggeration of individualism', rather than with a methodical, and therefore logical and constructive approach to form. Albers's course, although seemingly the antithesis of Itten's, was nevertheless based on the concept of learning through doing. 'The best education is one's own experience,' he wrote. 'Experimenting surpasses study.' Again, the approach to form was based on the exploration of the qualities and potential of materials; Albers's course, however, stressed the constructive rather than the expressive nature of materials, and results were achieved through self-discipline rather than self-expression. Justification was needed for every decision and process involved in the students' experimental constructions, since this encouraged 'responsibility and self-discipline – towards ourselves, the material and the work'. Economy both of materials and means was stressed, since what Albers described as 'thrift' was not only the antithesis of 'waste', but also made for 'an element of weightlessness', an essential quality in 'today's language of forms' in which every element should carry 'meaning'. . . . 'If in a form there is something that is not utilized, then the calculation has been wrong, for coincidence then plays a part and that is unjustified and unjustifiable. Moreover, it is senseless because it usually results from habit.' The course was carefully planned, therefore, in order to encourage the students to develop their 'spatial imagination', to 'think constructively' and to understand 'the sociological origins of our form language'. It was intended to eliminate dilettantism through creative experiment. 'This method', wrote Albers, 'stands in contrast to that of vocational school training which "inculcates" manual skills. . . . If one does "a bit of" cabinet-maker's work, "a bit of" tailoring, and "a bit of" book-binding, one arrives at dilettantism in the bad sense of the word. . . . "Also" sawing, "also" planing (the most difficult work in the cabinet-maker's shop), and "also" cutting cardboard and glueing remain unproductive, because these activities do nothing but keep one occupied. They do not satisfy the creative urge. Thus: no "fiddling around", but building. . . .'[30]

Albers's intention – to promote creativity through an a-historical and unpredetermined approach to form in design and architecture – was, of course, shared by his colleagues in the Bauhaus at that time. Albers was, perhaps, the most rigorous in his concentration on economy and efficiency, order and simplicity. According to Will Grohmann, he always 'limited himself to a minimum of means but not a minimum of meaning'[31] (Illus. 84). It is, however, not without significance that in spite of Albers's continued involvement with teaching (after he left the Bauhaus in 1933 to emigrate to the United States, he taught at the Black Mountain College, Harvard and Yale, as well as at the *Hochschule für Gestaltung* in Ulm), his reputation is now based on his work on colour theory and the series of paintings 'homage to the square', his main preoccupation from the 1950s until his death in 1977. These paintings were, according to Albers 'my own work'. 'In my own work,' he wrote, 'I am content to compete with myself and to search with simple palette and with simple colour for manifold instrumentation. So I dare further variants.'[32] Albers's approach, therefore, was the antithesis of that of Moholy-Nagy. To achieve what he described as a 'meaningful approach to the production of form', Albers concentrated on the specific in order to achieve the universal. However, he could only achieve this to his own satisfaction through painting, and the problem of the painter's involvement in design for the real world remained. His work as a designer in both Weimar and Dessau demonstrates his eclecticism as well as his growing concentration on simplicity of form and the minimum use of materials. It is not surprising, therefore, that in 1925 he designed a type-face (based on the elementary forms of the circle, triangle and square) for advertising purposes.

PRINTING AND COMMERCIAL ART

Whereas in Weimar the limited facilities of the printing workshop had been used for 'fine art' graphics and Bauhaus posters, in Dessau typography, and various aspects of 'commercial art' – advertising and exhibition design – became major (and lucrative) components of the curriculum. Expediency, of course, demanded that the school should advertise its products; at the same time, however, its philosophy required what Herbert Bayer described as a 'functional' and 'objective approach' to graphic and typographic communication, so that 'the essential aspects of the problem are understood before and during the design process'.[33] The fact that two terms of the Preliminary Course in Dessau were devoted to 'lettering' indicates the importance of these developments in the Bauhaus programme. Joost Schmidt, who also ran the sculpture (or plastic) workshop in Dessau, was in charge of this aspect of the course, and its objective, according to the curriculum was the 'mastery of letter forms and simple colour – areas – designs (preparation for instruction in the commercial art department)'.[34]

Joost Schmidt, who has been described as 'the forgotten Bauhäusler', had been a student in the Art Academy in Weimar before the war, and returned there in 1919 to join the sculpture workshop. Like Albers, his first major commission involved work for the Sommerfeld House – in his case the intricate geometric wood-carving on the doors and staircase. He also designed mural reliefs for the van de Velde building in 1923, as well as one of the most striking posters for the 1923 exhibition. He had no formal training in lettering, however, although he had worked on private commissions for Otto Dörfner. According to his widow, Hélène Schmidt-Nonne: 'The students were so poor that money had to be earned somehow. Schmidtchen earned himself a few extra marks by helping Otto Dörfner . . . to decorate such personal and celebration documents as congratulation cards, jubilee certificates and the like. The lettering was quite fancy and had to be applied with gold leaf on parchment. To acquire the necessary skill for this task, Schmidt borrowed some of those beautifully decorated medieval books that were in the Weimar State Library and diligently copied the hand-written script during his spare hours at home. So you see, he was really self-taught here.'[35]

Self-taught in the monastic tradition (it says a great deal for the Weimar State Library that Schmidt was apparently able to borrow their medieval books), he then transferred his concentration on the unity of image and text to the more iconoclastic formulas introduced by van Doesburg and Moholy-Nagy, and produced designs for advertising as well as posters before working on the Preliminary Course. His course in lettering involved the study not only of letter forms, but the optical, psychological, technical and economic influences on the development of these forms – in order to understand what he described as the 'socio-graphological form of expression'.[36] There were exercises in perspective, axonometric representation and colour theory – Schmidt obviously drew on his experiences as a sculptor as well as the ideological confrontations in Weimar in order to set the course within a theoretical and practical context. The course was compulsory for all students, but those who wanted to specialize in this area then went into the typographic and printing workshop, which was run by Herbert Bayer.

Bayer, who had been apprenticed to architects in Linz and Darmstadt, had already worked on minor graphic commissions – packaging, book-plates, stationery, etc. – before he became a student in the wall-painting workshop in Weimar. 'Weimar', he wrote, 'became the formative experience of my subsequent work,' and Gropius, who 'had already noticed my interest in graphics . . . encouraged its continuation with an occasional commission.'[37] Bayer's 'formative experience' as a graphic designer, however, was undoubtedly his introduction to De Stijl and Constructivist interpretations of visual communication (see page 118), as well as the impact of Moholy-Nagy, who saw 'the printer's work' as 'part of the foundation on which the **new world** will be built'.[38] Although Moholy had no formal connection with the typographic and printing workshop, he had anticipated its theory and practice through his own work on the design and layout of the Bauhaus Books, and his preoccupation with the unexploited potential of all forms of visual communication: photography and film, as well as print. Moholy saw typography as a means of both reflecting and initiating social change – a process, he believed, which was already being demonstrated by poster design. '. . . A new stage of development began with the first poster,' he wrote in 1924, '. . . one began to count on the fact that form, size, colour and arrangement of the typographical material (letters and signs) contain a strong visual impact. The organization of these possible visual effects gives a visual validity to the content of the message as well; this means that by means of printing the content is also being defined pictorially. . . . This . . . is the essential task of visual-typographical design.' The medium, therefore, became the message: a fact which, according to Moholy, had already been acknowledged by 'newspapers, posters and job printing, since typographical progress has been almost entirely devoted to this area'.[39] In this instance, Moholy's interpretation of 'typographical progress' referred to technical innovations within the printing industry which had been developed to meet the needs of mass-communication; at grass roots level, attempts had been made to integrate word and image for maximum visual impact. Book design and layout, on the other hand, had remained static, and 'the majority of our books today have come no further in their typographical, visual, synoptical form than the Gutenberg production, despite the technological transformation in their manufacture'.

While acknowledging 'the purity of visual effect' that could be achieved by the use of conventional type-faces and type-setting, Moholy believed that books could be designed to acknowledge 'the new dimension of life' and that 'the grey text will change into a coloured picture book and will be understood as a continuous visual design'.[40] The design and layout of the Bauhaus Books, which were planned in 1924 and published between 1925 and 1931, demonstrate Moholy's theories, with their asymmetrical layout, and the use of bold type, horizontal and vertical lines, circles and arrows (point and line and plane) for emphasis as well as visual continuity. His own book, *Malerei, Fotografie, Film (Painting, Photography, Film)* (1925) gave him the opportunity to present his theories through both text and imagery. With one exception, however, the photographs selected (including work by Moholy) concentrate on the unconventional presentation of conventional images: they demonstrate the diversity that can be achieved by the 'photo-eye', but they do not comment. The exception is 'The multi-millionaire' a photomontage by Hannah Höch – the distorted and magnified image of the ruler, who walks over a neo-classical city, surrounded by emblems of speed, industry, warfare and death. In 1924, however, Moholy, in spite of his social commitment, could not foresee the ambiguity of the 'visual validity' which he celebrated and he saw the power and potential of the camera as a harbinger of truth in mass communication. 'Men still kill one another,' he wrote. 'They have not yet understood how they live, why they live; politicians fail to observe that the earth is an entity; yet television (*Telehor*) has been invented: the "far seer" – tomorrow we will be able to look into the heart of our fellow-man, be everywhere and yet be alone; illustrated books, newspapers, magazines, are printed in millions. The unambiguousness of the real, the truth in the everyday situation is there for all classes. The hygiene of the optical, the health of the visible is slowly filtering through.'[41]

The fact that imagery could be manipulated for purposes of propaganda, and an entirely different interpretation of 'health and hygiene', could not be ignored later in the decade. In the mid-twenties, however, Bayer's murals still survived in Weimar, and Bayer himself was attempting to establish a systematic course of instruction in his new workshop, which was adequately, if not lavishly equipped. A professional printer and type-setter was employed to help the students, who produced work first for the school itself and then for commercial commissions. 'Their work,' according to Bayer, 'was not the fashionable and

abcdefghi
jklmnopqr
stuvwxyz

85 Universal type designed by Herbert Bayer, 1925

"aestheticizing" kind in the sense of "commercial graphics", but rather the kind based on the understanding of the purpose and a better utilization of typographical materials, which up to date had been enslaved in the traditions of antiquarian styles.' Their approach, he believed, 'led to a typography built on the inherent qualities of the material, from which a typesetting technique could be developed'.[42]

Bayer's conception of typography and layout was obviously influenced by Moholy-Nagy and the Constructivists; at the same time, however, his insistence on a systematic and, in his terms, logical approach to typography was reinforced by certain developments within the German printing industry. Bayer used DIN format paper sizes,[43] as well as grids for the organization of the material to be presented, and he limited the range of typefaces to sans-serifs. He then began working on the design of a 'new machine alphabet' (Illus. 85) that would meet the need for 'clarity, precision and abstract form'.[44] The alphabet had to be (a) simple in form 'for the sake of legibility'; (b) each letter was to be designed with 'basic geometric elements' in order to express harmony and proportion; (c) it had to be a sans-serif to avoid any association with 'a hand-written character', and (d) it had to be capable of adaptation for hand-writing and the typewriter. Moreover, capital letters (used for all nouns in German) were to be eliminated, again in the interests of economy as well as logic. 'Why do we write and speak with two different alphabets simultaneously?' he wrote. 'We do not speak with a capital "A" and a small "a"; to convey one sound we do not need large *and* small letter symbols. One sound, one symbol.'[45] Moholy-Nagy had also recommended the abolition of the use of capital letters, citing as precedents Jakob Grimm 'who had written all nouns with small initials' and the engineer Dr W. Porstmann, who had recommended the use of uniform lettering without capitals in a book on *Speech and Lettering*, published in 1920.[46] (Porstmann, whose theories were well known at the Bauhaus, recommended the 'development of a logical language through the means of writing – a 'world alphabet' that would develop from handwriting to the 'mechanization of writing'.)[47]

The ideal of a typographical 'esperanto', therefore, did not originate in the Bauhaus, and Bayer was formulating his own interpretation of the crusade for a 'new typography' that would 'express the spirit, the life and the visual sensibility of its day'.[48] Jan Tschichold, one of the most influential typographers of the twentieth century, had contributed an article on 'The New Typography' to the Leipzig Journal, *Elementare Typographie*, in 1925; Edward Johnston's sans-serif type-face for London Transport was introduced in 1916, and Gill Sans was designed in 1928. Compared with the work of these typographers, which had developed from calligraphy and lettering, Bayer's 'Universal Type', designed in 1925, seems contrived and mannered in its straitjacket of geometric curves and horizontal lines. It was not cast as a type-face, and it was seldom used, even by Bayer himself. It worked best in a display setting, for exhibition stands designed by the workshop, and it was most consistently used for covers of the magazine *Die Neue Linie*, becoming a component of the magazine's 'house style' throughout the thirties.

Before Bayer left the school in 1928, the workshop had several commissions for advertising and exhibition displays. In 1925, a range of stationery and advertising material was designed for the Fagus works – with type used horizontally and vertically and thick red lines delineating the text. Bayer and students in the workshop (notably Xanti Schawinsky) used photography and photo-montage in Bauhaus publicity material in the 1920s, but Bayer's major work in poster and publicity design was done in the 1930s, after he had left the school, and subsequently in the United States.

It is, however, interesting that in spite of his reputation as a graphic designer, Bayer considered himself first and foremost as a painter. 'I consider myself to be primarily a painter,' he wrote in his own book, 'and painting is the continuous link connecting the various facets of my work.'[49] Bayer's approach to poster and publicity design was founded in the skills he had acquired in the wall-painting workshop in Weimar, and therefore owe a great deal to Klee and Kandinsky's courses in perception and analytical drawing. In his book on his own work, published in 1967, Bayer provided a 'design analysis' of five of his posters, produced between 1926 and 1936, 'hoping to discover guidelines for a more precise visual language'. For as he pointed out, studies in psychology, perception and 'the physiology of the eye' could lead to a 'science of design' which would make advertising more effective.[50]

Questions of the morality of advertising did not inhibit Bauhaus designers in the twenties. According to Joost Schmidt, the purpose of advertising was to provide information through the presentation of facts and essential data.[51] Bayer believed that 'the keystone of contemporary civilization, industry, through its widespread and diversified contacts with the world, can become the promoter of significant art forms':[52] a variant, of course, of Gropius's slogan, Art and Technology: a new unity. The change from the concentration on the 'graphic arts' (Weimar) to 'commercial art' (Dessau), however, implied an ideal of collaboration with industry, rather than manipulation by industry, which could not be sustained in Germany in the thirties. The propaganda machine of the Third Reich exposed the naïvety of the concept of the collective that had sustained the school, and demonstrated the poverty of its ideal of a people's culture. 'It is you and your kind who sold revolutionary art down the river', a correspondent for the *Rote Fahne* (the *Red Flag*) told Moholy-Nagy in 1933, soon after the burning of the Reichstag. 'With your decadence and your precious experimentation you have destroyed the confidence of the masses in artists and writers. Because you fooled them they don't believe in art any more. . . . Go where you belong before they cut your throat – to the capitalists who finance Hindenberg and Bruhning, Hitler and the Bauhaus.'[53]

Pl. 10 (*Left*) Coffee pot in German silver, designed by Wilhelm Wagenfeld, 1923–4 (*Right*) Jug in German silver, W. Rössger and F. Marby, 1923–4 *Kunstsammlungen, Weimar*

Pl. 11 Cradle by Peter Keler, painted wood, 1922 *Kunstsammlungen, Weimar*

Pl. 12 Designs for kiosks, Herbert Bayer, 1924 (*Left*) Project for open streetcar station with news-stand (*Right*) Project for an exhibition stand *Victoria and Albert Museum, London*

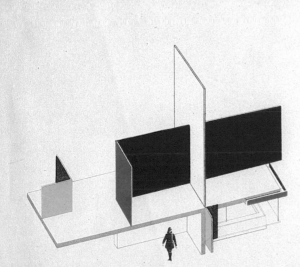

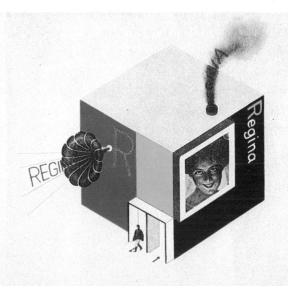

Pl. 13 (*Left*) Lecture theatre in Dessau, with tubular steel seating by Marcel Breuer and light fittings by the metal workshop. As restored in 1982 *Photograph Gillian Naylor*

Pl. 14 (*Below*) Bauhaus building, restored in 1982 *Photograph Gillian Naylor*

Pl. 15 (*Opposite*) Design for a carpet by Gunta Stölzl, watercolour, 1928 *Victoria and Albert Museum, London*

Pl. 16 Design for Jacquard woven hanging by Gunta
Stölzl, watercolour on graph paper, 1928
Victoria and Albert Museum, London

Pl. 17 Fabric samples produced by Bauhaus
staff and students *Victoria and Albert Museum,
London*

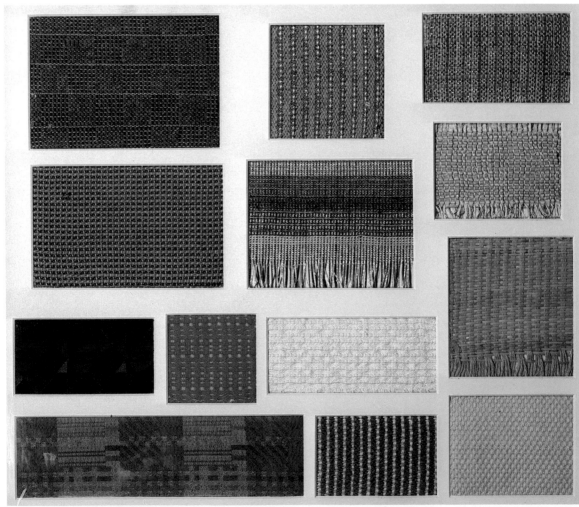

The Reichstag was burned down in March 1933, and in July 1933 the Bauhaus, then in Berlin under the direction of Mies van der Rohe, was closed by the Nazis. Of the original members of staff only Kandinsky and Albers remained, survivors of the ideological and political assaults on the school when Hannes Meyer took over the directorship in 1928.

Gropius had written to the authorities in Dessau in February 1928, asking for 'an early termination' of his contract (which still had two years to run), and proposing Hannes Meyer as his successor. He cited the increase in his 'public commitments' outside Dessau as the reason for his resignation (he had won first prize in a housing scheme for Karlsruhe and was also involved in the Siemenstadt housing complex in Berlin). After ten years' fighting for the survival of the school, Gropius obviously felt the need to concentrate on his architectural work, but the fact that the elections in December 1927 had resulted in a right-wing majority must have reinforced his decision to leave: he had had enough of coping with hostile bureaucracies. However his recommendation that Hannes Meyer (who had spent less than a year at the school) should replace him was obviously unpopular both with staff and students. 'You are still our guarantee that the Bauhaus will not become a school,' one of them said when the news was announced. 'For the sake of an idea we have starved here in Dessau. You cannot leave us now. If you do, the way will be open for reactionaries. Hannes Meyer may be quite a fine fellow; I don't want to say anything against him. But Hannes Meyer as director of the Bauhaus is a catastrophe.'[1]

When Gropius had appointed Hannes Meyer to run the architecture department, he obviously had him in mind as his successor. At that time Meyer's priorities as an architect, and his social commitment, seemed to reinforce the philosophies of the school. According to Oskar Schlemmer, who shared his house with him when he arrived, Meyer 'made a definite impression on the chief Bauhaus people, thanks to his sound opinions and winning ways'. Schlemmer's description of these 'sound opinions', however, immediately after Meyer's move to Dessau, gives some indication of future tensions. 'He was not interested in Klee; he says Klee must be in a perpetual trance; Feininger does not appeal to him, either. Kandinsky [does] because of his theoretical underpinnings. In terms of character he feels closest to Moholy, although he is very critical towards much about him – his manner (officious), his false teachings (which the students also see as such and reject); he was not interested in Muche's steel-construction new building, since steel is the least important element in it. Gropius can count himself fortunate to have this honest fellow as the latest feather in his cap.'[2]

The 'honest fellow', therefore, who had spelled out his convictions to Gropius before he agreed to run the school of architecture (see page 143), had weighed up the Bauhaus achievements in the light of these convictions, and found them wanting. Meyer's definition of design in *The New World* manifesto as 'the product of a formula: function multiplied by economics'[3] was too reductionist to be acceptable to the majority of students and staff; at the same time, however, Meyer was able to see the fallacies in the school's obsession with the 'type-form' as a model of the interaction between art and industry. As far as he was concerned there was too much 'art' and too amateurish an involvement with the processes of industry in the workshops. The result was a preoccupation with form that bore no relationship either to techniques of production or the demands of mass consumption. It was obvious that Meyer had made his priorities clear before he was appointed director, and that Gropius was, to a certain extent, in agreement with him. The beginning of the new academic year in October 1927 had coincided with the growing economic depression in Germany, as well as the swing to the right; the Bauhaus budget was again under threat. In a letter to Otto Meyer in January 1928, Schlemmer wrote: 'The Bauhaus will reorient itself in the direction of architecture, industrial production, and the intellectual aspect of technology. The painters are merely tolerated as a necessary evil now.'[4]

As far as the designers were concerned, this concentration on 'industrial production, and the intellectual aspect of technology' implied that the Bauhaus was in danger of becoming a trade school, and losing any autonomy it had gained in determining rather than interpreting the demands of industry. It is significant that Marcel Breuer, Herbert Bayer and Moholy-Nagy handed in their resignations before Gropius's decision to leave the school was announced. Breuer and Bayer (like Gropius) cited the growth of private commissions to justify their departure from Dessau: both went to Berlin, where Bayer became director of the Dorland advertising agency, while Breuer, whose work in tubular steel was for the most part a private, rather than a Bauhaus enterprise, aimed to continue this work, as well as set up an architectural practice. Nevertheless Breuer and Bayer had ideological as well as practical reasons for leaving the school, since, paradoxically, Meyer's stress on collective rather than individual endeavour implied a greater need for specialization. Breuer, for example, did not wish to be restricted to furniture design, and resented having to rely on the wall-painting workshop for the spatial organization of interiors, which, he believed, he could, and should, do himself.[5] Neither Breuer nor Bayer, however, made any overt statement about the direction the school was taking when they left. Moholy-Nagy, on the other hand, resigned on matters of principle, which he set down in a letter to the *Meisterrat* (governing masters) in January 1928. '. . . As soon as creating an object becomes a speciality, and work becomes trade,' he wrote, 'the process of education loses all vitality. There must be room for teaching the basic ideas which keep human content alert and vital. For this we fought and for this we exhausted ourselves. I can no longer keep up with the stronger and stronger tendency toward trade specialization in the workshops. . . . The spirit of construction for which I and others gave all we had – and gave it gladly – has been replaced by a tendency towards application. My realm was the construction of school and man.'[6]

It is, of course, ironic that it was Moholy, himself considered a philistine when he joined the school, who openly attacked and rejected Meyer's policies. For in theory the two men, as Schlemmer indicated, shared similar beliefs. Both had declared themselves Constructivists, and both claimed to be more concerned with social than with aesthetic issues in their conception of design. Their interpretation of the 'spirit of construction', however, was totally different, for Moholy's stress on 'man' rather than the 'product' implied an individualistic and empirical approach to design which Meyer could not countenance. Moholy would not accept traditional conceptions of 'art' in his own work and replaced them by experiments in photography and film; and in rejecting the mysticism of Itten, he had attempted to establish a factory 'aesthetic' in the metal workshops. As far as Meyer was concerned, however, this work, on the one hand experimental and on the other formalistic, was futile. It was based on intuition and individualism, it was directed at the avant-garde, and it was inspired by a pseudo-scientific method. For it was above all objective organization and method that Meyer wished to reinforce in the school. In Gropius's era, the painters had explored 'ways of seeing' in order to establish new, or non-historicist principles of design, and their concepts of form, colour, space and the nature of perception were reflected in attitudes to workshop production. The commercial success of some of the workshops, however, was of little interest to Meyer, since it was based on unrealistic conceptions of social needs. When Meyer was first appointed, however, the newly-formed architecture department was involved in embryonic sociological and technical research for the planning of the Dessau-Törten Siedlung, and Meyer's now notorious manifesto, *Bauen*,[7] could be interpreted as a more radical restatement of Gropius's intentions: '. . . The new house is a prefabricated building for site assembly; as such it is an industrial product and the work of a variety of specialists: economists, statisticians, hygienists, climatologists, industrial engineers, standardization experts, heating engineers . . . and the architect? . . . he was an artist and now becomes a specialist in organization! The new house is . . . primarily a social enterprise because it is – like every government standard – the standardized, industrial product of a nameless community of inventors.'

The manifesto concludes: **'Building is nothing but organization: social, technical, economical, psychological organization.'** This statement could be considered the logical conclusion of the stress on standards and standardization implicit in Gropius's pre-war theory, as well as in his more recent plans for the Dessau-Törten housing estate. The manifesto begins, however, with a denunciation of art which challenges the fundamental premise on which teaching at the school was based: 'All things in this world are a product of the formula: function times economy. All these things are, therefore, not works of art: all art is composition and, hence, is unsuited to achieve goals. All life is function and is therefore unartistic. The idea of the "composition of a harbour" is hilarious! But how is a town designed? Or the plan of a dwelling? Composition or function! Art or life???'

Meyer, like Georg Muche two years earlier, denied the conceptual links between art and design which the school had so carefully fostered, both in the structure and assumptions of its curriculum and in its teaching methods. He went further than Muche, however, in his polarization of 'art' and 'life', so that in theory the positions of the painters on the staff should have been precarious. Nevertheless Klee, Kandinsky, Albers, Schmidt and Schlemmer continued to teach on the Preliminary Course, and Klee and Kandinsky held 'free' painting classes, almost, it seems, in defiance of the régime. In 1929, for example,

Ernst Kallai, the Hungarian writer and theorist who was editor of the *Bauhaus Journal* from 1928 to 1929 wrote: 'It is . . . not without interest to observe that what goes on at the Bauhaus in Dessau is not only building and workshop production of objects of practical use. There is also painting. Cheek by jowl with the imposing concrete forms and glass expanses . . . in the shadow of these icily rational, purpose-dedicated spatial constructions that vaunt their industrial aesthetic. If the nocturnal devil of the legends were to peep into the cubicles and studios of the Bauhäusler, he would be astounded by the number of painters standing around, here and there, in front of their easels, dabbing at pictures.'[8] By encouraging free painting classes in the school, however, Meyer was, in effect 'marginalizing' art. He did not, of course, consider the establishment of a separate 'fine art' department, but he allowed art to develop as an end in itself, thus minimalizing the painters' influence on the workshops.

Since three influential teachers had left with Gropius, Meyer was able to restructure the courses and make his own appointments, as well as increase the number of visiting specialists. The work of the architecture department, with its stress on sociological and scientific research, became central to the school's activities. Ludwig Hilberseimer, a former member of the *Novembergruppe*, who had worked in Berlin as an architect and townplanner, took charge of the architecture programme; Anton Brenner, who had studied with Peter Behrens and worked with Ernst May in Frankfurt, joined the staff, as well as Edvard Heiberg, the Norwegian architect and theorist, and Alcar Rudelk, a construction engineer. Mart Stam, the Dutch architect (and Gropius's original choice as his successor) contributed regularly to the programme as a guest lecturer; visiting lecturers included Rudolph Carnap, Otto Neurath and Herbert Feigl, Viennese logical positivists, Karel Teige, the radical architect and designer from Prague, and for 'light relief' Hermann Finsterlin, Ernst Toller, Dziga Vertov and Piet Zwart. The teaching staff, therefore, was reinforced by leading radical architects, and the theoretical debates, as represented by the visiting lecturers, centred round the philosophy and convictions of radicals in Holland, Austria, Czechoslovakia and Russia. 'I never design alone,' wrote Hannes Meyer. 'All my designs have arisen from the very start out of collaboration with others. That is why I consider the choosing of suitable associates to be the most important act in preparing for a creative work in architecture. The more contrasted the abilities of the designing brigade, the greater its capabilities and creative power. . . .'[9]

The programme was based on an ideal of objective and systematic research into the social and biological factors governing design. These 'exact sciences', as Meyer described them, were, of course, in their infancy, although Hilberseimer, Brenner and Mart Stam, as well as Meyer himself, had personal experience of this analytical approach to architectural planning. Before embarking on a scheme the students were encouraged to consider various external factors relating to the site (Illus. 86): the movement of pedestrians, traffic, goods and services; the relationship of house to street, problems of noise, problems of smells (described by Meyer as 'olfactory relationships' – smoke, kitchen odours, dung piles

86 Schematic plan demonstrating the various factors that must be taken into account (movement, sun, light, etc.) when establishing ground plans for an apartment. Hannes Meyer, 1930 *Bauhaus-Archiv*

der grundriß errechnet sich aus folgenden faktoren

1. bewegungsfaktoren

der arbeitsplan ergibt die reihenfolge der
funktionen

kommen
gehen
anziehen   umziehen
geschütztes wohnen   baden   schlafen
ungeschütztes wohnen

3. sonnenberechnung

berechnet für ort:
breitengrad: 47.30
längengrad: 0.00

frühling und herbst.

winter.

sommer.

2. sonne

man braucht morgens sonne im schlafraum
man braucht abends sonne im wohnraum

daher
schlafräume nach osten
wohnräume nach westen

wohnen   schlafen

nachdem die wohnzellen
aneinander liegen müssen,
können sie:

1. vertikal erreichbar
sein.
es sind maximal zwei
wohnzellen an einer
zugang.-

1 und 2 gibt 4

2 und 3 gibt 5

2. horizontal
durch geschlos-
senen geschlos-
senen gang da
die wohnzelle
nur teil der
wohnräume im
hause.-

a. schlaf-
ankleide-
bade-raum
durch zu-
gang vom
wohraum
getrennt.-
forderung der
wohneinheit
nicht erfüllt.

b.
geschlossener
gang an o.seite.
forderung der
unmittelbarer
besonnung und
belüftung
erfüllt.

c.
gang über schlafraum
aufwand zu gross.

	wohnraum	balkon
besonnung in winter bis	16.15 uhr	16.15 uhr
besonnung in frühling und herbst	16.3o uhr	18.00 uhr
besonnung in sommer bis	15.1o uhr	16.3o uhr

konstruktion

trockenbauweise eisenskelett ausführung

luftbedarf des schlafzimmers.

1. luftwechselbedarf.
kohlensäureproduktion 0,015 cbm /st.
kohlensäuregehalt in 1 cbm zuluft 0,0004 cbm
zulässiger kohlensäuregehalt in 1 cbm raum-
luft 0,001 cbm.

$x = \frac{0,015}{0,001-0,0004} = 25 \text{cbm/st.}$

2. natürliche (selbst)belüftung.
der berechnung liegt nur die natürliche luft-
ausgleich zugrunde, der durch die undichtig-
keit der geschlossenen fenster verursacht
wird.
fensterfläche 1,98 qm. temperaturdiff. 3o.
rauminhalt des schlafzimmers und anschliessen-
den ankleideraumes 27,9 cbm.
überdruck der aussenluft 0,54 kg/qm.
luftdurchlässigkeit des fensters 8,65 cbm/st.

3. fensterlüftung.
frischluftbedarf 16.35 cbm/st.
luftgeschwindigkeit bei 10 temperaturdiff.
von 2,95 m/sec. ergibt einen lüftungsquer-
schnitt von 15,5 cm.
wirkungsgrad der lüftung klappen 72 %.
ergibt die faktische grösse von 26,56 cm.

blick-reich
beim erwachen

letzter strahl im wohnraum
letzter strahl auf dem balkon

strahl, frühling 6.3o uhr
strahl, sommer 6.3o uhr

grundriß der einzelwohnzelle

p. tschudinn - t. weber

and domestic animals), as well as light and heat (natural and artificial) and ventilation.[10] Then the requirements of living and communal areas had to be worked out in order to establish 'standard types for all vitally important individual spaces'.[11]

Naturally such investigations needed to be related to specific projects, such as the flats that were built on the Dessau-Törten estate, when Meyer joined the staff. The most important scheme, however, which involved both a practical and ideological commitment to the concept of the 'collective' was the design and building of the Trades Union School in Bernau, near Berlin. The German Trades Union Federation held a limited competition for the design of the school in 1927, inviting entries from Max Taut, Max Berg and Erich Mendelsohn, as well as Hannes Meyer. Meyer won the competition, and therefore brought the commission with him to Dessau. The school was intended for Trades Union members and officials attending short residential courses, and Meyer related the design and plan to its teaching curriculum. The school, consisting of residential blocks, teachers' accommodation, lecture theatre, seminar rooms, dining hall, kitchen and a gymnasium, was built near a lake in the forest of Bernau. The residential blocks were arranged to receive maximum light, the lecture hall was equipped with sophisticated visual aids, and the dining room faced the lake. Trades Union members attending the school, therefore, were presented with an ideal of practicality and order in the organization and planning of the various units of the building, as well as in the structuring of the courses they attended. According to Claude Schnaidt, 'One hundred and twenty students of both sexes were organized in twelve cells each of ten members. Two students roomed together and five of these groups of two formed a cell whose members lived together separate from the others. They ate together in the dining room, studied together in the lecture room, and formed a section in physical training. . . . The purpose of this rigid grouping was to give the individual worker . . . the opportunity to identify himself with the communal life of the school as quickly and as closely as possible through comradeship with his room-mate and through the life of the cells.'[12]

Meyer applied a similar rationalization to the organization of the courses at the Bauhaus (including the reintroduction of physical training and exercises – not, as with Itten, in order to heighten and co-ordinate the senses, but to counteract the 'one-sided emphasis on brain-work'). Four departments were established: building; advertising (which incorporated the graphic and printing workshops, as well as a new photography workshop under Walter Peterhans); interior design (metal workshop, wall-painting and furniture workshop), and the textile department. He revised the time-table, taking into account 'the capacity of the students to learn', so that 'the focal point of the week was three eight-hour days of workshop work';[13] he encouraged commissions 'which had the biggest contribution to make to the further development of traditional types of lamp, working chair, upholstery material, etc.';[14] he attempted to make the workshops self-supporting and he encouraged the students to collaborate on specific projects rather than work individually, and to form what he called 'vertical brigades' so that 'students in different years worked together and the older students helped the younger ones under the expert guidance of the master'.

Alfred Arndt, a former student in the wall-painting workshop, took charge of the interior design department; he was involved in the design of low-cost furniture for mass production in both wood and metal, and also encouraged the production of wallpapers, which were made and marketed by Rasch and Co. and brought in substantial royalties. 'In

1929 alone (the year they were introduced),' wrote Meyer, 'more than 20,000 rooms in Germany and neighbouring countries were papered with them. From the educational point of view, they provided an opportunity of dealing with the problem of "colour in the interior" as a general principle and also of making "hygiene in the worker's house" a reality, by producing cheap washable wallpapers.' The advertising department, run by Joost Schmidt, was also commercially successful, designing publicity material for Bauhaus projects as well as exhibitions and posters, etc., for a range of clients. The importance of photography in the work of this department was acknowledged by the appointment of Walter Peterhans in 1929: Peterhans had studied philosophy, mathematics and art history at Göttingen, and as with Lucia and Moholy-Nagy, his photographs rarely involved social comment. What impressed Meyer, however, was Peterhans's conception of photography as science rather than art: he taught 'photographic optics and chemistry in a three-year course for young people training to be camera reporters and advertising photographers'.[15] The textile department also increased its work with manufacturers, so that for a brief period the school achieved its aim of liaison with industry to mass-produce work at low cost. 'The annual production,' Hannes Meyer wrote in 1930, 'amounting to about RM 128,000 has been almost doubled. The number of students increased from 160–180 and we could control the intake only by fixing a limit to admissions. . . . In the last business year, RM 32,000 was paid out to students in the way of wages and this enabled those who were less well-off to study there. A Bauhaus travelling exhibition publicized our ideas in Basle, Breslau, Dessau, Essen, Mannheim and Zurich. . . . Industrial firms came along with urgent requests, engaged Bauhaus students on their staffs, and concluded licence agreements for Bauhaus fabrics, lamps, standard furniture and wallpapers. Thus there was every prospect of our finances being improved in future in the only really sound way, namely through self-help.'

This summary of the school's achievements is taken from Meyer's 'open letter' to the Mayor of Dessau, Fritz Hesse, after his dismissal without notice in the summer of 1930, three years before his contract was due to expire.[16] It was, of course, inevitable that Fascist politics in interwar Germany would eventually destroy a school which had been founded as a 'Cathedral of Socialism'. Nevertheless it was ironic that Meyer's policies for design and architecture, which coincided with a period of economic stabilization in Germany, were far from exceptional, and the commercial success of the school under his leadership was due in part to the recovery of German industry, and the encouragement, on the part of various state-funded organizations, of research into low-cost housing and standardization in the domestic market.

Meyer had, of course, made no attempt to conceal his political allegiances before Gropius nominated him as his successor; like Moholy-Nagy, he was a left-wing Constructivist; like Moholy he questioned the role that 'art' had to play in design, but unlike Moholy and the rest of the staff his approach to design was totally fundamentalist and totally unsentimental. 'Building is a biological and not an aesthetic process,' he wrote to Mayor Hesse. 'Building is not the embodiment of an individual passion but a collective action. Building is the social, psychological, technical and economic organization of the processes of life. Building is a demonstration of a philosophy of life and strongly held opinions are inseparable from strong work. I taught the students the connection between building and society, the path from formal intuition to scientific building research and the precedence of people's needs over luxuries. I taught them to despise the multifariousness of idealist reality and together we strove to attain the sole reality that can be mastered – that of the measurable, visible and ponderable.'[17]

Klee and Kandinsky, protagonists of the 'multifariousness of idealist reality' had looked for universal laws in nature and in art, but their expositions of analysis and synthesis were unquantifiable and therefore irrelevant. In fact, according to a group of students who published a proclamation in July 1930, the whole conception of the Preliminary Course was irrelevant. 'What is the content and purpose of analytical drawing? Still life, concise scheme, tensions, structural net, and as the ultimate objective – "free composition of three-dimensional, formal energy tensions". This kind of instruction is bound to lead to individual, abstract, creative work, as is borne out by the various distinctly individual renderings of one and the same still life.'[18] Meyer had, in fact, intended to introduce courses on Gestalt psychology, sociology and social economics in his attempt to convert the school from formalism to functionalism. As it was, his dismissal gave him the opportunity to denounce and renounce all that he had inherited from the 'Bauhaus condor, Gropius'. 'What did I find on my appointment? A Bauhaus whose reputation had vastly outrun its power of achievement and which was the object of unprecedented publicity. A "university of design" which made the shape of every tea-glass a problem in Constructivist aesthetics. A "cathedral of socialism" in which a medieval cult was practised with the revolutionaries of pre-war art, aided by a rising generation who were casting sly looks leftwards and yet hoped one day to be canonised in the same temple.

'Every path to a school of design which would satisfy the normal needs of life was barred by inbred theories. . . . The square was red. The circle was blue. The triangle was yellow. They sat and slept on furniture like coloured geometry. They lived in houses like coloured sculpture. What lay on the floor as carpets were the mental complexes of young girls. Everywhere art had a stranglehold on life. This resulted in the situation in which I found myself. As Director of the Bauhaus I was fighting against the Bauhaus style.'[19]

There is, of course, as much fiction as fact in this rhetoric: the medieval cults and constructivist tea-glasses were left behind in Weimar; the so-called 'mental complexes of young girls' had contributed to the revitalization of the weaving industry, and the other workshops had established links with industry before Meyer took over the school. There was, nevertheless, a Bauhaus 'style' which was, of course, not confined to the Bauhaus – the flat roof, white wall, steel and chrome furniture and sans-serif letter forms had become symbols of modernity and the rejection of tradition among the avant-garde throughout Europe in the 1920s and 1930s. Although Gropius insisted that the aim of the school was 'not to propagate any "style", system, dogma, formula or vogue',[20] the formal demonstration of its ideal of rationalization and standardization contributed to what Henry Russell Hitchcock and Philip Johnson were to define as 'The International Style' in their seminal book of 1932.

WEISSENHOF

According to Henry Russell Hitchcock 'The new style had won acclaim, if not acceptance, with the Werkbund exposition at Stuttgart in 1927';[21] the experimental houses and flats built at Weissenhof, on the outskirts of Stuttgart, had been designed by a group of European architects, including Le Corbusier, Oud and Mart Stam, as well as Gropius,

Bruno and Max Taut, Peter Behrens and Ludwig Hilberseimer. Mies van der Rohe was in charge of the scheme, which was sponsored by the Werkbund and the Stuttgart City Council, and which was intended to demonstrate the advantages and the versatility of the 'new architecture'. Weissenhof was the Werkbund's most ambitious project since the 1914 exhibition in Cologne, and reactions to the scheme reflect the polarization of social and political attitudes to design and architecture in Germany at that time. To 'independent' observers like Hitchcock and Johnson, Weissenhof was a justification of the ideals of the 'New Architecture'; to the radical left-wing it was a demonstration of misguided bourgeois idealism. Karel Teige, for example, the Czech Marxist, described the scheme as 'subordinate to the ideas of a bourgeois society' because the housing units were based on the concept of the family rather than the community.[22] Hermann Muthesius saw it as an exercise in *Stilarchitektur* – yet another style, so rigidly formalistic that the inhabitants of the houses were condemned to survive the German winter in an Arab village, in houses that allowed them no privacy, nor any means of individual expression.[23] The most vehement critics of Weissenhof, however, were the German Nationalists, members of the *Bund für Heimatschutz* (League for the Protection of the Homeland) and the *Kampfbund für Deutsche Kultur* (Fighting League for German Culture), who saw the buildings as 'nothing other than examples of objectivity, raped and diluted by internationalism'.[24] It is ironic, therefore, that the formalism and 'internationalism' associated with both Weissenhof and the Bauhaus was attacked by both left and right-wing critics, and that Hannes Meyer himself condemned 'the cry for an "international architecture"' as 'a dream of those building aesthetes, who, anxious to be thought in the forefront of fashion, conjure up for themselves a uniform world of buildings constructed of glass, concrete and steel, detached from social reality'.[25]

Meyer's interpretation of 'social reality', however, was too closely associated with left-wing politics for his paymasters in Dessau. Early in 1930, the right-wing Dessau press was accusing the Bauhaus of harbouring 'a communist cell', with the approval and support of its director. The city magistrate of Dessau, and the mayor, Fritz Hesse, who was responsible for the funding of the school, knew that it could not survive such accusations, and asked for Hannes Meyer's resignation. When Meyer refused to resign, he was dismissed, and his case then went to a court of arbitration. Meyer was accused of endangering the survival of the Bauhaus by 'politicizing' it. Unlike Gropius, who had always refused to allow any party political activities to take place within the school, Meyer, it was claimed, had encouraged the Communists, and the number of party members under his leadership had increased from seven to thirty-six. This 'cell' had disrupted the classes of those masters whose policies they did not agree with; they had published subversive issues of the *Bauhaus Journal*, and Meyer had personally contributed to a Communist-sponsored fund for the support of striking miners in Mansfield, England.[26] Meyer defended himself by maintaining that he had made no secret of his political allegiances when he was invited to be director of the school; that he was not a member of the Communist party; that he was a 'philosophical' rather than a practising Marxist, and that he supported 'cultural' rather than party politics. The publication in August 1930 of his 'open letter' to Fritz Hesse in the Berlin magazine *Das Tagebuch* did little to help his case, although it achieved maximum publicity. During the controversy Meyer received letters of support from Karel Teige in Prague, from Josef Frank in Vienna, from Emil Rasch, the director of the wallpaper factory, and most surprisingly from Paul Klee, who had accepted a post in the Düsseldorf Academy. 'You must not think' Meyer replied 'that I am in any way embittered. On the contrary the events have revived powers that I have had to stifle in Dessau. I feel younger and more ready for battle than ever. . . . You know that we will always reach out our hands to each other over the barriers that divide us. I will always remain grateful to you.'[27]

Meyer resigned as director of the Bauhaus during the course of the tribunal, and in October 1930 went to Moscow, with a group of his students, to take up a post as professor at the Higher Institute for Architecture and Building there. Since Meyer aroused so much controversy, on ideological as well as personal and political grounds during his two years as director of the school, it is not easy to evaluate his achievements there. There is no doubt that his policies were successful on a practical level, and that under his direction the workshops produced designs in keeping with the requirements of German industry and the domestic market: the Bauhaus did, in fact, become a competent 'trade school', with, at last, an active architecture department. His design theory at that time, however, was so totally materialistic and reductionist that it is difficult to take it seriously; nevertheless he identified and challenged some of the uneasy assumptions about radicalism in design on which teaching at the school was based. He was politically aware, although not politically astute, and he was prepared to sacrifice the school for his convictions. Gropius, for his part, could never forgive him for this; in a letter to Tomas Maldonado, who was having his own problems as director of the Ulm School of Design in post-war Germany, he wrote: 'I erred in my judgement of his character and I am to blame that he became my successor. . . . His strategy and tactics were too petty; he was a radical petit bourgeois. His philosophy culminates in the assertion that "life is oxygen plus sugar plus starch plus protein", to which Mies promptly retorted: "Try stirring all that together: it stinks".'[28]

At the same time it is to Meyer's credit that he did have the courage of his political convictions; he remained in Russia until 1936, when Stalinist policies made it impossible for him to work there; he then spent two years in Switzerland, and from there went to Mexico where he was involved with designs for housing, schools, hospitals and clinics until 1949. According to Gropius, while he was at Dessau, 'Meyer hoped confidentially, as we all did, for a favourable change in the situation'. There was, however, no possibility of a favourable change in Germany, and Mies van der Rohe, who took over as the impartial and a-political mediator after Meyer left the school, was equally unable to fight for its survival under the Nazi régime.

'Herr Oberbürgermeister! It is now your intention to exorcise the Spirit of Marxism from the Bauhaus I have so tainted. Morals, propriety, decency and order are to be ushered in again on the arm of the Muses. As my successor you have allowed Mies van der Rohe to be imposed upon you, on the advice of Gropius and not – as the articles prescribe – on the advice of the Bauhaus masters. . . . This infamous Marxism is to be fought, I suppose, with every weapon and thus the very life shaken out of the unsullied Bauhaus. Down with Marxism! And for this purpose who should you have chosen but Mies van der Rohe, who designed the memorial for Karl Liebknecht and Red Rosie!'[1]

When Hannes Meyer was dismissed, it was important for the school's survival that there should be no break in the leadership, and that some sort of order be restored as soon as possible. Gropius was invited to take charge again but, understandably, declined, and Mies van der Rohe was appointed director on 5 August 1930, during the litigation with Meyer. Like Gropius's monument to the *Marzgefällene* in Weimar, Mies's memorial to Karl Liebknecht and Rosa Luxemburg (completed in 1926 in Berlin, six years after their murder) was a reminder of his radicalism in the immediate post-war years, when Mies, together with Gropius, had been a member of the *Novembergruppe*, and a co-founder of the Ring group of architects. The Communist newspaper, *Die Rote Fahne* (The Red Flag) summed up Marxist reaction to this appointment: in spite of the memorial, Mies was not a Marxist; he was a confused idealist who, because of his lack of ideological commitment might well support the reactionary forces in Dessau.[2]

Mies's background and career, however, as well as his 'ideological commitment' was very similar to that of Gropius. He was born in Aachen in 1886 where his father was a master mason, and was first apprenticed as a furniture designer to Bruno Paul in Berlin. In 1908 he joined Gropius in Peter Behrens's office, and in 1911–12 worked on Behrens's neo-classical design for the German Embassy in St Petersburg. After the war he played a major role in the work of the *Novembergruppe*, organizing its exhibitions and producing his glass skyscraper projects in the early twenties. He was appointed vice-president of the Werkbund in 1926 and supervised the organization and construction of the Weissenhof Siedlung in 1927, as well as designing a block of flats there. None of these activities, of course, recommended him to the right wing. At the same time, however, he had designed the German Pavilion for the World Trade Fair in Barcelona in 1929 and the Tugendhat House in Brno in Czechoslovakia in 1930, and these commissions had gained him international prestige. 'In architecture', Philip Johnson wrote in 1933, 'there is only one man whom even the young men can defend and that is Mies van der Rohe. Mies has always kept out of politics and has always taken his stand against functionalism. No one can accuse Mies's houses of looking like factories.'[3]

To many of the students at the Bauhaus, however, whether or not Mies's houses looked like factories was immaterial, and his refusal to involve himself in politics was a betrayal rather than a virtue. They considered him a formalist and an élitist and 'held turbulent mass meetings in the Bauhaus canteen, at which they expressed indignation at the firing of Hannes and the hiring of Mies'.[4]

The first few months of Mies's directorship were so turbulent that the school was closed for a period and the ringleaders of the anti-Mies faction were expelled. When the school was reopened it was run on a strict timetable. 'We enter the building at 8 a.m., and at 5 p.m., after finishing with the day's course, we go back home again. . . . Many say that since the Bauhaus has become more like a technical school it has become much better than before. Mies is a wonderful architect, but as a man, and particularly as the Director, he is very reactionary. . . . There is simply no life left in the whole shebang.'[5] There was also very little money and a diminishing staff: Oskar Schlemmer had left to teach in Breslau in 1929; Paul Klee went to Düsseldorf in 1931, and Gunta Stölzl also left in 1931. Mies curtailed the workshop production, and concentrated on teaching architecture and interior design, with Lilly Reich, his partner in Berlin, Alfred Arndt and Ludwig Hilberseimer. Mies obviously spent a great deal of time with his architectural students; he gave them small-scale projects, mainly for housing. 'Mies van der Rohe continues to hold us to the small problem,' wrote Howard Dearnstyne, an American student, 'but that he is right in doing this is indicated by the fact that it takes weeks or months to do a small house of this nature in a decent way. The very simplicity of these houses is their chief difficulty. It's much easier to do a complicated affair than something clear and simple.'[6] This preoccupation with clarity, simplicity and formal perfection could be interpreted either as defiance or escapism in the Germany of the 1930s. Design and architecture could no longer be considered a-political, and the cultural storm-troopers of the Nazi party were demanding a demonstration of national values: folk art and architecture for the people and neo-classicism for the monuments of the Third Reich. In 1932 the National Socialists gained control of the Dessau city council and immediately launched a campaign to close the school. Paul Schultze-Naumburg, the author of *Art and Race*, was invited to inspect and report on the work there. Since he had replaced Otto Bartning as director of the Weimar school when the latter was dismissed in 1930, and had destroyed the murals there in an attempt to eradicate all traces of the former school and its philosophies, he could hardly be considered an impartial arbitrator. The school could not survive, and from April to August 1932, the council wrangled over the fate of the building as well as the staff and the students. All the teaching staff were dismissed but, on the insistence of Fritz Hesse, their salaries were paid until October, and royalties from Bauhaus products still went to the school. The building was to be destroyed. 'The disappearance of this so-called "Institute of Design" will mean the disappearance from German soil of one of the most prominent places of Jewish-Marxist "art" manifestation,' wrote the *Anhalter Tageszeitung*. 'May the total demolition follow soon, and may on the same spot where today stands the sombre glass palace of oriental taste, the "aquarium" as it has been popularly dubbed in Dessau, soon rise homesteads and parks that will provide the German people with homes and places for relaxation.'[7]

Fortunately it proved too expensive to destroy the building, although the workshop wing, badly damaged during the war, was bricked up in the immediate post-war period. The building was then used as a school, and was restored in 1976. In 1984, after further restoration, it was reopened as the Bauhaus – a school of design and architecture.

The expulsion from Dessau, however, was not the end of the school in Germany in the 'thirties. Thanks to the courage and tenacity of Fritz Hesse (who was arrested for allegedly mishandling the school's accounts), the staff were assured of some income, even if only for a brief period, and Mies decided to continue the school as a private institution and to transfer it to Berlin. In October 1932 he rented an empty telephone factory there; many of the students moved from Dessau, several more enrolled, and Mies was able to establish a teaching programme with Hilberseimer, Rudelt, Peterhans, Albers, Kandinsky and Hinnerk Scheper. As well as the courses in architecture, courses in city planning and interior design, commercial art, photography and weaving continued, and Kandinsky, in spite of some tensions with Mies, carried on with his theoretical courses. The Bauhaus had less than a year in Berlin, however; in April 1933, about six weeks after the burning of the Reichstag, the factory was raided by police and stormtroopers, who claimed to have found Communist documents there. (The raid was, in fact, instigated by the Dessau authorities who were hoping to find information to support their charges against Fritz Hesse.) Several of the students were arrested for not having correct identification papers, and the building was closed. Permission was granted to reopen it subject to the dismissal of Hilberseimer and Kandinsky, the 'vetting' of the remaining staff and the approval of a new curriculum. Obviously these conditions could not be met, and the faculty voted to dissolve the Bauhaus on 20 July 1933.

'The Klees finally left Dessau on 1 April. The Feiningers are in Deep. Their furniture left in storage, I gather. The only ones remaining in Dessau: the Schepers. . . . Yes, one wonders what the army of fired teachers will do? There are hardly any signs of concerted action. Each person is searching for a hole to crawl into, a spot all to himself.'[8]

Schlemmer's letter to Gunta Stölzl (who was safely established in Zurich) gives some indication of the shock and the rapidity of the Nazi takeover, and the apparent inability of the victims of its cultural vendettas to anticipate its ruthlessness. ('Kandinsky still cannot believe it has happened,' Schlemmer wrote.) As Gropius wrote in his letter to Tomas Maldonado, 'Meyer hoped confidently, as we all did, for a favourable change in the situation'. By 1933, however, it was obvious that there could be no favourable change; anyone associated with the Bauhaus was suspect, and all those who were able to left Germany.

Fortunately, thanks to Gropius's indefatigable promotion of the school, its activities were well known, and the architects and designers were welcomed as teachers, especially in the United States. Gropius and Marcel Breuer first emigrated to England; they were sponsored by Jack Pritchard, one of a few patrons of avant-garde design and architecture in England. Gropius worked in partnership with Maxwell Fry, designing a house in

Chelsea in 1935 and the Impington Village College in Cambridgeshire in 1936. Faber published his book, *The New Architecture and the Bauhaus* in 1935, so that Gropius's interpretation of the ideologies of the school was available to an English-speaking audience. In 1937 Gropius was appointed chairman of the Graduate School of Design in Harvard, and Marcel Breuer joined him there. Moholy-Nagy had set up a design office in Berlin after he left the Bauhaus, and spent a great deal of his time travelling – back to Hungary, to Paris, London and Holland (where he spent two years). He arrived in London with his second wife, Sibyl, in 1934, and was energetically occupied in advertising, photography and film (with Alexander Korda) until 1937, when he, too, emigrated to America with Gropius, Herbert Bayer and Xanti Schawinsky. He set up a New Bauhaus in Chicago, which in 1939 after various financial crises was reopened, under his directorship, as the School of Design. Mies van der Rohe remained in Germany until 1937, when he also emigrated to the United States. In 1938 he took charge of the Illinois Institute of Technology in Chicago; Ludwig Hilberseimer and Walter Peterhans joined him, together with Howard Dearnstyne, who had been his student in Dessau and Berlin. Josef and Anni Albers went to the States to work in the Black Mountain College, North Carolina. In 1950 Albers was appointed chairman of the Department of Design at Yale; in later years he concentrated on painting and his work on colour theory; Anni Albers consolidated her reputation as a weaver; and her book *On Weaving*, which was published in 1965, became a key text, promoting weaving both as an art form and as design.

Most of the painters, proscribed as 'degenerate' in Germany, were also forced to emigrate. Paul Klee and Kandinsky both left Germany: Klee was dismissed from his post in Düsseldorf in 1933, and returned to Switzerland, and the Kandinskys went to Paris. Lyonel Feininger, who had stayed on in Dessau (deprived of his master's house) returned to America in 1937, fifty years after his family had brought him to Germany. Johannes Itten left Berlin, where he had been running his own art school in 1931, and taught in the textile school in Krefeld until 1938. He then went to Zurich where he was in charge of the Arts and Crafts School and Museum. After leaving Itten's school in Berlin, Georg Muche taught at the Breslau Academy until 1931, when he was dismissed; he then went on to teach at Krefeld. Schlemmer, who had left the Bauhaus with relief in 1929 to teach at Breslau, was again without work when the Academy was closed in 1932; he taught in the State Art School in Berlin for a year and was dismissed in 1933. He stayed in Germany, taking what work he could (even camouflaging buildings) until 1930, when Kurt Herberts, who provided a '*Schindler's Ark*' for penniless and persecuted artists in his paint factory in Wuppertal, invited him to work there. As well as Schlemmer's friend, Willi Baumeister, Gerhard Marcks and Georg Muche worked at Wuppertal during the war, mixing and testing commercial paints.

Writing from Wuppertal to his wife in 1940, Schlemmer describes a visit to Krefeld: 'We also stopped by the museum, where an exhibition of arts and crafts is in progress: Wagenfeld (glass), Lindig (very lovely vases), wall hangings by Benita Otte. . . . Kadow, who directs one of the classes at the school, is likewise a Bauhaus product, as is his wife, who teaches silk embroidery. . . . Some of these people came for coffee at Muche's afterwards. . . . Isn't that amusing, so much Bauhaus all in one spot, and all of them productive people?'[9]

During the war years, however, as far as the historians and commentators who remained in Germany were concerned, the Bauhaus had not existed, and there are few references to the school in commentaries on design. Walter Passarge, for example, in *Deutsche Werkkunst der Gegenwart* (in the *Kunstbücher des Volkes – Art Books of the People –* series)[10] discusses work by Gerhard Marcks and Benita Koch-Otte, and illustrates designs by Otto Lindig and Wilhelm Wagenfeld. The Bauhaus is only mentioned once, however; these designers, as far as Passarge is concerned, trained at the State Bauhochschule in Weimar.

This attempted obliteration of 'modernism', on political as well as ideological grounds, was, in part, a justification for its promotion, especially in England. In 1933 Nikolaus Pevsner, himself a refugee from Nazi Germany, had arrived in England, and in 1936 he had published the first history of the Modern Movement. *Pioneers of the Modern Movement from William Morris to Walter Gropius*[11] set out to prove his thesis that 'the phase between William Morris and Walter Gropius is a historical unit', and that the social ideals of Morris had culminated in the achievements of Gropius. Pevsner's arguments are familiar as well as tendentious, and this is not the place to analyze them in detail. They are significant, however, in that they provided a theory that reinforced changing concepts of design in Britain, and Pevsner's subsequent book *An Enquiry into Industrial Art in England*[12] established a basis for the promotion of 'good design' that was to remain virtually unchallenged until the 1960s.

In 1953 Gropius, for example, wrote to Fritz Hesse (who had survived imprisonment and the war, and was reinstated as Mayor of Dessau): 'In retrospect one can hardly believe that in spite of difficulties the Bauhaus had made such an impression. When you live in Germany, you can hardly imagine how world-famous the Bauhaus has become, especially in the United States and England. In both countries the curriculums of the schools of art and architecture have followed the teachings of the Bauhaus, and the official state examination for architects contains the obligatory question, "What is the Bauhaus?" Therefore, it was all worthwhile, though neither you nor I knew beforehand the great and almost insurmountable difficulties we were going to have.'[13]

In America, however, long before Tom Wolfe was to challenge that 'figure of calm certitude at the centre of the maelstrom', Walter Gropius, the Silver Prince of the Bauhaus,[14] Gropius's own disciples were turning against him. 'Young architects went to study at his feet,' wrote Tom Wolfe, 'some, like Philip Johnson, didn't get up until decades later.' Philip Johnson, one of the first American pioneers of the pioneers, was one of the first to recant. In 1949 he told students at Yale University, 'I would rather sleep in the nave of Chartres Cathedral with the nearest john two blocks down the street than I would in a Harvard House with back to back bathrooms.'[15]

The subsequent stress on architecture as an art, the insistence on pluralism, complexity and contradiction in architecture is now as potent an ideal as that described by Robert Venturi as 'Modern architecture's cult of the minimum'. Venturi's *Complexity and Contradiction in Architecture*, published by the Museum of Modern Art in New York in 1966, reinforced the credo of the new generation. 'Architects', he wrote, 'can no longer afford to be intimidated by the puritanically moral language of orthodox Modern architecture. . . . I am for the richness of meaning rather than clarity of meaning; for the implicit function as well as the explicit function. I prefer "both – and" to "either – or". . . .'[16]

Pevsner was to condemn such heresies as 'anti-rationalist'. As far as he was concerned, 'what had been achieved in 1914 was *the* style of the century. It never occurred to me to look beyond. Here was the one and only style which fitted all those aspects which mattered, aspects of economy and sociology, of materials and function.[17]

Gropius, on the other hand, with a career of confounding critics behind him, was to relate the new developments to the ideologies he had helped to promote. 'In recent years', he said at the opening of the Fifty Years Bauhaus Exhibition in London in 1968 'a reaction against the Bauhaus was noticeable, but it dealt with surface appearances only. The complexity and psychological implications, as we developed them at the Bauhaus, were forgotten, and it was described as a simple-minded, purely utilitarian approach to design, devoid of an imagination that would give grace and beauty to life. . . . The slowly-developed attitude in the Bauhaus to *in*clude everything, to *ex*clude nothing which belongs to the totality of life, to say "and" instead of "either-or", has anticipated today's comeback to a total involvement as against narrow specialization.'

In spite of Gropius's efforts to emphasize the plurality and continued relevance of approaches represented by the individuals teaching at the Bauhaus, the school's achievements must be related to the social and political context that created it. It marked the culmination in the industrializing nations of Western Europe of more than half a century's attempts at social engineering through design reform. Its strengths, as well as its weakness, lay in the fact that it aimed to change the world through the discovery and application of 'universal' laws in art, architecture and design. Such Utopian concepts were, of course, not confined to the Bauhaus in the 1920s and '30s; they are also found in Dutch, Russian, Scandinavian and British theory. The pathos of such idealism has been revealed by subsequent events. The fact that the school was destroyed by Fascism may have enhanced its credibility in post-war Europe and the United States, but its ideal of universality was a myth and a mirage, shattered by war, politics and the demands of a consumer society. Today no designer or design organization could or would contemplate universal solutions to the problems of design for the real world. We are still in search of a theory, social commitment is still elusive, so we indulge in our fantasies, ironies and pastiche, which are more comforting (and more profitable) than that 'respect for stern realities' that Gropius demanded from architecture and design.

SOURCES AND NOTES

PART I SOURCES

1 EDUCATIONAL THEORY

1 Quoted from *Kunstschulreform 1900–1933* ed. Hans M. Wingler, Gebr. Mann, Studio Reihe, 1977, p. 28

2 Quoted from Marcel Franciscono *Walter Gropius and the Creation of the Bauhaus in Weimar* University of Illinois Press, 1971, p. 34

3 *Economical and Philosophical Notebooks* Marx-Engels Gesamtaufgabe, 144. Quoted from *Karl Marx: Selected Writings in Sociology and Social Philosophy* eds Bottomore and Rubel, Penguin Books, 1963, pp. 177–8

4 Maria Montessori's first *Casa dei Bambini* was opened in Rome in 1907

5 J. A. Lux *Das Neue Kunstgewerbe in Deutschland* Verlag von Klinkhardt und Bierman, Leipzig, 1908, p. 189. (On p. 191 Lux describes England as the 'motherland' of the modern movement)

6 See *inter alia: Die Kunst in der Schule* 1887; '*Der Praktische Zweck*' (*Dekorative Kunst* Bd 1) 1898. See also: Marcel Franciscono op. cit., pp. 182, 186; Joan Campbell *The German Werkbund* Princeton University Press, 1978, pp. 25, 44; Nikolaus Pevsner *Academies Past and Present* Da Capo Press, New York, 1973, p. 266; Fritz Stern *The Politics of Cultural Despair* University of California Press, 1961, pp. 174, 175; *Form and Function* eds Tim and Charlotte Benton with Dennis Sharp, Granada in assoc. with the Open University Press, 1975, pp. 9–11, 14–15

7 See *Kunstschulreform* op. cit., pp. 56–7

8 Fritz Stern op. cit., see the section on 'Julius Langbehn and Germanic Irrationalism'

9 Ibid. p. 147

10 Ibid. p. 149

11 *The Letters and Diaries of Oskar Schlemmer* selected and edited by Tut Schlemmer, Wesleyan University Press, 1972, p. 53

12 J. A. Lux op. cit., pp. 192–3, describes the conservatism of the State *Kunstschule* and *Kunstgewerbeschule* where 'the pressure of bureaucracy stifles fruitful experiment and encourages cautious clinging to the tried and tested'

13 For sources of information on the Debschitz-Schule, see the article by Helga Schmoll in *Kunstschulreform* op. cit., pp. 68–92

14 Hermann Obrist 'Ein Künstlerischer Kunstunterricht' 1900, published in *Neue Möglichkeiten in der Bildenden Kunst*, Leipzig, 1903, and *Kunstschulreform* op. cit., p. 83

15 Alexander Koch, who founded the *Zeitschrift für Innendekoration* (1890) and *Deutsche Kunst und Dekoration* (1897), owned a wallpaper factory in Darmstadt. See Alan Windsor *Peter Behrens Architect and Designer* The Architectural Press, 1981, p. 15

16 Taken from a collection of essays edited by Alexander Koch, 1901. Quoted by Alan Windsor op. cit., p. 16
17 See *Peter Behrens und Nürnberg* catalogue of exhibition at the Germanisches Nationalmuseum, Nürnberg, Prestel-Verlag, Munich, 1980
18 Alan Windsor op. cit., p. 262
19 Quoted from *Stadt* 10/82, p. 8. (Issue on Bruno Paul exhibition at the Hochschule der Künste, Berlin, 1982)
20 *Künstlerlehrzeit* (The Artist's Apprenticeship) (1917–18), and *Erziehung der Künstler an staatlichen Schulen* (The Education of the Artist in State Schools) (1919). Reprinted in *Stadt* 10/82, pp. 15–17
21 Joseph Popp *Bruno Paul* Verlag von F. Bruckmann, Munich, 1916, p. 5
22 *Erziehung der Künstler an staatlichen Schulen* op. cit., p. 17

2   CRAFT AND INDUSTRY

1 'Wohin treiben wir?' *Dekorative Kunst* 1898
2 C. R. Ashbee *Craftsmanship in Competitive Industry* Essex House Press, 1908
3 See Shulamit Volkov *The Rise of Popular Anti-Modernism in Germany: The Urban Master Artisans, 1873–1896* Princeton University Press, 1978
4 From W. O. Henderson *The Rise of German Industrial Power 1834–1914* Temple Smith, 1975, p. 150
5 Shulamit Volkov op. cit., note 14, p. 39
6 Ibid. p. 241
7 Ibid. p. 352
8 J. A. Lux *Das Neue Kunstgewerbe in Deutschland* Verlag von Klinkhardt und Bierman, Leipzig, 1908, p. 121
9 Ibid. pp. 127, 128
10 *Kunst und Alltag um 1900* Werkbund-Archiv Jahrbuch 3, ed. Eckhard Siepmann, Anabas Verlag, 1978, p. 217
11 Gottfried Semper *Wissenschaft, Industrie und Kunst* Vieweg and Son, Brunswick, 1852
12 *Kleine Schriften* eds M. and H. Semper, W. Spemann, Berlin and Stuttgart, 1884
13 *Wissenschaft, Industrie und Kunst* quoted from Hans M. Wingler *The Bauhaus* MIT Press, 1969, p. 18
14 Ibid. p. 18
15 W. O. Henderson, op. cit., gives a clear account of the State and private support that secured the survival of German industry in periods of recession, as well as the cartels that were formed to control output and pool research. For his description of Emil Rathenau's contributions to the establishment and success of AEG see pp. 194–8
16 Quoted from W. O. Henderson op. cit., pp. 195–6
17 For details of Behrens's association with AEG see Alan Windsor *Peter Behrens Architect and Designer* The Architectural Press, 1981, pp. 77–105. See also *Industrie Kultur, Peter Behrens und die AEG 1907–1914* (catalogue), Electa, Milan, 1978
18 Alan Windsor op. cit., p. 79
19 Ibid. p. 102
20 Walter Gropius *The New Architecture and the Bauhaus* Faber and Faber, 1935, p. 47
21 Reprinted in *Form and Function* eds Tim and Charlotte Benton with Dennis Sharp, Granada in assoc. with the Open University Press, 1975, pp. 188–90

3   THE WERKBUND

1 *Das Englische Haus* Wasmuth, Berlin, 1904–5. English translation Granada, 1979
2 Quoted from *Form and Function* eds Tim and Charlotte Benton with Dennis Sharp, Granada in assoc. with the Open University Press, 1975, pp. 34–5
3 Extracts from *Stilarchitektur und Baukunst* are published in J. Posener *Anfänge des Funktionalismus, von Arts and Crafts zum Deutschen Werkbund* Verlag Ullstein, 1964, pp. 150–75
4 Joan Campbell *The German Werkbund: The Politics of Reform in the Applied Arts* Princeton University Press, 1978, p. 16

5 *Deutscher Werkbund Yearbook 1912* and *Form and Function* op. cit., pp. 48–51
6 From Joan Campbell op. cit., p. 57
7 Van de Velde describes the genesis of his manifesto in his *Geschichte meines Lebens* ed. Hans Curjel, R. Piper, 1962, pp. 361–2
8 Ulrich Conrads *Programmes and Manifestoes of Twentieth-Century Architecture* Lund Humphries, 1970, reprints both statements, pp. 28–31
9 Julius Posener op. cit., pp. 199–205
10 Marcel Franciscono *Walter Gropius and the Creation of the Bauhaus in Weimar* University of Illinois Press, 1971, p. 278
11 Quoted from Wolfgang Pehnt *Expressionist Architecture* Thames and Hudson, 1973, p. 30
12 Julius Posener op. cit., pp. 228–9

PART II   THE BAUHAUS IN WEIMAR

1   WAR AND REVOLUTION

1 See Joan Campbell *The German Werkbund: The Politics of Reform in the Applied Arts* Princeton University Press, 1978, p. 82
2 William Carr *A History of Germany 1815–1945* Edward Arnold, 1969, p. 231
3 See Marcel Franciscono *Walter Gropius and the Creation of the Bauhaus in Weimar* University of Illinois Press, 1971, p. 34
4 Hans M. Wingler *The Bauhaus* MIT Press, 1969, p. 21
5 Karl-Heinz Hüter *Das Bauhaus in Weimar* Akademie Verlag, Berlin, 1976, p. 11
6 H. M. Wingler op. cit., p. 22
7 Ibid. pp. 123–4; Karl-Heinz Hüter op. cit., pp. 201–3
8 It seems that Endell was the favoured candidate in Weimar. In a letter (of July 1915) van de Velde tells Gropius that the Weimar authorities, in spite of his strong support of Gropius, are 'engaged in negotiations with Endell'. H. M. Wingler op. cit., p. 21
9 H. M. Wingler op. cit., pp. 26–7
10 Quoted from Frank Whitford *Bauhaus* Thames and Hudson, 1984, p. 202
11 Published by the Photographischen Gesellschaft in Charlottenburg, 1919
12 Reprinted in Wingler op. cit., pp. 31–3

2   THE CATHEDRAL OF SOCIALISM

1 Hans M. Wingler *The Bauhaus* MIT Press, 1969, p. 33
2 Ibid. p. 40. For a full account and documentation of the 'Gross Affair' see Karl-Heinz Hüter *Das Bauhaus in Weimar* Akademie Verlag, Berlin, 1976, pp. 20–3
3 Hans M. Wingler op. cit., p. 41
4 Ibid. p. 34. Max Thedy had been deputy director of the Academy
5 K. H. Hüter op. cit., pp. 210–11; H. M. Wingler op. cit. (extracts), p. 36
6 H. M. Wingler op. cit., p. 37
7 K. H. Hüter op. cit., p. 218
8 H. M. Wingler op. cit., pp. 42–3

3   THE WORKSHOPS

1 See Walther Scheidig *Crafts of the Weimar Bauhaus* Studio Vista, 1967, p. 13
2 *The Letters and Diaries of Oskar Schlemmer* selected and edited by Tut Schlemmer, Wesleyan University Press, 1972, p. 86
3 Ibid. p. 96
4 Marcel Franciscono *Walter Gropius and the Creation of the Bauhaus in Weimar* University of Illinois Press, 1971, p. 174

5 Ibid.
6 W. Scheidig op. cit., p. 21
7 Tut Schlemmer op. cit., pp. 98–9
8 Hans M. Wingler *The Bauhaus* MIT Press, 1969, pp. 44–8
9 Le Corbusier *Towards a New Architecture* Architectural Press, 1927; 1970 edition, p. 24. First published as *Vers une Architecture* Editions Crès, Paris, 1923
10 Translated as *The Theory and Organization of the Bauhaus* and reprinted in *Bauhaus 1919–1928* eds H. Bayer, Walter Gropius, Ise Gropius, Museum of Modern Art, New York, 1938. English edition Secker and Warburg, 1975, p. 29
11 Tut Schlemmer op. cit., p. 101
12 Walter Gropius *The New Architecture and the Bauhaus* English translation Faber and Faber, 1935, p. 75

4   JOHANNES ITTEN AND THE BASIC COURSE

1 Johannes Itten *Design and Form: The Basic Course at the Bauhaus* Thames and Hudson, 1964, p. 7
2 *The Letters and Diaries of Oskar Schlemmer* selected and edited by Tut Schlemmer, Wesleyan University Press, 1972, p. 54
3 Johannes Itten op. cit., p. 8
4 Ibid. p. 8
5 Rainer Wick *Bauhaus Pädagogik* DuMont Buchverlag, 1982, p. 80
6 Ibid. p. 81
7 Hans M. Wingler *The Bauhaus* MIT Press, 1969, p. 44
8 Johannes Itten op. cit., pp. 9, 10
9 Ibid. p. 9
10 Ibid. p. 11
11 Ibid. p. 79
12 Ibid. p. 46
13 Ibid. p. 80
14 *Bauhaus and Bauhaus People* ed. Eckhard Neumann, Van Nostrand Reinhold, 1970, p. 38
15 Ibid. p. 40
16 Ibid. p. 45
17 Ibid. p. 49
18 Ibid. p. 48
19 Lothar Schreyer *Erinnerungen an Sturm und Bauhaus* Albert Langen Verlag, Munich, 1956, p. 194
20 Tut Schlemmer op. cit., pp. 99–101
21 The correspondence is published in Marcel Franciscono *Walter Gropius and the Creation of the Bauhaus in Weimar* University of Illinois Press, 1971, pp. 290–7
22 Excerpts of notes reprinted in H. M. Wingler op. cit., pp. 51–2
23 H. M. Wingler op. cit., p. 54

5   CLAIMS FOR ART

KANDINSKY AND KLEE

1 Hans M. Wingler *The Bauhaus* MIT Press, 1969, p. 51
2 Karl-Heinz Hüter *Das Bauhaus in Weimar* Akademie Verlag, Berlin, 1976, p. 15
3 *Kandinsky: Complete Writings on Art* eds Kenneth C. Lindsay and Peter Vergo, Faber and Faber, 1982, p. 362
4 Ibid. p. 359
5 Ibid. p. 343
6 Peg Weiss *Kandinsky in Munich* Princeton University Press, 1979, p. 15
7 *Kandinsky: Complete Writings* op. cit., pp. 355–82. Quotations from *Rückblicke* (Reminiscences)
8 Ibid. p. 135
9 Ibid. pp. 154–5

10 Ibid. p. 154. See also *Arnold Schönberg/Wassily Kandinsky Letters, Pictures and Documents* ed. J. Hahl-Kock, Faber and Faber, 1984
11 Ibid. p. 149
12 Ibid. p. 176
13 Ibid. p. 197
14 Ibid. p. 82
15 Ibid. p. 219
16 *Kandinsky: Complete Writings* op. cit., p. 476. Charles-André Julien interviewed Kandinsky in Russia in 1921; the interview was not published, however, until 1969
17 Ibid. p. 477
18 Programme for the Institute of Artistic Culture, ibid. pp. 455–72
19 Quoted from *Art of the Avant-Garde in Russia: Selections from the George Costakis Collection* (catalogue) Solomon R. Guggenheim Foundation, 1981, p. 25
20 See *Modern Art and Modernism* eds Francis Frascina and Charles Harrison, Harper and Row, 1982, pp. 136–42
21 First published in *Staatliches Bauhaus Weimar 1919–1923* Bauhaus Press, 1923. See H. M. Wingler op. cit., p. 74
22 *Kandinsky: Complete Writings* op. cit., p. 245
23 For a detailed analysis of Kandinsky's teaching at the Bauhaus, see Rainer Wick *Bauhaus Pädagogik* DuMont Buchverlag, 1982, pp. 174–212
24 *Kandinsky: Complete Writings* op. cit., p. 747
25 *The Diaries of Paul Klee* ed. Felix Klee, The University of California Press, Los Angeles, 1964. No. 903
26 Ibid. No. 53
27 Ibid. No. 1008
28 Paul Klee *On Modern Art* Faber and Faber, 1953, p. 45
29 *The Diaries of Paul Klee* op. cit.
30 Ibid. No. 926
31 *Letters and Diaries of Oskar Schlemmer* selected and edited by Tut Schlemmer, Wesleyan University Press, 1972, p. 41
32 Ibid. p. 72
33 Ibid. p. 99
34 Rainer Wick op. cit., p. 216
35 Quoted from Werner Haftmann *The Mind and Work of Paul Klee* Faber and Faber, 1957, p. 83
36 Paul Klee *On Modern Art* op. cit. pp. 14–16
37 Paul Klee *The Thinking Eye* ed. Jürg Spiller, Wittenborn, New York and Lund Humphries, London, 1961, p. 67
38 Ibid. p. 76
39 *The Diaries of Paul Klee* op. cit. No. 670
40 Wilhelm Worringer *Abstraction and Empathy* English edition Routledge and Kegan Paul, 1963
41 *The Diaries of Paul Klee* op. cit. No. 952
42 Marianne Teuber 'New Aspects of Paul Klee's Bauhaus Style', *Paul Klee Paintings and Watercolours from the Bauhaus Years 1921–31* Des Moines Art Center, 1973, pp. 6–17
43 Produced by Jürgen Maesemaer, Schwerbe & Co. AG, Basle/Stuttgart, 1979
44 *Kandinsky: Complete Writings* op. cit., p. 602
45 Ibid. p. 162

VAN DOESBURG AND MOHOLY-NAGY

1 The article is unsigned but undoubtedly by Le Corbusier
2 *De Stijl* Vol. 1
3 'The Will to Style: A New Form of Expression of Life, Art and Technology', *De Stijl* Vol. V, Sept. 1922; quoted from *Form and Function* eds Tim and Charlotte Benton with Dennis Sharp, Granada in assoc. with the Open University Press, 1975, pp.92–4

4 Joost Baljeu *Theo van Doesburg* Studio Vista, 1974, p. 41

5 Ibid. p. 41

6 *Der Moderne Zweckbau* was first published in 1926. As Ulrich Conrads points out in his Introduction to the 1964 reprint (Verlag Ullstein), it was one of the first books to demonstrate a theory of 'modern' architecture, and the delay in its publication obscured its originality.

7 Ibid. p. 68

8 Quoted from Nancy J. Troy *The De Stijl Environment* MIT Press, 1983, p. 86

9 Quoted from Joost Baljeu op. cit., p. 43

10 Quotations from 'The New Aesthetics and its Realization' *De Stijl* Vol. VI, March 1923. Reprinted Joost Baljeu op. cit., pp. 127–31

11 'The Significance of Colour for Interior and Exterior Architecture' *Werkblad* Vol. IV no. 21. Quoted from Joost Baljeu op. cit., pp. 137–40

12 Ibid. p. 149

13 'The Will To Style' *De Stijl* Vol. V, Sept. 1922; quoted from *Form and Function* op. cit., p. 93

14 Ibid. pp. 94–5

15 See Karl-Heinz Hüter *Das Bauhaus in Weimar* Akademie Verlag, Berlin, 1976, p. 269

16 H. M. Wingler *The Bauhaus* MIT Press, 1969, p. 56

17 *De Stijl* Vol. IV, April 1922. Extracts in *The Tradition of Constructivism* ed. Stephen Bann, Thames and Hudson, 1974, pp. 58–62

18 Stephen Bann op. cit., p. 68

19 Ibid. p. 23

20 Joost Baljeu op. cit., p. 134

21 Quotations from Laszlo Moholy-Nagy *The New Vision and Abstract of an Artist* George Wittenborn Inc., 1947, pp. 68, 71

22 Quoted from Frank Whitford *Bauhaus* Thames and Hudson, 1984, p. 127

23 Laszlo Moholy-Nagy op. cit., p. 72

24 Reprinted in Stephen Bann op. cit., pp. 51–2

25 H. M. Wingler op. cit., p. 51

26 Laszlo Moholy-Nagy op. cit., p. 75

27 *Form and Function* op. cit., pp. 95, 96

28 Sibyl Moholy-Nagy *Moholy-Nagy: Experiment in Totality* MIT Press, 1969, p. 39

29 Lothar Schreyer *Erinnerungen an Sturm und Bauhaus* Albert Langen Verlag, Munich, 1956, pp. 238 and 242

30 Writing to Otto Meyer in June 1923, Schlemmer told him that the students were only waiting for the exhibition to be over before they went to Gropius to ask him to get rid of the 'corridor-masters', so called 'because one meets them in the Bauhaus corridor, never in the workshops'. *The Letters and Diaries of Oskar Schlemmer* op. cit., p. 139

31 Lucia Moholy-Nagy *Marginal Notes* Scherpe Verlag, Krefeld, 1972, pp. 54–5

32 *Bauhaus 1919–1928* eds Herbert Bayer, Walter Gropius, Ise Gropius, Museum of Modern Art, New York, 1938. English edition Secker and Warburg, 1975, p. 89

33 *Bauhaus and Bauhaus People* ed. Eckhard Neumann, Van Nostrand Reinhold, 1970, pp. 180, 181

34 *Fifty Years Bauhaus* (catalogue) Royal Academy of Art, 1968, p. 36

35 George Rickey *Constructivism, Origins and Evolution* Studio Vista, 1967, p. 46

36 First published in *Zeitschrift für Sozialforschung* Vol. V no. 1, 1936. Reprinted in Walter Benjamin *Illuminations* Fontana, 1973, p. 236

37 Laszlo Moholy-Nagy *Painting, Photography, Film* Bauhaus Book, 1925; Lund Humphries, 1969, pp. 35 and 45

38 Ibid. Essay by Otto Stelzer p. 146

39 Laszlo Moholy-Nagy *The New Vision* op. cit., p. 79

40 Lucia Moholy-Nagy op. cit., p. 76

41 Laszlo Moholy-Nagy *The New Vision* op. cit., p. 79

42 Walter Gropius *The New Architecture and the Bauhaus* Faber and Faber, 1935, pp. 55, 56. Also introduction to *Neue Arbeiten der Bauhauswerkstätten* Bauhaus Book, 1925; facsimile reprint, Florian Kupferberg Verlag, Mainz, 1981

6   CRISIS AND CONSOLIDATION

1 See Karl-Heinz Hüter *Das Bauhaus in Weimar* Akademie Verlag, Berlin, 1976, pp. 34–40 and 243–52; and Hans M. Wingler *The Bauhaus* MIT Press, 1969, p. 61

2 H. M. Wingler op. cit., p. 56

3 *The Letters and Diaries of Oskar Schlemmer* selected and edited by Tut Schlemmer, Wesleyan University Press, 1972, p. 135

4 Ibid. p. 130

5 Since the house has been destroyed, one has to judge by photographs

6 H. M. Wingler op. cit., p. 18

7 *G. Rietveld Architect* (catalogue) Arts Council, 1972 (unpaginated)

8 Erich Dieckmann *Möbelbau* Julius Hoffmann Verlag, Stuttgart, 1931

9 *Form und Zweck Fachzeitschrift für Industrielle Formgestaltung* Issue 3, 1979, p. 13

10 H. M. Wingler op. cit., p. 308

11 'Die Entwicklung der Bauhausweberei' *Bauhaus Journal* No. 5, 1931. Reprinted in *Form und Zweck* op. cit., pp. 32–5

12 *Bauhaus 1919–1928* eds Herbert Bayer, Walter Gropius, Ise Gropius, Museum of Modern Art, New York, 1938. English edition Secker and Warburg, 1975, p. 141

13 *Bauhaus Journal no. 2* 1931, quoted from Wingler op. cit., p. 465

14 H. M. Wingler op. cit., p. 314

15 Sibyl Moholy-Nagy *Moholy-Nagy: Experiment in Totality* MIT Press, 1969, p. 38

16 *Form und Zweck* op. cit., pp. 56, 57

17 Ibid. p. 69

18 *Bauhaus and Bauhaus People* ed. Eckhard Neumann, Van Nostrand Reinhold, 1970, p. 98

19 *Bauhaus 1919–1928* op. cit., p. 134

20 Ibid. p. 134

21 Wilhelm Wagenfeld 'Das Staatliche Bauhaus – die Jahre in Weimar' *Form 37* March 1967, pp. 17–19

22 Georg Muche *Das Künstlerische Werk* (catalogue) Bauhaus-Archiv, 1980, p. 24

23 Ibid. pp. 32–3

24 *Bauhaus 1919–1928* op. cit., p. 93

25 Article in *Neue Frauenkleidung und Frauenkultur*, 1924, reprinted in *Form und Zweck* op. cit., p. 7

26 Georg Muche op. cit., p. 27

27 Ibid. pp. 41–3

28 H. M. Wingler op. cit., p. 64

29 *The Letters and Diaries of Oskar Schlemmer* op. cit., p. 82

30 Ibid. p. 74

31 Ibid. p. 132

32 H. M. Wingler op. cit., p. 67. In this context it is perhaps worth noting that Walter Passarge published a book, *Deutsche Werkkunst der Gegenwart* (German Applied Art of the Present) in c. 1940, which included work by Bauhaus trained designers, without any reference to the school's activities before the 1930s (See page 179)

33 H. M. Wingler *Graphic Work from the Bauhaus* Lund Humphries, 1969, p. 18

34 Laszlo Moholy-Nagy *Vision in Motion* Paul Theobald & Co., Chicago, 1947; 1965 edition, p. 299

35 H. M. Wingler *The Bauhaus* op. cit., p. 81

36 *The Letters and Diaries of Oskar Schlemmer* op. cit., p. 154

37 See K. H. Hüter op. cit., p. 259

PART III   THE BAUHAUS IN DESSAU

1   DESSAU: THE GREAT TRANSFORMATION

1 *Bauhaus 1919–1928* eds Herbert Bayer, Walter Gropius, Ise Gropius, Museum of Modern Art, New York, 1938. English edition Secker and Warburg, 1975, p. 97

2 Hans M. Wingler *The Bauhaus* MIT Press, 1969, p. 97

3 *Bauhaus and Bauhaus People* ed. Eckhard Neumann, Van Nostrand Reinhold, 1970, p. 157

4 H. M. Wingler op. cit., p. 110; see also introduction to *Neue Arbeiten der Bauhauswerkstätten* (New Work from the Bauhaus Workshops) which was published as a Bauhaus Book in 1925

5 Walter Gropius *The New Architecture and the Bauhaus* Faber and Faber, 1935, p. 20

6 Ibid. p. 78

7 Ibid. p. 89

8 *Kandinsky: Complete Writings on Art* eds Kenneth C. Lindsay and Peter Vergo, Faber and Faber, 1982, pp. 702–5

9 Ibid. p. 729

10 H. M. Wingler op. cit., p. 145

11 Herbert Read *Art and Industry* Faber and Faber, 1934; quoted from revised edition, 1956, pp. 63, 64

12 H. M. Wingler op. cit., pp. 113–14; *Form and Function* eds Tim and Charlotte Benton with Dennis Sharp, Granada in assoc. with the Open University Press, 1975, pp. 151–2

2   DESSAU AND ARCHITECTURE

1 Walter Gropius *The New Architecture and the Bauhaus* Faber and Faber, 1935, pp. 99 and 96

2 *Bauhausbauten Dessau* (Dessau Bauhaus Building) first published in 1930 as the twelfth Bauhaus Book; reprinted 1974, Kupferberg Verlag, p. 12

3 Ibid. p. 20

4 Walter Gropius op. cit., p. 19

5 Ibid. p. 82

6 H. M. Wingler *The Bauhaus* MIT Press, 1969, p. 125

7 *Bauhausbauten Dessau* op. cit., pp. 100, 101

8 H. M. Wingler op. cit., p. 120

9 Ibid. p. 124. Comment by the art and architectural critic, Max Osborn.

10 Ibid. pp. 126–7

11 *Bauhausbauten Dessau* op. cit., p. 155

12 H. M. Wingler op. cit., p. 416

13 *Bauhaus Kolloquium, Wissenschaftliche Zeitschrift der Hochschule für Architektur und Bauwesen* Weimar, 1979, pp. 351–55

14 Hannes Meyer *Bauen und Gesellschaft* VEB Verlag der Kunst, Dresden, 1980, p. 10

15 Claude Schnaidt *Hannes Meyer: buildings, projects and writings* Verlag Gerd Hatje, Stuttgart, 1965, p. 15

16 *Form and Function* eds Tim and Charlotte Benton with Dennis Sharp, Granada in assoc. with the Open University Press, 1975, pp. 106–9

17 Hannes Meyer op. cit., pp. 41–3

18 Ibid. p. 44. *ABC* was a manifesto published by the Dutch architect Mart Stam in Basle in 1926

3   FROM WORKSHOP TO LABORATORY

1 Statement by the International Faction of Constructivists, Congress of International Progressive Artists 1922; *The Tradition of Constructivism* ed. Stephen Bann, Thames and Hudson, 1974, p. 68

2 *Kandinsky: Complete Writings on Art* eds Kenneth C. Lindsay and Peter Vergo, Faber and Faber, 1982, p. 734. Article 'Bare Wall', published in *Das Kunstnarr*, 1929

3 *The Letters and Diaries of Oskar Schlemmer* selected and edited by Tut Schlemmer, Wesleyan University Press, 1972, p. 228

4 Laszlo Moholy-Nagy *The New Vision and Abstract of an Artist* George Wittenborn Inc., 1947, p. 31

5 Ibid. p. 29 (Raoul France's book was published in Stuttgart in 1920)

6 Laszlo Moholy-Nagy *Vision in Motion* Paul Theobald and Co., 1947, pp. 33, 34, 55

7 Sibyl Moholy-Nagy *Moholy-Nagy: Experiment in Totality* MIT Press, 1969, pp. 43, 44

8 Laszlo Moholy-Nagy *The New Vision* op. cit., p. 89

9 Sibyl Moholy-Nagy op. cit., p. 44

10 Ibid. p. 41

11 *Bauhaus 1919–1928* eds Herbert Bayer, Walter Gropius, Ise Gropius, Museum of Modern Art, New York, 1938. English edition Secker and Warburg, 1975, pp. 122–3

12 Laszlo Moholy-Nagy *The New Vision* op. cit., p. 30

13 John Heskett *Industrial Design* Thames and Hudson, 1980, pp. 78–9

14 *Bauhaus and Bauhaus People* ed. Eckhard Neumann, Van Nostrand Reinhold, 1970, p. 98

15 Ibid. p. 98

16 Quoted in *Das Bauhaus 1919–1928* op. cit., p. 126

17 Marcel Breuer 'Metal Furniture' *Innenraume* Werner Graff, Stuttgart, 1928, quoted from *Form and Function* eds Tim and Charlotte Benton with Dennis Sharp, Granada in assoc. with the Open University Press, 1975, p. 226

18 Quoted from Christopher Wilk *Marcel Breuer: Furniture and Interiors* The Architectural Press, 1981, p. 37. See also *Stuhle aus Stahl, Metallmöbel 1925–1940* Jan van Geest and Otakov Máčel, Cologne, 1980, p. 64

19 Christopher Wilk op. cit., pp. 38, 188

20 *Form and Function* op. cit., p. 226

21 Quoted from Hans M. Wingler *The Bauhaus* MIT Press, 1969, p. 452

22 Christopher Wilk op. cit., gives a detailed account of Breuer's contracts with Standard-Möbel and Thonet, and the problems of copyright involved, pp. 73–8. See also *Stuhle aus Stahl* op. cit.

23 Quoted from Christopher Wilk op. cit., p. 184

24 '*Offset, Buch und Werbekunst*' quoted from H. M. Wingler op. cit., p. 116

25 Gunta Stölzl; quoted from H. M. Wingler op. cit., p. 174

26 *The Letters and Diaries of Oskar Schlemmer* selected and edited by Tut Schlemmer, Wesleyan University Press, 1972, p. 186

27 *Bauhaus 1919–1928* op. cit., pp. 141–2

28 H. M. Wingler op. cit., pp. 116–17

29 Ibid. p. 142

30 Ibid. pp. 142–3

31 Quoted from *Albers* catalogue, Gimpel Fils, London, 1961

32 Ibid.

33 H. M. Wingler op. cit., p. 135

34 Ibid. p. 145

35 Interview with Basil Gilbert, *Bauhaus and Bauhaus People* op. cit., p. 125

36 See H. M. Wingler op. cit., p. 161

37 Herbert Bayer *Herbert Bayer* Studio Vista, 1967, pp. 10–11

38 Laszlo Moholy-Nagy *Painting, Photography, Film* Bauhaus Book no. 8, 1925, Lund Humphries, 1969, p. 38

39 Idem, '*Modern Typography, Aims, Practice, Criticism*' written in 1924 and published in *Offset, Buch und Werbekunst* 1926. Quoted from H. M. Wingler op. cit., p. 81

40 Ibid.

41 Laszlo Moholy-Nagy *Painting, Photography, Film* op. cit., p. 35

42 Herbert Bayer 'Typography and Commercial Art Forms' *Bauhaus Journal* Vol. 2, no. 1, 1928. Quoted from H. M. Wingler op. cit., p. 135

43 The DIN (German Industrial Standard) format for the standardization of paper sizes was introduced in 1922

44 H. M. Wingler op. cit., p. 135

45 Herbert Bayer 'Towards a New Alphabet: the "Universal Type"' 1925. From Herbert Bayer op. cit., p. 26

46 H. M. Wingler op. cit., p. 114

47 See Herbert Bayer *Das Künstlerische Werk 1918–1938* (catalogue) Bauhaus-Archiv, 1982, p. 118

48 Jan Tschichold *Typographische Gestaltung* 1935, translated as *Asymmetric Typography* Faber and Faber, 1967, p. 19

49 Herbert Bayer op. cit., p. 12

50 Ibid. pp. 46–7

51 Rainer Wick *Bauhaus Pädagogik* DuMont Buchverlag, 1982, p. 294
52 *Herbert Bayer* op. cit., p. 86
53 Sibyl Moholy-Nagy op. cit., p. 88

4   HANNES MEYER: FORMALISM OR FUNCTIONALISM?

1 Quoted from H. M. Wingler *The Bauhaus* MIT Press, 1969, p. 136. Also described in *The Letters and Diaries of Oskar Schlemmer* selected and edited by Tut Schlemmer, Wesleyan University Press, 1972, p. 225
2 Tut Schlemmer op. cit., pp. 198, 202
3 *Form and Function* eds Tim and Charlotte Benton with Dennis Sharp, Granada in assoc. with the Open University Press, 1975, p. 107
4 Tut Schlemmer op. cit., p. 221
5 See Christopher Wilk *Marcel Breuer: Furniture and Interiors* The Architectural Press, 1981, pp. 84, 85
6 Sibyl Moholy-Nagy *Moholy-Nagy: Experiment in Totality* MIT Press, 1969, pp. 46, 47
7 *Bauhaus Journal* Dessau, Vol. 2, no. 4, 1928, pp. 12–13; quoted from H. M. Wingler op. cit., pp. 153–5. (The original is without capital letters and printed in different weights of type to emphasize main points)
8 'Der Kunstnarr' April 1929. Quoted from *Kandinsky: Complete Writings on Art* eds Kenneth C. Lindsay and Peter Vergo, Faber and Faber, 1982, p. 731
9 Quoted from Claude Schnaidt *Hannes Meyer: buildings, projects and writings* Verlag Gerd Hatje, Stuttgart, 1965, p. 27
10 See H. M. Wingler *The Bauhaus* MIT Press, 1969, pp. 488–9
11 Claude Schnaidt op. cit., p. 27
12 Ibid. p. 43
13 Ibid. p. 103
14 Ibid. p. 109 (quoting Meyer's article 'Bauhaus Dessau: My Experience of a Polytechnic Education', published 1940)
15 Ibid. p. 109
16 First printed in the magazine *Das Tagebuch* August 1930; reprinted in Claude Schnaidt op. cit., pp. 101–5
17 Ibid. p. 103
18 H. M. Wingler op. cit., p. 172
19 Claude Schnaidt op. cit., p. 103
20 Walter Gropius *The New Architecture and the Bauhaus* Faber and Faber, 1935, p. 92
21 Henry Russell Hitchcock and Philip Johnson *The International Style* W. W. Norton & Co., 1932; revised edition 1966, p. viii
22 Karel Teige 'Contemporary International Architecture' 1928, *Red* (Prague), No. 5, 1928. Quoted from *Form and Function* op. cit., p. 200
23 Hermann Muthesius *Die neue Bauweise* 1927; extract in Julius Posener *Anfänge des Funktionalismus* Verlag Ullstein, Frankfurt, 1964, p. 228
24 Paul Schmitthenner *Tradition and New Buildings* Deutsche Kulturwacht, 1933. Quoted from *Form and Function* op. cit., p. 211
25 Claude Schnaidt op. cit., p. 55
26 Ironic at the time of writing (author)
27 Hannes Meyer *Bauen und Gesellschaft* VEB Verlag der Kunst, Dresden, 1980, pp. 73–8
28 Claude Schnaidt op. cit., p. 123. Quoted from correspondence between Walter Gropius and Tomas Maldonado, *Ulm Magazine*

5   CONFRONTATION AND COLLAPSE

1 Claude Schnaidt *Hannes Meyer: buildings, projects, writings* Verlag Gerd Hatje, Stuttgart, 1965, p. 105
2 *Die Rote Fahne* 28 September 1930
3 Philip Johnson 'Architecture and the Third Reich' *Hound and Horn* New York, 1933; quoted from *Form and Function* eds Tim and Charlotte Benton with Dennis Sharp, Granada in assoc. with the Open University Press, 1975, p. 208

4 Howard Dearnstyne *Bauhaus and Bauhaus People* ed. Eckhard Neumann, Van Nostrand Reinhold, 1970, p. 214

5 Hans M. Wingler *The Bauhaus* MIT Press, 1969, p. 175 (letter from a Swiss architectural student)

6 Howard Dearnstyne op. cit., p. 216

7 *Anhalter Tageszeitung* 10 July 1932. Quoted from Wingler op. cit., p. 177

8 Letter to Gunta Stölzl, 16 June 1933 *The Letters and Diaries of Oskar Schlemmer* selected and edited by Tut Schlemmer, Wesleyan University Press, 1972, p. 312

9 Ibid. p. 384

10 Walter Passarge *Deutsche Werkkunst der Gegenwart* Rembrandt Verlag, Berlin, n.d. (probably *c.* 1940)

11 Reprinted and revised as *Pioneers of Modern Design* Penguin Books, 1960. Numerous subsequent editions

12 Nikolaus Pevsner *An Enquiry into Industrial Art in England* Cambridge University Press, 1937

13 *Bauhaus and Bauhaus People* ed. Eckhard Neumann, Van Nostrand Reinhold, 1970, p. 145

14 Tom Wolfe *From Bauhaus to Our House* Jonathan Cape, 1982, pp. 10, 11

15 Vincent Scully *Journal of the Society of Architectural Historians* March 1965, p. 46

16 Robert Venturi *Complexity and Contradiction in Architecture* Museum of Modern Art, New York, 1966, pp. 22–3

17 Nikolaus Pevsner 'Architecture in our time, the Anti-Pioneers', *The Listener* December 1966, p. 953

SELECT BIBLIOGRAPHY

Relevant articles and books are referred to in the *Sources and Notes;* the information is repeated here where key texts are involved.

Adler, Bruno *Das Weimarer Bauhaus* Bauhaus-Archiv, Darmstadt, 1963

Argan, Giulio C. *Walter Gropius und das Bauhaus* Rowoht, Hamburg, 1962

Baljeu, Joost *Theo Van Doesburg* Studio Vista, London, 1974

Banham, Reyner *Theory and Design in the First Machine Age* Architectural Press, London, 1960; MIT Press, Cambridge, Mass., 1980

Bann, Stephen (ed.) *The Tradition of Constructivism* Thames & Hudson, London, 1974

Bayer, Herbert *Herbert Bayer* Studio Vista, London/Reinhold, New York, 1967

Bayer, Herbert, Gropius, Walter, Gropius, Ise (eds) *Bauhaus 1919–1928* Museum of Modern Art, New York, 1938, 1972; Secker and Warburg, London, 1975

Benton, Tim and Charlotte, with Sharp, Dennis (eds) *Form and Function* Granada, in association with Open University Press, London, 1975

Behne, Adolf *Der Moderne Zweckbau* Drei Masken Verlag, Munich, 1926; reprinted Ullstein, Frankfurt, 1964

Behr, Adalbert *Das Bauhaus Dessau* Leipzig, 1980

Berghahn, V. R. *Modern Germany* Cambridge University Press, 1982

Blake, Peter *Marcel Breuer, Architect and Designer* Museum of Modern Art, New York, 1949

Blake, Peter (ed.) *Marcel Breuer: Sun and Shadow* Dodd, Mead & Co., New York, 1955

Blake, Peter *Mies van der Rohe: Architecture and Structure* Pelican Books, London, 1963

Blaser, Werner *Mies van der Rohe, Furniture and Interiors* Academy Editions, London, 1982

Breuer, Marcel *Marcel Breuer: buildings and projects, 1921–1961* Thames & Hudson, London, 1962

Burckhart, L. (ed.) *The Werkbund* Design Council, London, 1980

Campbell, Joan *The German Werkbund: The Politics of Reform in the Applied Arts* Princeton University Press, 1978

Carr, William *A History of Germany, 1815–1945* Edward Arnold, London, 1969; St Martin, New York, 1979

Franciscono, M. *Walter Gropius and the Creation of the Bauhaus in Weimar* University of Illinois Press, 1971

Gay, Peter *Weimar Culture* Secker and Warburg, London, 1969; Greenwood, USA, 1981

Giedion, Sigfried *Walter Gropius: Work and Teamwork* Reinhold, New York, 1954

Gomringer, Eugen *Josef Albers* Wittenborn, New York, 1968

Gropius, Walter *The New Architecture and the Bauhaus* Faber and Faber, London, 1935; MIT Press, Cambridge, Mass., 1965; (ed.) *Internationale Architektur* (Bauhaus Book 1) Albert Langen Verlag, Munich, 1925; (ed.) *Neue Arbeiten der Bauhauswerkstätten* (Bauhaus Book 7) Albert Langen Verlag, Munich, 1925; reprinted by Florian Kupferberg, Mainz, 1981; *Bauhausbauten Dessau* (Bauhaus Book 12) Albert Langen Verlag, Munich, 1930; reprinted by Florian Kupferberg, Mainz, 1974

Henderson, W. O. *The Rise of German Industrial Power 1834–1914* Temple Smith, London, 1975; University of California Press, 1976

Heskett, John *Industrial Design* Thames & Hudson, London, 1980; Oxford University Press, New York, 1980

Hirschfeld-Mack, Ludwig *The Bauhaus: an introductory survey* Longmans, London, 1963

Hitchcock, H. R. and Johnson, P. *The International Style* Norton & Co., New York and London, 1932

Hüter, Karl-Heinz *Das Bauhaus in Weimar* Akademie Verlag, Berlin, 1976

Itten, Johannes *Design and Form: The Basic Course at the Bauhaus* Thames & Hudson, London, 1964; Reinhold, New York, 1975 (Eng. edition); *Mein Vorkurs am Bauhaus: Gestaltungs und Formlehre* Otto Maier, Ravensburg, 1963; *The Art of Colour* Reinhold, New York, 1961

Junghans, Kurt *Das Deutsche Werkbund: sein erstes Jahrzehnt* Henschelverlag, Berlin, 1982

Klee, Felix (ed.) *The Diaries of Paul Klee* University of California Press, 1964

Klee, Paul *On Modern Art* Faber & Faber, London, 1948; *Pedagogical Sketchbook* Faber and Faber, London, 1953; *Pädagogisches Skizzenbuch* (Bauhaus Book 2) Albert Langen Verlag, Munich, 1925

Lane, Barbara Miller *Architecture and Politics in Germany, 1918–1945* Harvard University Press, 1971

Laqueur, W. *Weimar, a cultural history* Weidenfeld & Nicolson, London, 1974; Perigee Books, New York, 1976

Lindsay, Kenneth C. and Vergo, Peter (eds) *Kandinsky: Complete Writings on Art* (2 vols) Faber and Faber, London, 1982; Twayne, G. K. Hall, Boston, 1982

Meyer, Hannes *Bauen und Gesellschaft* VEB Verlag der Kunst, Dresden, 1980

Moholy-Nagy, Laszlo *The New Vision and Abstract of an Artist* George Wittenborn Inc., New York, 1947; *Vision in Motion* Paul Theobald, Chicago, 1947; *Painting, Photography, Film* Lund Humphries, London, 1969; *Malerei, Fotographie, Film* (Bauhaus Book 8) Albert Langen Verlag, Munich, 1925

Moholy-Nagy, Lucia *Marginal Notes* Scherpe Verlag, Krefeld, 1972

Moholy-Nagy, Sibyl *Moholy-Nagy: Experiment in Totality* MIT Press, 1969

Muthesius, Hermann *Das Englische Haus* Wasmuth, Berlin, 1904–5; *The English House* Granada, London, 1979; Rizzoli International, 1979

Neumann, Eckhardt (ed.) *Bauhaus and Bauhaus People* Van Nostrand Reinhold, New York, 1970

Pehnt, Wolfgang *Expressionist Architecture* Thames & Hudson, London, 1973

Pevsner, Nikolaus *Academies of Art, Past and Present* Da Capo Press, New York, 1973; *Pioneers of the Modern Movement* 1936; revised as *Pioneers of Modern Design* Penguin Books, 1960; *An Enquiry into Industrial Art in England* Cambridge University Press, 1937

Posener, Julius *Anfänge des Funktionalismus, von Arts and Crafts zum Deutschen Werkbund* Frankfurt and Berlin, Ullstein, 1964

Read, Herbert *Art and Industry* Faber and Faber, London, 1934; Horizon, New York, 1983

Roters, Eberhard *Painters at the Bauhaus* A. Zwemmer, London, 1969

Schädlich, Christian *Bauhaus Weimar, 1919–25* Weimar, 1980

Scheidig, Walther *Crafts of the Weimar Bauhaus* Studio Vista, London/Reinhold, New York, 1967

Schlemmer, Tut (ed.) *The Letters and Diaries of Oskar Schlemmer* Wesleyan University Press, 1972

Schnaidt, Claude *Hannes Meyer: buildings, projects and writings* Verlag Gerd Hatje, Stuttgart, 1965

Schreyer, Lothar *Erinnerungen an Sturm und Bauhaus* Albert Langen Verlag, Munich, 1956

Selle, Gert *Ideologie und Utopia des Designs* DuMont, Cologne, 1968; *Die Geschichte des Designs in Deutschland von 1870 bis heute* DuMont, Cologne, 1978

Semper, Gottfried *Wissenschaft, Industrie und Kunst* Vieweg and Son, Brunswick, 1852

Semper, M. & H. (eds) *Kleine Schriften* W. Spemann, Berlin and Stuttgart, 1884

Siepmann, E. (ed.) *The Thinking Eye* Paul Klee, Lund Humphries, London, 1961

Stern, Fritz *The Politics of Cultural Despair* University of California Press, 1961

Troy, Nancy *The De Stijl Environment* MIT Press, 1983

Van Doesburg, Theo *Principles of Neo-Plastic Art* (*Grundbegriffe der neuen gestaltenden Kunst* Bauhaus Book 6, 1925) Lund Humphries, London, 1969

Volkov, Shulamit *The Rise of Popular Anti-Modernism in Germany, the Urban Master Artisans, 1873–1896* Princeton University Press, 1978

Weiss, Peg *Kandinsky in Munich* Princeton University Press, 1979

Whitford, Frank *Bauhaus* Thames and Hudson, London, 1984

Wick, Rainer *Bauhaus Pädagogik* DuMont, Cologne, 1982

Wilk, Christopher *Marcel Breuer: Furniture and Interiors* Architectural Press, London, 1981; Museum of Modern Art, New York, 1981

Willett, John *The New Sobriety, Art and Politics in the Weimar Period 1917–1933* Thames and Hudson London, 1978; Pantheon, New York, 1980; *The Weimar Years* Thames and Hudson, London, 1974

Windsor, Alan *Peter Behrens: Architect and Designer* The Architectural Press, London, 1981; Watson-Guptill, New York, 1982

Wingler, Hans M. *The Bauhaus* (English adaptation), MIT Press, 1969. (First published as *Das Bauhaus* Verlag Gebr. Rasch & Co and M. DuMont Schauberg, Cologne, 1962.); *Graphic Work from the Bauhaus* Lund Humphries, London, 1969; *Kleine Bauhaus Fibel* Bauhaus-Archiv, Berlin, 1979

Wingler, Hans M. (ed.) *Kunstschulreform 1900–1933* Gebr. Mann, Studio Reihe, Berlin, 1977

Wolfe, Tom *From Bauhaus to our house* Farrar, Straus & Giroux, New York, 1981; Jonathan Cape, London, 1982

MAGAZINES AND JOURNALS

Form und Zweck, Fachzeitschrift für Industrielle Formgestaltung Issue 3, 1979

Bauhaus Kolloquium, Wissenschaftliche Zeitschrift der Hochschule für Architektur und Bauwesen Weimar, 1979

Bauhaus Journal (*Zeitschrift für Gestaltung*) Quarterly, 1926–31

Jahrbücher des Deutschen Werkbundes 1912–17

CATALOGUES

Herbert Bayer Das Künstlerische Werk, 1918–1938 Bauhaus-Archiv, Berlin, 1982

Bauhaus Weimar Werkstättarbeiten Kunstsammlungen zu Weimar (selection of work from the Weimar Kunstsammlung collection) Weimar

Fifty Years Bauhaus Royal Academy of Art, London, 1968

Industriekultur, Peter Behrens und die AEG 1907–1914 Electa International, Milan, 1978

Georg Muche Das künstlerische Werk, 1918–1938 Bauhaus-Archiv, Berlin, 1980

Hermann Muthesius Akademie der Künste, Berlin, 1977

Paris-Berlin Centre Georges Pompidou, Paris, 1978

Sammlung Bauhaus-Archiv Museum (Catalogue of the Bauhaus-Archiv Museum, Berlin), 1981

Aalto, Alvar 152
Abstract of an Artist (Moholy-Nagy) 99
Abstraction and Empathy (Lipps) 92
AEG (Allgemeine Elektricitäts Gesellschaft) 32, 34, 36, 46, 48, 95
Aesthetik: Psychologie der Schönen und der Kunst (Lipps) 91
Albers, Anni *83*, 109, 155, 178
Albers, Josef 9, *82*, *84*, 100, 101, 104, 105, 107, 108, 115, 116, 125, 146, 152, 155–6, 157, 165, 167, 177, 178
Arbeitsrat für Kunst 54–7 passim, 60, 74, 104
Arndt, Alfred 152, 170, 176
Arp, Hans 50, 97, 98
Art and Race (Schultze-Naumburg) 176
Art Education Movement 16, 17
Art Nouveau 14, 18, 21, 25
Artist's Colony, Darmstadt 21
Arts and Crafts Movement 25, 26, 43
Ashbee, C. R. 25
Avenarius, Ferdinand 17
Ažbè, Anton 17, 84

Baillie Scott, M. H. 12
Bartning, Otto 55, 125, 176
Bauhaus, The (Wingler) 10
Bauhaus 1919–1928 (Bayer et al, eds) 10, 100, 124, 146, 147
Bauhaus Archiv 10, 11
Bauhaus Books 10, 92, 108, 119, 126, 157, 158
Bauhaus in Weimar, Das (Hüter) 10
Bauhaus Journal 127, 138, 141, 168, 173
Bauhaus-Weimar 1919–1925 (Schädlich) 10
Bauhausbauten Dessau 129
Baumeister, Willi 178
Bauwelt, Die 117
Bayer, Herbert 9, *52*, *53*, *85*, 118, 119, 125, 156–60 passim, 166, 178, Pl. 12

Beckmann, Max 50
Behne, Adolf 54, 55, 94–5, 98, 117
Behrens, Peter *9*, *15*, *16*, *17*, 21–2, 23, 28, 34, 36, 40, 46, 48, 55, 66, 85, 122, 168, 173, 175, Pl. 1
Benirschke, Max 22
Benjamin, Walter 101
Benton, Charlotte 127
Benton, Tim 127
Berg, Alban 75
Berg, Max 170
Berger, Otti 155
Berlage, H. P. 22, 94, 122
Berlin Academy of Fine Art 15, 50
Berlin Handelshochschule 39
Berlin Kunstgewerbe Museum 23, 50
Berlin Museum 23, 53
Berlin State Art School 178
Bertsch, Karl 28
Bing, Samuel 25
Black Mountain College 156, 178
Blaue Reiter 85, 88, 92
Bode, Wilhelm von 23, 24, 53, 57
Bogler, Theo 72
Bonset, I. K.
    see Van Doesburg, Theo
Börner, Hélène 67, 108
Brandt, Marianne 77, 111–12, 146–7, 148, Pl. 8
Brenner, Anton 168
Breslau Academy 178
Breuer, Marcel 9, *43*, *51*, *63*, 72, *78–81*, 104–8 passim, 115, 116, 125, 129, 138, 143, 148–53 passim, 166, 177, 178, Pl. 6, Pl. 13
Breuer, Robert 43
Bronstein, M. *37*
Brücke, Die 40
Bruckmann, Peter 39
Bruckmüller, Josef 22
Buscher, Alma *45*, 107, 108, 115, 116
Busoni, Ferruccio 121

Camini, Aldo 97
Campbell, Joan 40
Carnap, Rudolph 168

Carr, William 48
Citroen, Paul *39*, 78–9, 100
Cizek, Franz 76
Cobden-Sanderson, Thomas 43
Complexity and Contradiction in Architecture (Venturi) 179
Constructivism 95, 97, 99–100, 101, 104, 107, 119, 127, 142, 145, 157, 159, 167, 172
Cubism 57, 98
Cuypers 22

Dada 97
Dalcroze, Emil-Jaques 31
Damaschke, Adolf 142
Dearnstyne, Howard 176, 178
Debschitz-Schule 18, *19*, *20*, 85
Dekorative Kunst 24
Dell, Christian 110–11, 112, 125, 146, 147
Design and Form: The Basic Course at the Bauhaus (Itten) 77
Deutsche Stil, Der (Naumann) 46
Deutsche Werkkunst der Gegenwart (Passarge) 179
Deutsches Warenbuch 23, 48
Deutscher Werkbund
    see Werkbund
Development of Modern Industrial Architecture (Gropius) 46
Dieckmann, Erich 107, 108, 115, 116
Dörfner, Otto 157
Durch Kunst zum Leben (Kunowski) 17
Dürerbund 17

Ebert, Friedrich 49
Eckmann, Otto 34
Einstein, Albert 122
Elementare Typographie 160
Endell, August 20, 44, 46, 50, 53
Englische Haus, Das (Muthesius) 37, 39
Enquiry into Industrial Art in England, An (Pevsner) 179
Esprit Nouveau, L' 93

'Exact Experiments in the Realm of Art' (Klee) 127
Expressionism 57, 66, 77, 98

Feigl, Herbert 168
Feininger, Lyonel 9, *26*, *54*, *55*, 57, 58, 60, 66, 68, 74, 81, 97, 100, 101, 102, 104, 119, 124, 132, 138, 144, 165, 177, 178
'Fine Art and Industrial Form' (Muche) 114, 127, 141
Finsterlin, Hermann 55, 168
Fischer, Theodor 40, 66
Forbat, Fred 94
Form and Function (ed. Benton) 127
Francé, Raoul H. 145
Franciscono, M. 46
Frank, Josef 173
Froebel, Friedrich 15, 16, 146
From the Easel to the Machine (Tarabukin) 86–7
'From Wine Jugs to Lighting Fixtures' (Moholy-Nagy) 146
Fry, Maxwell 177
Futurism 98, 119, 142

Gaertner, Eduard *25*
Gebhard, Ernst 116
'Glass Chain' 54
Greil, Dr Max 103–4
Grimm, Jakob 159
Grohmann, Will 156
Gropius, Carl Wilhelm 50
Gropius, Ferdinand 50
Gropius, Martin (Walter's father) 50
Gropius, Martin (Walter's great-uncle) 50
Gropius, Walter *3*, 9, 14, 15, 20, *21*, 22, *22*, 23, *24*, 36, 40, *43*, 44, 46, 49, 50, 52–8 *passim*, 60, *61*–7, 65–6, 67, *69*, 72, 74, 75, 76, 81, 82, 83, 87, 89, 93–9 *passim*, 102–5 *passim*, 112, 114, 117, 118, 121, 122, 124–7 *passim*, 129, 132, 138, 140–46 *passim*, 150, 153, 157, 160, 165–8 *passim*, 171–5 *passim*, 177–80 *passim*
Gross, Hans 60
Grünewald 77

Harvard Graduate School of Design 178
Harvard University 156
Hausmann, Raoul 98
Heckel, Ernst 40, 55
Heiberg, Edvard 168
Helmholtz, Hermann von 92
Herberts, Kurt 178
Herfurth, Dr Emil 66, 103
Heskett, John 11, 146
Hesse, Ernst Ludwig, Grand Duke of 21
Hesse, Fritz 124, 153, 171, 173, 176, 177, 179
Hilberseimer, Ludwig 168, 173, 176, 177, 178
Hindemith, Paul 121
Hirschfeld-Mack, Ludwig 119

Hitchcock, Henry Russell 172, 173
Hitler, Adolf 26, 160
Höch, Hannah 158
Hoffmann, Josef 22, 39, 46, 122
Hölzel, Adolf 17, 75, 77, 88
Huszar, Vilmos 93, 96, 103
Hüter, Dr Karl-Heinz 10, 11, 50

Idee und Aufbau des Staatlichen Bauhauses in Weimar (Gropius) 10, 74, 93
Illinois Institute of Technology 178
Industrial Design (Heskett) 146
Inkhuk (Institute of Artistic Culture) 86, 87, 92
Institute of Social Research, Frankfurt 122
International Style 46
Itten, Johannes 9, 17, 60, 75–9 *passim*, 81–2, 83, 84, 90, 93–6 *passim*, 99, 100, 101, 106, 110, 111, 114, 142, 153, 155, 167, 170, 178

Ja! Stimmen des Arbeitsrat für Kunst in Berlin 55
Jensen 43
Johnson, Edward 160
Johnson, Philip 172, 173, 176, 179
Jucker, Karl J. *48*, 112
Jugend 23, 24
Jugendstil 14, 15, 18, 20, 21, 23, 24, 28, 34, 39
Julien, Charles-André 86, 87
Jungnik, Hedwig 109, Pl. 9

Kadow 178
Kallai, Ernst 168
Kandinsky, Wassily 9, 17, 22, *72*, 83–8 *passim*, 90–94 *passim*, 96, 98, 99, 101, 102, 108, 117, 118, 119, 121, 122, 125, 127, 132, 138, 143, 145, 146, 149, 155, 160, 165, 167, 172, 177, 178, Pl. 3
Kapp, Wolfgang 49, 58, 66
Kassàk, Ludwig 98
Keler, Peter 108, Pl. 11
Kerkovius, Ida 75
Kirchner, Ernst 40
Klee, Felix 78
Klee, Paul 9, *40*, *41*, 68, 74, 81, 83, 84, 87–93 *passim*, 96, 98, 101, 102, 105, 110, 117, 119, 126, 127, 132, 155, 160, 165, 167, 172, 174, 176, 177, 178, Pl. 4
Klein, César *28*, 55
Kok, Anthony 93, 95
Kokoschka, Oskar 75, 98
Korda, Alexander 178
Krefeld Textile School 153
Krehan, Max 67, 72, Pl. 2
Kreubel, Dr 60
Krupps 32, 46, 142
Kubin, Alfred 89
Kunowski, Gertrud von 17
Kunowski, Lothar von 17
Kunstakademie 24

Kunstgewerbeschule 15, 16, 18, 20, 21, 24, 26, 34, 39, 52, 56, 57, 65, 67, 72, 74, 76, 85, 142

Langbehn, Julius 17, 18, 60
Lauweriks, J. L. M. 22, 95, 105
Le Corbusier 36, 39, 73–4, 93, 96, 117, 151, 152, 172
Leck, Bart van der 93
Leudesdorff, L. *38*
Lichtwark, Alfred 16, 17
Liebknecht, Karl 48, 58, 175
Lindig, Otto *34*, *35*, 72, 125, 178, 179
Lipps, Theodor 91, 92
Lissitzky, El 97, 98
Little Articles on Big Questions (Kandinsky) 87
Loos, Adolf 39, 75
Luckhardt Brothers 55
Lux, J. A. 16, 29
Luxemburg, Rosa 48, 58, 175
Luz, Martha 18

MA 98, 99
Macke, August 88
Mackensen, Fritz 52
Mahler, Alma 65, 75
Mahler, Gustav 65
Maldonado, Tomas 174, 177
Malerei, Fotografie, Film (Moholy-Nagy) 158
Marby, F. Pl. 10
Marc, Franz 88, 98
Marcks, Gerhard *28*, *29*, 55, 60, 65, 70, 72, 125, 178, 179, Pl.2
Marx, Karl 16
May, Ernst 138, 168
Mazdaznan 77, 78–9, 81
Mendelsohn, Eric 55, 170
Messel, Alfred 34
Metzendorf, Georg 46, 142
Meyer, Adolf *21*, 22, *22*, 36, *43*, 46, *48*, 50, 55, 94, 95, 104, 105, 114, 125, 129
Meyer, Hannes 9, 10, *86*, 127, 142–3, 146, 165–8 *passim*, 170–77 *passim*
Meyer, Otto 68, 117, 121, 166
Mies van der Rohe 36, 55, 165, 173–8 *passim*
Modern Movement 14, 179
Moderne Zweckbau, Der (Behne) 94
Moholy-Nagy, Laszlo 9, *42*, 83, 97–102 *passim*, 112, 119, 122, 125, 132, 143–7 *passim*, 156–60 *passim*, 165, 166, 167, 171, Pl. 5
Moholy-Nagy, Lucia 97, 100, 149, 171, 178
Moholy-Nagy, Sibyl 178
Molnar, Farkas 129
Mondrian, Piet 93, 94, 127
Montessori, Maria 16, 146
Morris, William 16, 20, 25, 29, 32, 70, 109, 146, 155, 179
Moscow Academy 86, 87
Muche, Georg 9, *49*, 70, *73*, *76*, 81, 90, 109, 114–17 *passim*, 125, 127,

128, 129, 132, 141, 142, 144, 153,
166, 167, 168, 178
Munch, Edvard 98
Munich Academy 100
Munich Secession 84
Münter, Gabriele 85
Museum of Modern Art, New York
10, 179
Muthesius, Günther *18*
Muthesius, Hermann *18*, *20*, 21, 37,
39, 40, 42, 43, 46, 48, 53, 54, 104,
125, 173

Naumann, Friedrich 46
Neue Arbeiten der Bauhaus-
Werkstätten 108
Neu Linie, Die 160
Neufert, Ernst 129
Neurath, Otto 168
New Architecture and the Bauhaus,
The (Gropius) 10, 36, 126, 129,
132, 178
'New Typography, The'
(Tschichold) 160
New Vision, The 98, 145
'New World, The' (Hannes Meyer)
142, 143, 166
Nolde, Emil 55
Novembergruppe 54, 55, 57, 74, 168,
175

Obrist, Hermann *4*, 18, 19–20, 44,
46, 50, 54, 85
Olbrich, Josef 39
On Modern Art (Klee) 90
On Weaving (Anni Albers) 178
Op Art 155
Ostwald, Wilhelm 46
Otte, Benita 116, 178, 179
Oud, J. J. P. 40, 93, 94, 95, 117, 121,
172

Paedagogical Sketchbook (Klee)
92
Pankok, Bernhard 20
Pap, Gyula 110, 111
Passarge, Walter 118, 179
Paul, Bruno 5, 6, 23–4, 28, 31, 40,
57, 65, 107, 115, 175
Paulick, Richard 76, 141
Pechstein, Max 55
Pédagogie (Le Corbusier) 93
Peterhans, Walter 170, 171, 177,
178
Pevsner, Nikolaus 179–80
Pflänze als Erfinder, Die (Francé)
145
Phalanx group 85
Pioneers of the Modern Movement
from William Morris to Walter
Gropius (Pevsner) 179
Poelzig, Hans 44, 54, 55, 141
Point and Line to Plane (Kandinsky)
92, 126
Popp, Joseph 24
Portsmann, Dr W. 159
Pritchard, Jack 177
Puni, Ivan 98

Rasch, Emil 174
Rathenau, Emil 34, 36
Rathenau, Walther 34, 48
Raumaesthetik und geometrische-
optische Täuschungen (Lipps) 91
Read, Sir Herbert 127
Redslob, Dr Edwin 114
Reich, Lilly 176
Rembrandt Als Erzieher (Langbehn)
17
Richter, Hans 50, 97
Rickey, George 101
Riemerschmid, Richard 7, *8, 10, 11*,
20, 28, 31, 40, 46, 66, 107, 115
Rietveld, Gerrit 106, Pl. 7
Ring group 175
Romanticism 77
Rössger, W. Pl. 10
Ruchet, Bertha 20
Rudelk, Alcar 168, 177
Ruskin, John 14, 16, 29, 32, 70

Saxe-Weimar, Grand Duke of 15, 50
Schädlich, Professor Christian 10, 11
Schawinsky, Xanti 160, 178
Scheidig 72
Scheper, Hinnerk 125, 177
Schiele, Egon 98
Schinkel, Karl Friedrich 40, 50
Schlemmer, Oskar 2, 9, 10, 11, 17,
18, 67–9, 72, 74, 75, 81, 83, 84,
88–9, 104, 105, 110, 117–18, 121,
122, 132, 143, 145, 153, 165, 166,
167, 176, 177, 178
Schlemmer, Tut 125
Schmidt, Joost 104, 105, 118, 119,
125, 156, 157, 160, 167, 171
Schmidt, Karl 29, 31
Schmidt-Nonne, Hélène 154–5, 157
Schmidt-Rottluff, Karl 40
Schnaidt, Claude 142, 170
Schönberg, Arnold 75, 85, 122
Schreyer, Lothar 81, 100
Schultze-Naumburg, Paul 28, 40,
118, 176
Schumacher, Fritz 40, 66
Schwechten, Franz 34
Semper, Gottfried 32–3, 43
Simplicissimus 20, 23, 24
Slutzky, Naum 47
Sommerfeld, Adolf 104, 115
Spartacus League 48
Speech and Lettering (Porstmann) 159
Stam, Mart 95, 168, 172
Statutes of the Staatliches Bauhaus in
Weimar 72
Steiner, Rudolf 143
Stelzer, Otto 101
Stern, Fritz 17
Stijl, De 74, 93, 94, 95, 106, 107,
119, 127, 157
Stijl, De (magazine) 93, 94, 97, 98,
103, 106
Stilarchitektur und Baukunst
(Muthesius) 37, 39
Stölzl, Gunta 9, 108–9, 125, 128,
152, 153–4, 155, 176, 177, Pl. 15,
Pl. 16

Stravinsky, Igor 121
Sturm, Der 75, 98, 102
Stuttgart Academy 75, 88
Surrealists 16

Tarabukin, Nikolai 86
Taut, Bruno 40, 44, 54, 55, 94, 173
Taut, Max 55, 170, 173
Technische Hochschule 24, 40
Teige, Karel 168, 173
Tenner 103
Tessenow, Heinrich 31
Teuber, Marianne 92
Thedy, Max 66, 105
Theosophical Society 22
Thinking Eye, The (Klee) 90
Tiffany, Louis Comfort 43
Toller, Ernst 168
Triadic Ballet 117, 121
Tschichold, Jan 159–60
Typenmöbel 23, 24, 107
Tzara, Tristan 97

Über das geistige in der Kunst
(Kandinsky) 85, 86, 92, 93
Ulm School of Design 174

Value of Theoretical Instruction in
Painting, The (Kandinsky) 126
Van de Velde, Henry 15, 18–19, 20,
20, 23, 43, 44, 46, 50, 52, 67, 72,
90, 108, 110, 117, 118, 119, 157
Van Doesburg, Theo 9, 74, 83, 93–8
passim, 106, 119, 157
Vantongerloo, Georges 93
Venturi, Robert 179
Vereinigten Werkstätten für Kunst in
Handwerk 23, 28, 39, 154
Vereinigung für angewandte Kunst 85
Vertov, Dziga 168
Victoria, Queen 21
Vienna Secession 22
Vision in Motion (Moholy Nagy) 145
Vkhutemas 87
Vogel, Hans 95
Volkov, Shulamit 26
Von Debschitz, Wilhelm 18, 20

Wagenfeld, Wilhelm *48*, *77*, 112,
178, 179, Pl. 10
Walden, Herwarth 98
Weidensee, Reinhold 107
Weimar Art Academy 50, 52, 157
Weimar School of Arts and Crafts 50
Weimar State Bauhochschule 179
Weimar State Library 157
Weiss, Peg 84
Werkbund 17, 19, 21, 23, 24, 36, 37,
39, 40, 43, 44, 46, 48, 50, 53, 54,
66, 70, 107, 152, 172, 173, 175
Werkbund Yearbook *19*, 46
Werkstätte für Kunst in Handwerk,
Dresden 12, *13*, 29, 31, 39
Werkstätte für Wohnungseinrichtung
28, 39
Wilk, Christopher 149
Will to Style, The (Van Doesburg)
94

Wils, Jan 93, 117
Windsor, Alan 36
Wingler, Hans M. 10, 11, 108, 110,
    127, 147
Wissenschaft, Industrie und Kunst
    (Semper) 32
Wittwer, Hans 142
Wo Stehen Wir? (Muthesius) 40, 43
Wolfe, Tom 179
Worringer, Wilhelm 92

Yale University 156, 178, 179

Zachmann, Josef 81, 105, 107
Zevi, Bruno 94
Zwart, Piet 168